Margaret Thaler Singer
with Janja Lalich

Foreword by Robert Jay Lifton

Cults in Our Midst

Cults in Our Midst

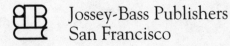

Jossey-Bass Publishers
San Francisco

For sales outside the United States, please contact your local Paramount Publishing International Office.

Substantial discounts on bulk quantities of Jossey-Bass books are available to corporations, professional associations, and other organizations. For details and discount information, contact the special sales department at Jossey-Bass Inc., Publishers.
(415) 433–1740; Fax (800) 605–2665.

 Manufactured in the United States of America on Lyons Falls Pathfinder Tradebook. This paper is acid-free and 100 percent totally chlorine-free.

Credits are on page 381.

Library of Congress Cataloging-in-Publication Data

Singer, Margaret Thaler.
  Cults in our midst / Margaret Thaler Singer with Janja Lalich.
      p.   cm.—(The Jossey-Bass social and behavioral science series)
  Includes bibliographical references and index.
  ISBN 0-7879-0051-6
  1. Cults—Controversial literature. 2. Psychology, Religious. 3. Persuasion (Psychology) 4. United States—Religion—1960– I. Lalich, Janja. II. Title. III. Series.
BP603. S56 1994
291.9—dc20

94-33598
CIP

FIRST EDITION
HB Printing 10 9 8 7 6 5 4 3 2 1

Code 9508

Contents

Foreword

Margaret Thaler Singer stands alone in her extraordinary knowledge of the psychology of cults. Over decades, she has brought to the subject a rare combination of professional skill and personal courage.

Singer recognizes the complexities of the cult phenomenon. She is aware of a continuum from relatively innocuous if one-sided efforts at persuasion at one end to systematic thought-reform procedures on the other. She is also aware that psychological manipulation is the heart of the matter, with or without the use of physical violence. At the same time she knows well that the more general issue of totalistic groups transcends any professional discipline and has to do with larger social and historical forces.

I have been preoccupied with questions of totalism from the time of my study of Chinese thought reform in the mid 1950s, and came full circle in returning to the subject when studying Nazi doctors in the late 1970s and early 1980s. Totalism is likely to emerge during periods of historical—or psychohistorical—dislocation, in which there is a breakdown of the symbols and structures that guide the human life cycle. Contributing to this dislocation is the mass media revolution, which creates the remarkable possibility of any one of us, at any moment, having access to any image or idea originating anywhere in the contemporary world or from any cultural moment of the entire human past. Still another powerful influence furthers our dislocation: awareness of our late-twentieth-century technological capacity to annihilate ourselves as a species, and to do so with neither purpose nor redemption. What result from these historical forces are widespread feelings that we are losing our psychological moorings. We feel ourselves buffeted about by unmanageable currents and radical social uncertainties.

A major response to this confusion has been the contemporary worldwide epidemic of fundamentalism. That movement, broadly understood, derives from a fear of the loss of "fundamentals," giving rise to a demand for absolute dogma and a monolithic self—all rendered sacred in the name of a past of perfect harmony that never was.

What we call cults represent an important expression of fundamentalism. One person's cult, of course, is another's religion—or, for that matter, political or commercial organization. One must make careful distinctions, as Singer cautions us, and judge each group by its own behavior. I define cults in terms of a cluster of groups with certain characteristics. First, all cults have a charismatic leader, who himself or herself increasingly becomes the object of worship, and in many cases, the dispenser of immortality. Spiritual ideas of a general kind give way to this deification of the leader. Second, in cults there occurs a series of psychological processes that can be associated with what has been called "coercive persuasion" or "thought reform," as described in some detail in this book. And third, there is a pattern of manipulation and exploitation from above (by leaders and ruling coteries) and idealism from below (on the part of supplicants and recruits).

But neither fundamentalism nor cult formation should be seen as the last word. There is an alternative, much more hopeful pattern that arises from the same historical soil. I have in mind a tendency toward a more open and flexible self that can be in tune with the larger uncertainties that surround us. I have named it the *protean self* after Proteus, the Greek sea god of many forms.

The protean self, in contrast to the fundamentalist or cult self, is open and many-sided; rather than narrowly prescribed, it calls forth odd combinations, and includes important elements of humor and mockery. The protean self is not without its difficulties in its constant quest for an ethical core. But it has the virtue of avoiding absolutes and dead ends and holding out an ever-present possibility of transformation and change.

Indeed, I believe this pattern of proteanism to be a primary response to our present historical situation. Tendencies toward fundamentalism and cult formation are best understood as reactions against proteanism. These reactions can be fierce, as we well know. But it is also true that even fundamentalists are susceptible to protean tendencies, as recent work at the Center on Violence and Human Survival has shown. That is why people leave cults or cease to be fundamentalists.

Since history, like individual life, is forward-moving, the returns are never quite in. Much of the unease in our present world has to do with a struggle between protean and fundamentalist tendencies, as epitomized in the bizarre "death sentence" applied to the writer Salman Rushdie by the Islamic fundamentalist Ayatollah Khomeini.

Much that Margaret Thaler Singer writes in *Cults in Our Midst* echoes this struggle. We do well to learn all we can from her hard-won experience on preserving the freedom of the mind.

New York, New York   Robert Jay Lifton
January 1995   John Jay College
                                  City University of New York

To my parents,
    Margaret McDonough Thaler and Raymond Willard Thaler
To my children,
    Sam and Martha
And to my husband, Jay

Acknowledgments

Over the years many colleagues have shared ideas, research, and insights that have been important to the work I have done in examining cults and their practices and helping former members of cults. Most especially, I acknowledge the contributions of Robert Jay Lifton, Laura Nader, Richard Ofshe, Morton Reiser, David McKay Rioch, Edgar Schein, Louis Jolyon West, and Lyman Wynne.

I could never have accomplished so much without all the assistance of the American Family Foundation and the Cult Awareness Network— their enthusiastic support and help in providing referrals, locating source materials, supplying literature and reprints of articles, and sponsoring annual conferences that bring together so many people who are interested in this social problem. I also thank the people at the Spiritual Counterfeits Project for their graciousness in allowing me use of their library and resources, and want to thank our many friends and colleagues around the world who generously provided documentation materials.

My warmest thanks and deepest appreciation go to the more than three thousand cult victims who shared their stories, their pain, and their healing with me, helping me to learn about cults and the harm they have brought upon so many.

This book could not have been written without the encouragement, prodding, quick wit, and intelligent pen of my collaborator, Janja Lalich. The book began with the two of us clicking out a proposal one afternoon at the computer on my dining room table, and from then on, we worked together like lifelong pals. Thank you, Janja.

Finally, both Janja and I wish to thank Alan Rinzler, our editor at Jossey-Bass. His dedication to this project was apparent from the start, and throughout he was swift to respond with urgings and remarks that inspired us to do better.

Berkeley, California   Margaret Thaler Singer
January 1995

Introduction

I have always been interested in words: how words create mental pictures, how those pictures stir emotions and call up other ideas and feelings, and how people use words to entertain, educate, and influence one another. When I was very young, I made lists of new words as I learned them. By age ten I had begun to notice the conversational skills of my relatives, the wonderful ways they could recount events from their past. I became curious as to why certain relatives were so good at telling stories of long-ago life, of faraway places and people. How did the good storytellers make things come alive in word pictures?

By the time I entered college I had practiced storytelling and studied conversations. Now, I wanted to learn how speakers used words, reasoning, and voice persuasively. So I got involved in college debate, oratory, and extemporaneous speaking and found that my favorite classes were propaganda analysis and logic, for those classes dissected language and reasoning.

I became a clinical psychologist, and again, language and communication were central to much of the research I did. After a number of years at the University of Colorado School of Medicine, Department of Psychiatry, I went to Washington, D.C., as a senior psychologist in the laboratory of psychology at the Walter Reed Army Institute of Research. There, among other things, I worked with people who were studying prisoners of war from the Korean War. I became knowledgeable about, and intrigued with, the forms of coercive persuasion, or thought-reform programs, that not only prisoners of war but also civilians in a variety of milieus had been exposed to in the Far East. I also interviewed a number of Jesuit priests who had been exposed to thought-reform processes while imprisoned in mainland China.

As a result of this work, I became familiar with the history of coercive persuasion in many settings throughout history. Later, laboratory studies done by social psychologists, field studies of influence done by anthropologists, and propaganda analyses done by political and linguistic analysts all came to be of use as I studied how current cults and other groups using thought-reform processes induce attitude and behavior changes in their members, how they use words to persuade, control, and even damage people. In the 1960s, I began to hear from families who had missing members—usually the missing person was young, between eighteen and twenty-five years old, and had become involved with one or another of the cultic groups that were just taking hold in those years. The family, and others who knew the person, told about a sudden change in personality, a new way of talking, a restriction of emotions, a splitting from family and the past. I recognized what sounded like the effects of a thought-reform program or the type of intense persuasion and social controls that I had studied for so long, things that until then we thought happened more often in faraway places. But here it was right at home.

I began interviewing as many families of cult members as I could, and as many members of the new cultic groups as I could find on the University of California's Berkeley campus. People who had emerged from the groups also began contacting me. What I learned was that there was a plethora of groups using intense, well-packaged psychological and social control methods.

Meanwhile, former cult members were telling me of their dismal contacts with clergy and mental health professionals who didn't know about social influence programs, psychological adaptations to the stresses of life in closed intense high-control groups, or the pains of life after leaving a cult. In 1979, I wrote the first article to appear in the popular press designed to help those leaving cults. It was called "Coming Out of the Cults" and appeared in *Psychology Today*. Having counseled so many ex-members by that point in time, I hoped such an article would be of use to cult veterans who had no one they could talk to about their time in the cult and the multitude of problems they faced on leaving the group.

Hundreds of former cult members have told me how useful the article was when they were given a copy by an exit counselor, therapist, or friend.

Since that time, I have interviewed and worked with more than three thousand current and former members of cults and groups that use thought-reform processes. I have also interviewed hundreds of families who have lost loved ones to cults. Because of my familiarity with intense influence situations, in 1976 I was called to be a court-appointed examiner of Patricia Hearst, who had been kidnapped and held prisoner by a radical terrorist cult and later was tried as a bank robber, after having been forced by the cult to participate in its activities. I have also counseled many survivors of Jonestown and the families of the Peoples Temple members who died there in 1978, as well as families of the Branch Davidians who died in Waco in 1993. I have been an expert witness in numerous cases in which former members sued their cults for damages.

Thus *Cults in Our Midst* is based not only on my fifty years as a psychologist doing research and clinical work but also on my lengthy observations of the direct social and psychological impacts of cult techniques and thought-reform processes on large numbers of individuals.

There are many definitions and views of what a cult is, and sometimes writers, scholars, and even former members avoid the term altogether. The term *cult* tends to imply something weird, something other than normal, something that is not us. But as *Cults in Our Midst* will show, cults are far from marginal, and those who join them are no different from you or me. The issues they represent are basic to our society, to our understanding of each other, and to our accepting our vulnerabilities and the potential for abuse within our world.

In this book, I will use *cult* and *cultic group* to refer to any one of a large number of groups that have sprung up in our society and that are similar in the way they originate, their power structure, and their governance. Cults range from the relatively benign to those that exercise extraordinary control over members' lives and use thought-reform processes to influence and control members. While the conduct of certain cults causes nonmembers to criticize them, the term cult is not in itself pejorative but simply descriptive. It denotes a group that forms around a person who claims he or she has a special mission or knowledge, which will be shared with those who turn over most of their decision making to that self-appointed leader.

Cults come in all sizes, form around any theme, and recruit persons of all ages and backgrounds. Not all cults are religious, as some people think. Their reasons for existing may concern religion, life-style, politics, or assorted philosophies. Not everyone who is approached by a cult recruiter joins, and of those who join, not all stay forever. Cults vary in how much financial and political power they wield. Some are local phenomena with only a dozen members. Others have thousands of members, operate multinational businesses, and control complex multimillion- if not multibillion-dollar organizations.

Cults are not always easy to recognize at first glance. Most people have a general grasp of what a cult is and are aware of the rise of cultic groups in the past decades. However, what people are not generally aware of is how cults achieve the control of people's lives that they appear to have.

In my study of cults, I find that the personality, preferences, and desires of the leader are central in the evolution of any of these groups. Cults are truly *personality cults*. Because cult structure is basically authoritarian, the personality of the leader is all important. Cults come to reflect the ideas, style, and whims of the leader and become extensions of the leader.

Legend has it that all cult leaders are charismatic. In reality, charisma is less important than skills of persuasion and the ability to manipulate others. In order to start a group, a leader has to have ways of convincing others to follow him or her, and such leaders tend not to relinquish their control. Cult leadership can be a heady role when the leader comes to see the amount of control he or she holds and how easily he or she can influence followers.

Cults present a consumer issue as well as the philosophical issue of whether one person should have near-total control over others. From the consumer vantage point, how can a potential cult member learn what really occurs during membership? Allegations abound that there are deceptions during the recruitment phase and that new members are not at all aware of what will be expected after they affiliate with a cultic group. More than one former cult member has told me that once caught up in the group, he or she found it something far different than it appeared at first.

In order to understand how someone can be hoodwinked to such a degree that she or he gives up job, family, and the freedom of self-determination, we must look at the social and psychological influence techniques used by cults and cultic groups. This process of planned, covert, coordinated influence—popularly called brainwashing or mind control or, more technically, thought reform—is the route by which the cult leader gains control.

Sometimes people laugh when I tell them about the content of certain cultic groups or show films about the groups. For example, I tell them about assisting former members of a horse cult, an outer-space cult, a sports cult, a weight-lifting cult, a music camp cult, a diet cult, and a hair-dressing cult.

While such groups may sound odd, *Cults in Our Midst* is not about weird people who join crazy groups. It's about how all of us, at various times, can fall into vulnerable states during which another person can wield more influence over us than at other times. We are all more vulnerable to flattery, deception, lures, and enticements when we are lonely, sad, and feeling needy. In such periods of transient vulnerability, most of us are more manipulable, more suggestible, and more likely to be deceived by the flattery and inducement of designing persons.

Modern-day cults and thought-reform groups tend to offer apparent utopias, places where all humankind's ills will be cured. The cults' lure is, if you just come along, all will be fine, and everyone will live happily ever after.

Down through time, people have written about such promised utopias, but they have also described their downsides, which might be called negative utopias. In 1949, George Orwell wrote about the negative utopia he feared would evolve, perhaps by 1984. Others before him, such as Daniel Defoe, Aldous Huxley, and Jack London, had also written about negative utopias in which political systems gradually curbed and eventually stifled people's most central capacities for reasoning creatively, scientifically, and compassionately. In these real or imagined centralized governments, torture, drugs, and mysterious, esoteric techniques were the feared methods by which people might be controlled.

Orwell's genius was in sensing that combinations of social and psychological techniques are easier, more effective, and cheaper than the gun-to-the-head methods of coercion. Social and psychological persuasion is also less likely to attract attention and thus is less apt to mobilize opposition early and easily from those being manipulated. Orwell reasoned that if a government could control all media and interpersonal communication while simultaneously forcing citizens to speak in a politically controlled jargon, it could blunt independent thinking. If thought could be controlled, then rebellious actions against a regime could be prevented. Not only in his book *Nineteen Eighty-Four* but also in his essays on politics and the English language, Orwell emphasized the power of words. Words represent thoughts, and without the capability to express thoughts, people lose access to their own thinking.

When the year 1984 arrived, various totalitarian governments were controlling and censoring the media and squelching dissenting individuals. And over the years, many versions of Orwell's Big Brother, Newspeak, and Thought Police, some more ominous and subtle than others, have appeared here and elsewhere throughout the world. Orwell's predictions may never come to pass completely because of the wondrous properties of the human mind when it remains free to reason. But his ideas still serve as a warning of the extent to which people's thinking can be influenced.

Since the 1960s, there has been a burgeoning not of governments but of independent entrepreneurial groups that go into the mind-manipulation and personality-change business. Myriads of false messiahs, quacks, and leaders of cults and thought-reform groups have emerged who use Orwellian mind-manipulation techniques. They recruit the curious, the unaffiliated, the trusting, and the altruistic. They promise intellectual, spiritual, political, social, and self-actualization utopias. These modern-day pied pipers offer, among other things, pathways to God, salvation, revolution, personal development, enlightenment, perfect health, psychological growth, egalitarianism, channels to speak with 35,000-year-old "entities," life in ecospheres, and contact with extraterrestrial beings.

There is truly a smorgasbord of spiritual, psychological, political, and other types of cults and cultic groups seeking adherents and devotees. Contrary to the myth that those who join cults are seekers, it is the cults that go out and actively and aggressively find followers. Eventually, these groups subject their followers to mind-numbing treatments that block critical and evaluative thinking and subjugate independent choice in a context of a strictly enforced hierarchy.

The wisdom of the ages is that most manipulation is subtle and covert. When Orwell drew on this wisdom, he envisioned the evolution of an insidious but successful mind and opinion manipulator. He would appear as a smiling, seemingly beneficent Big Brother. But instead of one Big Brother, we see hordes of Big Brothers in the world today. Many of them are cult leaders.

In the following pages, Janja Lalich and I hope to convey an understanding of the cult phenomenon in our society, so that you and those around you may take heed and be warned. It is not a pretty picture, but I believe it is one that desperately needs to be looked at.

Readers should know that a number of cults are highly litigious and use their wealth and power to harass and curb critics. Citizens, academics, journalists, former cult members and their parents, and publications ranging from *Time* magazine to the *Journal of the American Medical Association* have been the targets of legal suits brought by various wealthy cults in efforts to intimidate and silence critics. Defending himself or herself against the false accusations made by some of these cults can break the ordinary person. It appears that winning is not the most important goal for the cults. Their motivation appears rather to be to harass, financially destroy, and silence criticism.

Last year alone, one large cult was involved in approximately two hundred suits with government entities, critics, and ex-members who spoke out about their time in the group. You'll learn more about these types of threats and intimidating acts when you read Chapter Nine.

For these reasons, and because I want to keep on helping ex-members of cults understand what happened to them and how to overcome some of the long-lasting damage cult behavior has brought into their lives, I have elected to write generically of cults, so that my energies can continue to be directed to studying cults and helping cult victims. Throughout, names of some individuals have been changed, and names of groups and some other individuals have sometimes had to be omitted.

Without the citizenry being aware of the power and control certain cults are wielding, democracy and freedom can be curbed one step at a time. Cults by their very structure and nature are not democratic, do not promote freedom of speech and freedom of expression, and are the antithesis of structures in which full human growth can develop.

There are cults in our midst, more than the average citizen realizes. And these powerful groups infiltrate many areas of our lives.

Cults in Our Midst

PART ONE

What Are Cults?

1

Defining Cults

Twice in less than fifteen years we have been shown the deadly ends to which cult followers can be led. In 1978, aerial photos of 912 brightly clad followers of Jim Jones, dead by cyanide-laced drinks and gunshots in a steamy Guyanese jungle, were shown in magazines and on television, reappearing with each subsequent anniversary of the end of Jonestown. And in early 1993, television news programs showed the Koresh cult's shoot-out, then several weeks later its flaming end on the Texas plains. How many more Jonestowns and Wacos will have to occur before we realize how vulnerable all humans are to influence? In the time between these two episodes, nearly a hundred cult children and mothers died from lack of care in Indiana and there were reports of numerous other children and adults abused in cults. A California-based cult tried to murder a lawyer by placing a rattlesnake in his mailbox, because he'd won three cases against the group. The Rajneesh cult in Oregon attempted to poison the water supply in the town of The Dalles and harm public officials in Wasco and Jefferson Counties for carrying out the laws of the state, which the group didn't want applied to them. Cult members who once were ordinary citizens have been persuaded by each of these and other groups to carry out group whims—including murder, suicide, and other violent acts—at the behest of the cult leader.

The cults whose names you tend to recognize are more visible because of their size, their flagrant behavior, and for some, their self-destructive tendencies. But there are many other groups that are subtle and sophisticated, yet just as insistent and just as dangerous. A multitude of cultic groups is actively recruiting, flourishing, and gaining money and power in the United States and throughout the world. These groups exploit and abuse their members or followers through deliberate mind manipulations, or thought-reform processes. These mind manipulations can be used in a number of contexts or settings.

In this book, we will be looking at two main categories of groups. The first is made up of the cults and cultlike groups who expose their recruits and members to organized psychological and social persuasion processes designed to produce attitudinal changes and to establish remarkable degrees of control by the group over these recruits' and members' lives. These cults deceive, manipulate, and exploit their members and hope to keep them for as long as possible.

The second category consists of the commercially sold large group awareness training programs and other "self-improvement," psychology-based, or miscellaneous organizations that use similar intense coordinated persuasion processes but ordinarily do not intend to keep their customers for long periods of membership. They prefer that adherents buy more courses and products and bring in more customers, staying around for perhaps a year or two.

Thus, groups in both categories use thought-reform processes. The originators of cults and thought-reform groups tend to conjure up coordinated programs of coercive influence and behavioral control using ages-old persuasion techniques in order to change people's attitudes around a vast array of philosophies, theories, and practices. These masterful manipulators appear to be aware that they need to put into place a packaged set of influence techniques, tactics, and strategies in order to convince others to follow them and go along with their bidding. Not every one of these groups meets the definition of a cult, but along with cults, all of them use thought-reform techniques in recruiting, changing, and exploiting followers. (See Chapter Three for a more detailed discussion of thought-reform processes.)

Do you have any idea how many cultic groups are disguised as legitimate enterprises—as restaurants, self-help groups, business training workshops, prosperity clubs, psychotherapy clinics, martial arts centers, diet plans, campus activities, and political organizations? Rather than withering away, as many people believe, cults and groups using thought-reform processes have grown like mushrooms after a rainstorm.

Currently, depending on how one defines a cult, there are anywhere from three thousand to five thousand cults in the United States alone. Over the past two decades as many as twenty million people have been involved for varying periods of time in one or another of these groups. And not only are the cult members affected, but millions more family members and loved ones worry and wonder, sometimes for years, about what has happened to their relatives or friends.

Not everyone who is approached by a cult recruiter ends up joining the group, and not everyone who joins stays forever. But enough do join and stay for long enough periods of time to make cults a pressing societal problem that merits serious inspection. And I'm not talking about a problem that can be dealt with by a philosophical debate or a hot exposé on a television talk show. The threat presented by cults goes much deeper than that. I'm talking about the very real threats to public health, mental health, political power, and democratic freedoms—as well as growing concerns over consumer issues—that become apparent as we learn how these manipulative and often unethical groups and programs have spread into not just the nooks and crannies but also the major sectors and institutions of our society.

Cults are no longer solely a concern for parents who observe their idealistic, and in some cases disaffected, young adult children being recruited, as was the case in the 1960s and 1970s. For in the 1980s and 1990s, we have seen cults seduce people of all ages and all income brackets. In the past, cults gained a foothold by attracting the so-called marginal people—the unaffiliated, the disenchanted, the disgruntled of each generation. But today's cultic groups have so professionalized their approaches and techniques of persuasion that they are moving well beyond the fringe and into the mainstream. They want you.

I have interviewed more than three thousand persons who have been in one or another—or in some cases in several—of the multitude of cults in the United States, as well as hundreds of relatives of cult members. I've also studied dozens of persons who have been involved with other high-control groups and numerous individuals, usually women, who have had their lives taken over by a single individual who controlled them as much as if they had been in a cult. From this life experience and more than fifty years of study, research, and clinical practice, I can only say that whenever I think I've heard it all, along comes new evidence that is even more outlandish than the last.

In this book, I attempt to explain how ordinary citizens leave their everyday lives and become part of groups that carry out acts ranging from bizarre and unethical to self-destructive and murderous. Cults seem to have no end to their peculiar practices. Cult leaders seem to have no end to their unconscionable behaviors and their capacity to abuse their followers. Cult members seem to have a stamina almost beyond human comprehension. And after they leave cults, former members clearly have a boundless spirit and unbeatable will to heal themselves, reclaim their independence, and come out on the positive side of horrific experiences—a spirit and a will that I can only admire and uphold, more and more with each person I meet.

Definitions and Characteristics

The noun *cult* tends to impart an image of a static organization. But like people in other groupings, people in a cult interact in special ways, and these ways change across time. It is in their inner workings that cults tend to be unusual, so it's not always easy to grasp the differences between an open society or organization and a cult. Sometimes people fail to consider how cults work because they mistakenly either write cults off as filled with a bunch of crazies or think cults are just like the regular groups they attend, such as the local Rotary Club, the PTA, or the Loyal Order of Moose.

The usual dictionary definitions of a cult are descriptive of certain aspects. But I also want to convey what life in various cults consists of and to convey a more dynamic picture of the processes that go on.

I prefer to use the phrase "cultic relationships" to signify more precisely the processes and interactions that go on in a cult. A cultic relationship is one in which a person intentionally induces others to become totally or nearly totally dependent on him or her for almost all major life decisions, and inculcates in these followers a belief that he or she has some special talent, gift, or knowledge.

For our purposes, the label *cult* refers to three factors:

1. The origin of the group and role of the leader
2. The power structure, or relationship between the leader (or leaders) and the followers
3. The use of a coordinated program of persuasion (which is called thought reform, or, more commonly, brainwashing)

What is labeled a cult by one researcher may not be identified as such by another. For example, some researchers count only religion-based groups, discounting the myriad cults formed around a variety of doctrines, theories, and practices. Using the three factors of leader, structure, and thought reform allows us to assess the cultic nature of a particular group or situation regardless of its belief system. So let's expand on these three factors to amplify our understanding.

Origin of the Group and Role of the Leader

In most cases, there is one person, typically the founder, at the top of the cult's structure, and decision making centers in him. (There are some female cult leaders, but most are male, and so for simplicity cult leaders will be referred to as male throughout this book.) These leaders typically have the following characteristics.

Cult leaders are self-appointed, persuasive persons who claim to have a special mission in life or to have special knowledge. For example, leaders of flying-saucer cults often claim that beings from outer space have commissioned them to lead people to special places to await a spaceship. Other leaders claim to have rediscovered ancient ways to produce enlightenment or cure disease, while yet others claim to have developed inventive scientific, humanistic, or social plans that will lead followers to "new levels" of awareness, success, or personal and political power.

Cult leaders tend to be determined and domineering and are often described as charismatic. These leaders need to have enough personal drive, charm, or other pulling power to attract, control, and manage their flocks. They persuade devotees to drop their families, jobs, careers, and friends to follow them. Overtly or covertly, in most cases they eventually take over control of their followers' possessions, money, and lives.

Cult leaders center veneration on themselves. Priests, rabbis, ministers, democratic leaders, and leaders of genuinely altruistic movements keep the veneration of adherents focused on God, abstract principles, or the group's purpose. Cult leaders, in contrast, keep the focus of love, devotion, and allegiance on themselves. In many cults, for example, spouses are forced to separate or parents forced to give up their children as a test of their devotion to their leader.

Structure: Relationship Between Leader and Followers

For a simple visual portrayal of a cult, imagine an inverted T. The leader is alone at the top, and the followers are all at the bottom.

Cults are authoritarian in structure. The leader is regarded as the supreme authority although he may delegate certain power to a few subordinates for the purpose of seeing that members adhere to his wishes and rules. There is no appeal outside of the leader's system to greater systems of justice. For example, if a schoolteacher feels unjustly treated by a principal, he or she can appeal to another authority. In a cult, the leader has the only and final ruling on all matters.

Cults appear to be innovative and exclusive. Cult leaders claim to be breaking with tradition, offering something novel, and instituting the only viable system for change that will solve life's problems or the world's ills. For example, an Arizona-based group purports to have found immortality and tells its followers that they too will live forever—but only by staying with the leaders, known by the initials of their first names, CBJ (Charles, BernaDeane, and James). CBJ is reported to have thirty thousand followers worldwide. Meanwhile, another group professes that by living with the group and learning a secret breathing method members will eventually be able to live on air alone. Almost all cults make the claim that their members are "chosen," "select," or "special," while nonmembers are considered lesser beings.

Cults tend to have a double set of ethics. Members are urged to be open and honest within the group and to confess all to the leader. At the same time, members are encouraged to deceive and manipulate nonmembers. In contrast, established religions and ethical groups teach members to be honest and truthful to all and to abide by one set of ethics. The overriding philosophy in cults, however, is that the ends justify the means, a view that allows cults to establish their own brand of morality, outside normal social bounds.

For example, one large group introduced the concept of "heavenly deception," another introduced "transcendental trickery," and some of the neo-Christian groups introduced terms such as "talking to the Babylonians" or referred to outsiders as the "systemites." Language such as this is meant to justify a double set of ethics, making it acceptable for members to deceive nonmembers.

Coordinated Program of Persuasion

Later, I will describe specific techniques of exploitative persuasion, that is, the various thought-reform processes used by cult leaders and cultlike groups to induce people to join, stay, and obey. Here, I describe general characteristics of this crucial factor in the definition of cults.

Cults tend to be totalistic, or all-encompassing, in controlling their members' behavior and also ideologically totalistic, exhibiting zealotry and extremism in their worldview. Eventually, and usually sooner rather than later, most cults expect members to devote increasing time, energy, and money or other resources to the professed goals of the group, stating or implying that a total commitment is required to reach some state such as "enlightenment." The form of that commitment will vary from group to group: more courses, more meditation, more quotas, more cult-related activities, more donations. Cults are known to dictate what members wear and eat and when and where they work, sleep, and bathe as well as what they should believe, think, and say. On most matters, cults promote what we usually call black-and-white thinking, an all-or-nothing point of view.

Cults tend to require members to undergo a major disruption or change in life-style. Many cults put great pressure on new members to leave their families, friends, and jobs to become immersed in the group's major purpose. This isolation tactic is one of the cults' most common mechanisms of control and enforced dependency.

Cults Are Not All Alike

Cults are not uniform nor are they static. Cults exist on a continuum of degrees of influence, from more to less extreme. There are live-in and live-out cults. Groups vary in levels of membership and degrees of involvement: for example, members on the periphery of a group usually are not privy to the costs, contents, and obligations of the later stages of membership and have little knowledge of the real purposes of the group or the amount of power wielded by the leader. Even within the same cult, rules, restrictions, and requirements may change from year to year, or from location to location, depending on outside pressures, local leadership, and the fancies of the leader.

The manner in which controls are put into place, the extent of control over details of members' behavior, and the blatancy of these controls also vary from cult to cult. In most live-in cults, every detail of life comes under group scrutiny. For example, there are dress codes, food restrictions, and enforced marriages or relationships. In such cults, the members generally live together at the headquarters or at specified locations around the country or overseas and work for cult-owned enterprises. However, there are also cults whose devotees appear to remain active in quite a few major aspects of the outside world, earning a living outside the cult. But for all practical purposes these individuals also live under rules governing such crucial features of their personal life as the people with whom they associate, what happens to their money, whether they raise their own children, and where they live.

Cults basically have only two purposes: recruiting new members and fund-raising. Established religions and altruistic movements may also recruit and raise funds. Their sole purpose, however, is not simply to grow larger and wealthier; such groups have as goals bettering the lives of their members or humankind in general, either in this world or in a world to come. A cult may claim to make social contributions, but in actuality these remain mere claims or gestures. In the end, all work and all funds, even token gestures of altruism, serve the cult. (In Chapter Four, I explore further these very significant differences between cults and legitimate social, business, or religious groups.)

In sum, the term *cult* is merely descriptive, not pejorative. It refers to the origins, social structure, and power structure of a group. The conduct of certain cults, however—especially groups that tend to overtly exploit and abuse people and engage in deceptive, unethical, and illegal conduct—does provoke the surrounding society into a critical stance.

Although cults have existed at different times in the United States, aggressive recruitment by certain cults in the late sixties drew some public attention to cults. Then the tragic mass suicide-murders in Jonestown in 1978 focused intense, worldwide attention on the cult phenomenon. People began to wonder how someone could get such total control of people that they would drink cyanide on his instructions. They saw other leaders marrying thousands of strangers in mass weddings. They read of a leader requiring his followers to switch marital partners and then submit to vasectomies. They learned of another leader instituting a "flirty fishing" policy that had women followers going into the streets as prostitutes to lure males to the group gatherings where they could be led to join the cult.

Various researchers' reports indicate that it's fair to estimate that between two million and five million Americans are involved in cults at any one time. Naturally, membership counts are rough. Some cults puff up their membership rolls in order to seem larger and more effective than they really are; others count as members every person who ever had any contact with the group, perhaps by signing a group-sponsored petition, buying a raffle ticket on the street, taking a personality test, or purchasing a book. Another group classifies as associate members everyone who ever signed a 3 × 5 card at a free dinner. Another counts as associates all who have attended a lecture, while some groups count only persons who have advanced through an initiation ceremony. Still other groups are highly secretive about their membership, revealing little or no reliable information. And there are countless groups, with anywhere from two or three followers to a dozen or more, that we learn about only indirectly or from members who leave. In general, cults do not stand up to be counted.

Cult Types

Remembering that many of the better-known cults in the late 1960s and early 1970s tended to be religious cults, some people today mistakenly think that all cults are religious. Another factor that may feed the idea that all cults are religious is that many of these groups incorporate as churches, because of tax and legal benefits given religious entities. However, it is not at all the case that all cults are religious. A cult can be formed around any content: politics, religion, commerce, self-improvement techniques, health fads, the stuff of science fiction, psychology, outer-space phenomena, meditation, martial arts, environmental life-styles, and so on. Yet the misconception that all cults are religious has left many unaware not only of the variety of cult contents but also of the plethora of cults, large and small, that has spread throughout our society.

Today, in fact, the fastest-growing cultic groups, competing with the religious cults for members, are those centered around New Age thinking and certain personal improvement training, life-styles, or prosperity programs. These latter cults are most likely to be the kind you or your friends may have come across or been influenced by, perhaps even seduced by, for a period of time.

A pied piper with sufficient determination and a touch of charm, charisma, seduction, or simply good sales skills can, with enough time and effort, secure a following around almost any topic. Regardless of the type of cult they have fostered, cult leaders induce the sad, the lonely, and the disaffiliated to join, as well as those who merely are available and who respond to an invitation at some vulnerable point in their lives.

In the United States, there are at least ten major types of cults, each with its own beliefs, practices, and social mores. The list below is not exhaustive, but most cults can be classified under one of the following headings:

1. Neo-Christian religious
2. Hindu and Eastern religious

3. Occult, witchcraft, and satanist
4. Spiritualist
5. Zen and other Sino-Japanese philosophical-mystical orientation
6. Racial
7. Flying saucer and other outer-space phenomena
8. Psychology or psychotherapeutic
9. Political
10. Self-help, self-improvement, and life-style systems

Cult names suggest further groupings and emphases. Some cults start their names with "The," implying that theirs is the only way to be, to think, or to live. Examples include The True Believers, The Way International, The Walk, The Process, The Foundation, The Body, The Farm, The Assembly.

Others groups emphasize the concept of family: The Family, The Love Family, The Family of Love, The Rainbow Family, The Forever Family, The Christ Family, The Lyman Family, The Manson Family.

Images of siblings provide other family models, such as Brother Julius, Brother Evangelist, Brother David, Great White Brotherhood, and countless other brotherhoods (or sometimes sisterhoods).

Many groups are designated simply as churches or temples: the Peoples Temple for example, or the Church of Armageddon—with such variations as the Word of . . . , or the People of . . . , or using Bible in the name.

New Age and psychotherapy groups take names such as The Center for Feeling Therapy, the Sullivanians, Alive Polarity Fellowship, Direct Centering, est, Sun Arts, Arica, and Silva Mind Control.

There is a plethora of Eastern-based groups, whose names are often formed around the name of the guru or mission. Both personal and other kinds of names abound in groups representing a variety of philosophies: Alamo Christian Foundation (Tony and Susan Alamo Foundation), Ecclesia Athletic Association, Bubba Free John and the Dawn Horse Communion, Emissaries of Divine Light, Kashi Ranch, Blue White Dove Foundation, and the No Name Group.

This kind of listing could go on and on, exposing the sheer numbers and scope of the cults around us. Yet, on one level, all cults are a variation on a single theme. And ultimately, that theme has nothing to do with belief. In cultic groups, the belief system— whether religious, psychotherapeutic, political, New Age, or com- mercial—ends up being a tool to serve the leader's desires, whims, and hidden agendas. The ideology is a double-edged sword: it is the glue that binds the member to the group, and it is a tool exploited by the leader to achieve his goals.

To understand cults we must examine structure and practice, not beliefs. As will be explained in later chapters, it is the thought- reform techniques used by skillful manipulators to ensure compli- ance and obedience among their followers that is, in the final analysis, what makes cults so worrisome and harmful.

Who Joins Cults?

When we hear of cults, scams, and individuals' being controlled and influenced by others, we instinctively try to separate ourselves from those persons. It seems a point of valor and self-esteem to insist that "no one could get *me* to do such things" when hearing about situations of intense influence. Just as most soldiers believe bullets will hit only others, most people tend to believe that their own minds and thought processes are invulnerable. "Other people can be manipulated, but not me," they declare.

The "Not Me" Myth

People like to think that their opinions, values, and ideas are invi- olate and totally self-regulated. They may grudgingly admit that they're influenced slightly by advertising. Beyond that, they want to preserve the myth that other people are weak-minded and easily influenced while they are strong-minded. Even though we all know human minds are open to influence—whether or not that is a comfortable thought—most of us defensively and haughtily proclaim, "Only crazy, stupid, needy people join cults. No one could ever get me to commit suicide or beat my kids or give my wife over to a cult leader. No one could ever talk me into anything like that."

As I hear people say that, I silently ask, "You want to bet?"

People also cherish a fantasy that manipulators confront, browbeat, and argue people into doing their bidding. They envision Big Brother wearing storm trooper boots, holding a gun to people's heads, and forcing them to change their beliefs, alter their personalities, and accept new ideologies.

The average person looks down on those who get involved in cults, get taken in a scam by some operator who bilks people, or remain in an abusive group or relationship for long periods. That only happens to weak and silly people, the person boasts, generating for herself or himself a category called "not me" in which to place the victims of cults, scams, and intense influence. There is an almost universal aversion to accepting the idea that we ourselves are vulnerable to persuasion. I have heard this from journalists, college professors, neighbors, passengers seated next to me on a plane, people I talk with in the street, graduate students, gardeners, salesclerks. Neither education, age, nor social class protects a person from this false sense of invulnerability.

Several years ago when I was lecturing in Switzerland, a Swiss psychiatrist opened the program by saying: "We have such an educated, close-knit, middle-class society, we have no cults here. Cults will never get an inroad in this country." I then provided literature containing the street addresses of various large, internationally known cults, as well as many small ones, operating in Zurich and other Swiss cities. Few, if any, countries in the world are without cults.

Yes, You

Despite the myth that normal people don't get sucked into cults, it has become clear over the years that everyone is susceptible to the lure of these master manipulators. In fact, the majority of adolescents and adults in cults come from middle-class backgrounds, are fairly well educated, and are not seriously disturbed prior to joining.

Research indicates that approximately two-thirds of those who have joined cults came from normal, functioning families and were demonstrating age-appropriate behavior around the same time they entered a cult. Of the remaining third, only about 5 to 6 percent had major psychological difficulties prior to joining a cult. The remaining portion of the third had diagnosable depressions related to personal loss (for example, a death in the family, failure to be admitted to a preferred university or training program, or a broken romance) or were struggling with age-related sexual and career dilemmas.

Certain family backgrounds may render some young people more vulnerable than others to the lure of cults. Cults offer instant, simplistic, and focused solutions to life's problems. Some families unwittingly foster a combination of indecisiveness and rebelliousness that makes the cult seem like a perfect solution to the young person seeking escape from the frustrations of the family situation. In such families, children are often constantly encouraged to be adventurous, be activists, be independent, go against the grain, or buck the system. Yet whenever the offspring become active, or choose an affiliation or rebel in some way, they are berated by these same parents for choosing the wrong activity or friends, doing the wrong thing, making the wrong decision. Pushing their children too much and too quickly to grow up and be adult, some parents tend to be less than helpful to these young people facing a variety of decisions. The children feel left to their own devices, and at the same time lack confidence in their own decision-making abilities.

A number of cult members are found to come from such family backgrounds.

Another kind of vulnerability, or stress factor, evolves when a person, especially an adolescent or young adult, feels overwhelmed by the sheer number of choices he or she needs to make, the ambiguity of life at this age, the complexity of the world, and the amount of conflict associated with many aspects of daily life. In addition to facing pressing personal decisions, many adolescents are attempting to come to grips with their overall values, beliefs, and purposes.

Many former cult members report that certain classes they took late in high school and early in college contributed greatly to their bewilderment. They commonly describe classes, teachers, and experiences that they felt destabilized their views of the world, leaving them frightened by the complexity of making seemingly endless decisions. Feeling lost and alone, they felt a need to find affiliation and some simple ways to make their lives work. Without intending to make such a choice, they found themselves swept along into a group that offered simple and guaranteed paths to follow, as was the case for the following student.

"Mary," an undergraduate on a campus of a large state university, was feeling low; she didn't know what she wanted to do when finished with college. But most of all, she was in three courses—psychology, sociology, and political science— in which the teachers were young, radical, and disturbing to Mary's outlook on life. She had begun the classes expecting to learn historical facts, read works of famous persons, and have good class discussions. But this year, things were different.

The personal outlooks and worldviews of the instructors seemed overwhelmingly pessimistic, nihilistic, and demoralizing to her. Each in his own way told her there is no reality: everyone sees whatever he or she thinks he or she sees, all things are relative, there is no right and wrong, and so on. The psychology instructor was involved with a New Age group and had the class meditate lengthily as part of each class period. Mary found this puzzling, as it seemed the instructor was really teaching a religious philosophy rather than general psychology. But at least, she felt, it was not as demoralizing as the other courses in which she was told life is pointless and meaningless.

A man in the school cafeteria invited her to the place where he lived, which turned out to be the local ashram of a guru. There Mary was told there was one, true, easy path to follow, which the guru would share with her. After a number of visits, Mary dropped out of school and moved into the ashram. Ten years later, her parents finally lured her out of the group. In counseling afterward, Mary told me that the university instructors had so destabilized her world that the guru group sounded like a dream come true: it seemed to have a sense of purpose, meaningfulness, paths to follow, and things that were agreed upon as good and bad. She later realized that at the time she met the guru group she was an easy subject to recruit into their ways.

Mary was typical of many college students who lack the social or familial stability to fend off the seductive lure of simple answers and whose susceptibility to cult recruitment increases as their view of the world around them becomes unsettled.

Something similar happens to many adult joiners. Many adults today are overwhelmed by the confusion and apparent coldness of our society: the senseless violence, the rampant homelessness, the lack of meaning, the widespread loss of respect for authority figures, the vast numbers of unemployed and marginalized, the insecurity and instability of the job market, the loss of family communication, the lessening role of the established religions, the failing sense of community or even neighborhood. No less bewildered than the adolescents, many mature adults are finding less and less to hold onto in today's technoculture. What does this create but ripe recruits for the multitude of manipulators and swindlers?

Nevertheless, the fact remains that even apart from unsettling socioeconomic conditions and certain relevant family factors, *any* person who is in a vulnerable state, seeking companionship and a sense of meaning or in a period of transition or time of loss, is a good prospect for cult recruitment. Although most contemporary cults primarily recruit young adults, preferably single, some—especially the neo-Christian cults—seek entire families, and even the elderly are targets for some groups.

What do the cults offer to lonely, depressed, or uncertain persons? In one form or another, each cult purports to offer an improved state of mind, an expanded state of being, and a moral, spiritual, or political state of righteous certainty. That supposedly beneficial state can be reached only by following the narrowly prescribed pathways of a particular group master, guru, or trainer. To grasp that approach to life, the new recruit—the *babe*, the *preemie*, the *trial member*, the *spiritual god-child*, the *lower consciousness one*, as certain groups label the beginner—must surrender his or her critical mind, must yield to the flow of force, must have childlike trust and faith. (The special methods used to manipulate recruits into such an accepting state of mind will be explored in detail in later chapters.)

Why Do They Join?

Those of us who have studied the modern-day cults have found that it is not one type of person who gets enmeshed with cults, but rather a person who has a combination of factors occurring nearly simultaneously. I have found that two conditions make an individual especially vulnerable to cult recruiting: being depressed and being in between important affiliations. We can be especially vulnerable to persuasion and suggestion because of some loss or disappointment that has caused a depressed mood or even mild to moderate clinical depression. And we're especially prone to the cults' kind of influence when we're not engaged in a meaningful personal relationship, job, educational or training program, or some other life involvement.

Vulnerable individuals are lonely, in a transition between high school and college, between college and a job or graduate school, traveling away from home, arriving in a new location, recently jilted or divorced, fresh from losing a job, feeling overwhelmed about how things have been going, or not knowing what to do next in life. Unsettling personal occurrences are commonplace: A high school senior is rejected by the college of her choice. A man's mother dies. A woman decides to sell her condo and travel after an unhappy ending to a long-term relationship. At such times, we are all more open to persuasion, more suggestible, more willing to take something offered us without thinking there might be strings attached.

A depressed and temporarily unaffiliated person is more likely to resonate to the offerings of a cult recruiter, particularly if the offering fits in with a personal interest or if the person feels at liberty to check out the invitation. Some people will respond to printed notices on kiosks and bulletin boards, others to media ads offering lectures and group meetings. Besides tapping the responses to those luring but deceptive ads, cults also use one-on-one recruiting techniques. In most cases, the actual recruitment grows out of such one-on-one contact between a cult recruiter and a temporarily or situationally vulnerable person.

Some of the larger cults have training manuals for recruiters and carry out drills on where and how to approach prospects, much as sales trainers train new salespersons. For example, former cult members who had been involved in recruiting while in their various cults told me the following:

- One cult member was directed to get a job in the registrar's office at a nearby university and to target anyone who came to drop out of courses. Such persons were depressed and needy and more likely to accept invitations to the cult's house near the campus than someone doing well at school.

• A female recruiter was instructed to stand outside the student counseling service and invite the lonely to the cult for a dinner-lecture and evening of fellowship.

• A number of recruiters were sent to tourist attractions in San Francisco, such as Fisherman's Wharf, to the French Quarter in New Orleans, and to tour-bus stations in major cities to look for visitors with British flags on their backpacks who were alone. (The British flags identified English speakers; it is just too difficult for cult members who speak only English to persuade and manipulate someone who does not speak English.)

• Recruiters were sent to social events at various churches to approach people who were standing alone. The recruiter was to invite the person to come to have pie and ice cream or some similar treat or to offer the person a ride home—anything to ingratiate the recruiter with the person.

Each cult has its own lures and tactics for getting new members and recruiting its type of person. The techniques just outlined are used by cults targeting mostly the under-thirty crowd. They often use these young adults to solicit funds on the streets of cities around the world and to recruit yet more members. These cults engage in direct solicitation from the gullible public, whereas other cults turn to their own members as a means of getting money, seeking out, for example, the elderly with pensions or property or professionals with decent salaries and good connections. Other groups want to recruit members into their pay-as-you-go programs and therefore target employed persons with money-making skills, to whom the cults will sell "courses," gradually hooking these people into greater and greater commitment to the group, as well as selling them more and more expensive courses. Some of these recruits end up leaving their jobs and working for the cult to pay for the courses.

Courses used to lure people into cults have a wide range: how to communicate, how to "scientifically reduce stress in your life," how to manage your office and become a millionaire, how to "get in control of your life," how to become a martial arts teacher, how to "live forever," how to detect if you have been abducted by space creatures and join with others who have had that experience, how to reach perfect enlightenment and govern the world, how to live past lives, and on and on. The courses are as varied as the gimmicks around which cults are formed. Offerings are worded as if the group were specifically made to benefit you. You usually do not learn the full story (and real purpose) of the cult until long after becoming embedded in the group. One of the most central criticisms of the current crop of cults hinges on their deceptive recruiting methods.

Recently, I was consulted about two separate situations that I believe show the worldwide ramifications of this problem. First, I interviewed two Russian students who had been brought to the United States by a cultic group under false pretenses. They had been promised full scholarship to a U.S. university. Instead, once they got here, they were put out in tourist areas to recruit new members.

Then I talked with some people who were trying to help a German family who had come to Berkeley to speak with their son, who had come to the United States to work in a summer camp. While on vacation in San Francisco, the young man had been recruited into a large cultic group. For eighteen months the family attempted to contact him, finally coming to America. But even while here, they were never able to be alone with him. In the course of the family's visit to Berkeley, the group sent the son off, some hundred miles away. In desperation, the family began to picket the group's local house and called local television stations, but eventually, the family had to return to Germany with no resolution in sight.

Myth of the Seeker

Another myth surrounding those who join cults is that these people go out looking for cults. Cult apologists capitalize on this notion and claim people seek out the very group they end up in. Some of these apologists are academicians who describe cult members as "seekers," because these researchers only study members *after* they are already in the group. In their claim that the cult member went out looking for a guru or self-appointed messiah, the apologists avoid attributing any agency to the cult. Instead, they describe a cult as if it were the Washington Monument, sitting still, waiting for tourists to visit. In fact, the cult leader, after securing a few followers, trains them to go out and recruit new members. Voluminous popular and academic literature counters the seeker theory, calling attention to the active, sophisticated, and unrelenting proselytizing engaged in by the majority of today's cults.

As we have seen, a cult can be defined in many ways, but for our purposes and to explain most modern-day cults, it is necessary to think of a process, not an event, and to view life in the cult as a process. Processes evolve and unfold, something goes on between people. There is an interaction, a transaction, a relationship established.

The act of joining a cult results from a process put in motion by a cult recruiter. Cult practices make it clear that recruits are propagandized and socialized to accept the life conditions of the group. These conditions are revealed slowly, and the recruits do not know where they are going when they start. How can they be seekers for a particular result when they are unaware of the final patterns and contents of the group that they join?

Those who put forth the seeker theory tend to look only at preselected surface features of the cults and claim that members had set out searching for the specific group they became involved with. Seeker theorists fail to study cult actions, the persuasion and influence techniques used. In working with several thousand individuals who have been in cults, I have not been told by one of them that she or he went out looking for a guru to set her or him up in prostitution, flower selling, cocaine dealing, gun smuggling, child abuse, or living off garbage, which were the ways these various individuals had ended up while in the cult. They had not been seeking *that*.

Former cult members commonly reveal that they were looking for companionship or the chance to do something to benefit themselves and mankind. They say they were not looking for the particular cult they joined and were not intending to belong for a lifetime. Rather, they were actively and/or deceptively pressured to join, soon found themselves enmeshed in the group, were slowly cut off from their pasts and their families, and became totally dependent on the group.

Blaming the Victim

At a recent meeting of the American Psychiatric Association, a young psychiatrist approached several speakers on the platform who were about to conduct a seminar on cults. He confidently asked them if they were "going to explain why cults attract people with borderline personality disorders." He said he had not worked with any ex–cult members, but that he "knew" that only borderline or psychotic persons—"strictly pathological types"—joined cults. The speakers invited him to be sure to stay and hear the program.

Two well-known social phenomena—the *just world concept* and *blaming the victim*—can help us understand what is going on in reactions like the one of this psychiatrist. Social psychologists have studied both these widespread human reactions and trace their origins to primitive times.

Basic to the just world concept is the widely held belief that if a person obeys the rules of society, nothing bad will happen to him or her. Rule-breakers, on the other hand, get punished. Punishment comes in the form of bad luck, disasters, illness, and loss. Thus victims of any disaster, crime, illness, or misfortune automatically fall into the category of blameworthy people. This primitive reasoning goes something like this: "Since I feel protected from evil and misfortune if I just obey the rules—because it *is* a just world—then I can separate myself from those who come to harm. They must have done something bad to have bad things happen to them."

Blaming victims is an almost universal response to misfortune happening to others. Women who get raped are often blamed. People will say that the rape victim was wearing a short dress, was out after 10 P.M., or was in a neighborhood where she should not have been. Therefore the rape is her fault. The same attitude is often taken toward victims of muggings: "Well, he was wearing a good suit in a bad neighborhood." Any parent reading this realizes how often she or he has fussed at a child, blaming the young one for some misfortune. Across time, this same parent has no doubt been blamed for her or his own misfortunes. What husband has not said, "If you had not been driving in that part of town, you wouldn't have gotten a nail in your tire."? Or what wife has not said, "If you had worn your jacket, you wouldn't have caught a cold."?

Similarly, when somebody goes into a cult, the tendency is for the society to say that there must be something wrong with that person. There must be some personal defect, otherwise he or she would not have joined such a group. Since the public continues to regard cult members as stupid, crazy, and weak-minded, the near-universal public response is: "It's his fault. He went out looking for what he got." In our society, there is a strong taboo on being victimized through scams, influence, and deceptions, and breaking this taboo makes the cult victim even more scorned.

We also have a tendency to blame families and relatives, saying or implying that they must have failed in some way, otherwise their offspring would never have joined a cult. One woman came up to me at a talk I was giving in London and said, poignantly, "We parents are made to look like the abusers and the menace."

The tendency to blame victims prevents both lay and professional persons from seeing that most individuals who become involved in cultic relationships are a type of victim insufficiently recognized and understood. If a man in the jungle walks near a river and a crocodile bites his leg, the unlucky victim will be blamed for getting close enough to the water that a crocodile could harm him. Few will take the time to learn that the crocodile was lying in wait, hidden, and the man had no idea danger was so close. So, too, when an old lady is bilked out of her money by a swindler, her friends are prone to say it was her fault for being gullible. So it is also when a person becomes involved with a cult. The person is blamed for being a seeker, gullible, or mentally aberrant. The actions of the cult are overlooked in the appraisal.

The general public now recognizes four classes of victims. I don't encourage people to think of themselves as victims forever, as has become popular in certain segments of the self-help movement in the United States. Nevertheless, I think the victim analysis is helpful to show how getting duped by the cults is as common as buying a pair of shoes that don't fit.

The first class of victims includes the victims of violent crimes; the second class, the victims of natural disasters and serious illnesses; the third class, the victims of terrorists and kidnappers; and the fourth class, the victims of civil torts, able to seek redress through the courts for personal injuries, malpractice, and other wrongful things that have happened to them. But I see also a fifth class of victims: those who have been in situations of *enforced dependency* (as I call them) as a consequence of having been subjected to thought-reform processes. In essence, a thought-reform program is a behavioral reconstruction program, a program of systematic manipulation using psychological and social techniques (see Chapter Three). It is commonly known as brainwashing, and yes, it does exist. The cult member falls into this fifth class of victims.

We all are being influenced all the time. And we all are potentially vulnerable to a cult's pitch, especially as our society becomes more and more commercialized, violent and alienating, dishonest and corrupt, polarized and without structure. To counter the blaming mentality, we must, as a society, seek educational and informational preventive programs to teach about open versus deceptive recruitment and to expose the manipulative and unethical techniques used by various cults to keep members guiltily bound to the group.

If you buy a pair of shoes that don't fit, you can usually return them. But once you join a cult, it may be years before you get out.

For me, Waco was a replay of Jonestown, when 912 people died at the direction of their leader, Jim Jones, in a remote South American jungle. Jones also ordered the murder of U.S. Congressman Leo J. Ryan and four journalists who had gone to Guyana at the behest of relatives who had tried for years to get the world to heed the conditions of slavery under which their loved ones were held. Of those who were forced by Jones to drink cyanide-laced Fla-Vor-Aid, 276 were children, many of them sent to live with his group in California but then transported by Jones to the jungle where they died.

I was shocked when, less than six weeks after the Jonestown tragedy, a man at a party attended by university professors and their families remarked, "Those people in Jonestown really got what they were looking for. What kind of insanity leads people to join a cult like that? I guess cults keep some of the demented and stupid off the streets. No one could ever argue me into one of those groups." I talked with him about how cults evolve and operate. But he had said aloud what many people think: that only the demented and crazy get into cults.

For a time in 1993, David Koresh's cult in Waco became the center of attention, much as Jonestown had in 1978. A big splash in the news, then people back off from noticing the cults and the exploitative persuasion that surrounds us all. After the horror of Jonestown receded into the past, journalists asked, "Are cults still a big thing or did they die out after Jonestown?" Then after Waco, they asked, "How many more cults are there like that one?" But even when told there are many others, the journalists join the average person in not comprehending that—as we shall see in the chapters ahead—they or a member of their own families may already be enmeshed in a cult.

2

A Brief History of Cults

History tells us something about the periods when cults thrive. It appears that there have been legions of self-appointed messiahs, gurus, or pied pipers (I use the terms interchangeably) throughout time. But these types, ever present in our midst, only obtain substantial followings in certain periods. Traditionally, these periods have been marked by unusual social or political turbulence or breakdowns in the structure and rules of the prevailing society. Such are the times when cults flourish.

Pied pipers attract only modest followings in eras when a society is functioning in a way that conveys structure and a sense of social solidarity. Citizens understand their expected paths in these eras, and most members of society know the acceptable behaviors—whether they like them or not. However, when segments of society cannot see where they fit in, what the rules are, or what the socially agreed-upon answers to life's big questions are, then, like a dormant disease, the ever-present potential cult leaders take hold and lure followers to their causes.

These determined self-designated gurus seem always to be lurking on the sidelines ready to step in and offer answers to life's problems. They claim they have the only and sure way of life. They induce people to follow them by touting a special mission and special knowledge. The special mission is to preach the contents of a supposedly "secret" learning, which the leaders assert can only be revealed to those who join them.

Cult leaders usually claim that they have access to either ancient knowledge that they alone have reclaimed or new knowledge that they alone have discovered, or some blend of these two, and that this circumstance qualifies them for their special mission in life. Whether the lure is warmed-over ancient lore or the most avant-garde secrets of the universe, followers are expected to step into the elite compound, community, or sphere of the leader. To do so usually means leaving behind family and friends and forsaking most of the ordinary world. In return for participating in this elite group, followers are told that they will be let in on the special knowledge.

Historically, we have seen that as the fabric of a society unravels, self-appointed leaders easily recruit a following. People at a loss to make sense of the mayhem around them look for direction and become more approachable and vulnerable to the manipulations and exploitations of these skillful con artists. Certainty and simple solutions for the complex problems of decision making become attractive offerings in a world that appears to be unstable and rapidly changing.

For example, cults burgeoned after the fall of Rome. At the time of the French Revolution, cults spread not only in France but across Europe. When the Industrial Revolution came to England, cults spread once again as thousands of people moved into the larger centers where industries were building. European colonization resulted in the emergence of various cults in other parts of the world as well.

Cults sprang up in Japan after World War II, when the social structure in the defeated country left many people not knowing where they fit in or how to make decisions in the new and puzzling world around them. Some of these Japanese-based cults have now spread into other countries. And most recently, we see cults swarming to and emerging in Eastern Europe, where the breakup of the Communist regimes has left a social and ideological void—and once again, masses of people vulnerable and susceptible to the cults' lure.

Cults in the 1800s

A comparison is often made between the rise of contemporary cults (from the 1960s onward) and the Second Great Awakening, a religious upheaval that occurred in the United States between 1820 and 1860. At that time, as now, there were rapid social and economic shifts in U.S. society, giving rise to a period of uncertainty, schism, and reorganization.

In looking at what occurred during the Second Great Awakening, we can gain some insight into why cults have taken hold and flourished over the past three decades. And although the Second Great Awakening gave rise primarily to religious groups, I emphasize once again that not all cults, especially today, are religious and therefore need to be analyzed from a perspective of religious history or sociology of religion. My purpose in describing this earlier era is to show the link between cults and socioeconomic changes and how both religious and secular cults emerge in periods of change and instability, conditions that are certainly present in our world today. As I will stress throughout, whether the group in question is popularly called a cult, a sect, a new religious movement, a New Age group, or a thought-reform group is not my concern. My focus is on groups that exhibit the three factors discussed in Chapter One concerning the role of the leader, the group's structure, and the use of a coordinated persuasion program meant to bring about behavioral change.

New religious sects arise when segments of society feel their religious needs are not fulfilled by the mainstream religions. In part, the marginal groups at the time of the Second Great Awakening—blacks, women, and young people—were those who joined and, in some cases, came to lead various sects. Other evidence indicates that people affected by urbanization, geographical relocation, and the mechanization of their jobs were most sympathetic to the new religious groups. Ultimately, a broad segment of the population became involved in the revivalist movement. This matches our experience: initially, the present-day cults attracted marginal populations, but now they are successfully recruiting among all segments of society.

As a result of socioeconomic changes in the 1800s, the U.S. evangelical movement shifted from a minor religious trend into a major religious expression. Personal conversion, or a person's actual involvement in his or her own salvation, became the most important religious act. Faith was no longer a matter of waiting but of initiation. Revivals became the norm and were carried on throughout the country. The revivalists then set off the next stage of development. Revival meetings and the preachers who led them were controversial and engaged in ideological confrontation, causing schisms within denominations to occur everywhere. The polarization of ministries and congregations, accusations of factionalizing, and ensuing in-fighting led to groups splitting from the smallest to the largest congregations.

As a result, many new religious sects emerged throughout this period. So long as the economic and social environment was unstable, there was a need for and interest in new ideas and new movements. The beliefs, practices, and impact of the sects varied greatly. Some were radical, others conservative; some strict, others loosely bound; some held close to their parent institution, others flung themselves far afield; some were short lived, others survived to be among us today. These sects of the 1800s can be categorized according to their purposes and beliefs.

Regenerative sects merely wanted to make changes within a particular denomination. They were seen as the least divisive of the sects and appeared to represent a fight between new and old schools of thought. Examples of this category are the Presbyterian new school, the Congregational new school, the Methodist Episcopal Church, and the Lutheran General Synod.

Schismatic sects stood for radical transformations in beliefs and permanent separation from their parent denomination. They provided actual alternatives for their followers. Most were evangelical, adopting narrow interpretations of the Bible and strict codes of behavior. Included here are the Missouri Synod and the Millerite, Mennonite, Shaker, Unitarian, Universalist, and Seventh-Day Adventist sects.

Cultic sects substituted their own beliefs for Christianity and from the start were completely independent of established religion. These groups offered new and unique ways of viewing the world, sometimes with scientific or pseudoscientific interpretations. They also formulated new ways to classify physical and psychic phenomena. This category includes spiritualism, Swedenborgianism, Mesmerism, phrenology, homeopathy, and astrology. Most of these groups were not cohesive and were somewhat vague in their ideology. Although no strong institutions came out of the cultic sects, their impact was to greatly broaden the spectrum of what is called religion in America.

Quasi-religious sects touted specific political or social beliefs with an accompanying structure, and minimized traditional religion. Here are classed communal and socialist movements such as Owenism, Fourierism, and the Oneida Community as well as abolitionism and agrarian reform. In these movements, secular ideas dominated, and these groups were considered the most radical.

The westward movement in the United States swept countless religious sects and cults across the nation. In the hundred years after the gold rush, at least fifty well-defined and well-studied utopian cults were established in California alone. The majority were religious and lasted on the average about twenty years, with the secular variety usually enduring only half that long. Most purported to offer health benefits of one kind or another. Many similar cults were established elsewhere in the United States, some becoming transformed by their own success. For example, the Oneida Community and the Amana Society were two major cults that evolved into enterprises far different from their founders' intent.

Oneida Community

Founded in Oneida, New York, in 1848, the Oneida Community was a utopian settlement that experimented with religious and social theories. Starting at age twenty, founder John Humphrey Noyes experienced several conversions and revelations. A lawyer trained at Dartmouth, he left the field of law and went on to the Yale Divinity School. While there, he had a revelation that told him that anyone who gave himself completely to God could live without sin, or, in other words, become perfect. So he gave himself to God and from that time on considered himself perfect.

The first members of his community were his immediate family and in-laws. In time, others joined. By 1849 there were 140 members; in 1880 there were 288. The members were sometimes called Perfectionists, because of their belief in the possibility of reaching perfection. They lived a simple life, with early morning prayer followed by work in the fields, and Bible study and mutual criticism in the evenings. The community was established on the principles of Bible-based communism: all property was held in common. Members also favored the practice of "complex marriage," or free love, and rejected monogamy. Complex marriage meant that all adult members were considered married to each other, and children were raised collectively.

The idea for complex marriage apparently came to Noyes for mundane not spiritual reasons. Noyes, already married to a wealthy woman who shared his views and backed him financially, began to covet the wife of another Oneidan. Through fancy talking and "praise be's," Noyes managed to convince his own wife and the other couple of the saintliness of complex marriage. This perhaps more than any other ideology became the hallmark of the Oneida Community for the next thirty years and caused varying degrees of controversy in the surrounding communities.

It didn't take long for the Oneida Community to evolve into a tightly structured system, with Noyes at the helm deciding who would pair with whom, when children should be born, and so on. Reportedly, Noyes made sure to pair himself at least once with every woman. On the surface the Oneidans appeared tranquil and productive. The community gradually flourished financially due to varied industries, including the manufacture of steel traps and silverware. Faced with increasing hostility toward the Oneidan's marriage system from neighbors and with other social forces, however, Noyes feared for his life and fled to Canada.

In 1881, the Oneidans abolished complex marriage and several other practices of communistic sharing. The community also reorganized as a joint-stock company at that time, officially ending the social experiment. The company continued to operate and has remained a successful commercial enterprise, widely known today for the manufacture of silver plate.

Amana Society

The Amana Society, or the Society of True Inspiration, is the last surviving branch of a pietistic, separatist sect that espoused a primitive form of Christianity and formed an utopian organization. The sect was founded in Germany in 1714. In 1842, one of the leaders, Christian Metz, took eight hundred members out of Germany and settled in Ebenezer, New York. In 1855, they moved to Iowa and took the corporate name Amana Church Society. The community adopted a system of pure communism administered by church elders and maintained seven communal villages for ninety years.

The belief held by this group was that God spoke to them through "an inspired instrument," originally Christian Metz. The instrument was known to shake sometimes for an hour before receiving God's message, which most often was some form of urgent appeal to the followers to live an even holier life. The person who was seen as inspired was regarded as the spiritual leader, the only one worthy of receiving divine guidance. This ideology held the group together and was the justification for certain demands and rules of behavior.

The Amanites rejected anything that was considered "worldly," such as sports, modern dancing, card playing, and personal adornment. Members did not leave the community without special permission, and interactions with visitors and nonmembers were restricted and controlled. Celibacy was preferred, and those who remained celibate were awarded privileged status. Once engaged, couples were to wait two years before getting married. Like the Oneidans, Amanites practiced mutual criticism, often in public sessions.

With the advancement of technology, transportation, and industry, the outside world encroached more and more on this isolated and insular community. As their relationship to the external world changed, the Amanites were also forced to change. In 1932, the community was reorganized as the new Amana Society, with a church group and an industrial group. Many communistic practices were dropped, and all members were issued stock in the profit-sharing society, with more than $33 million worth of assets being split among its members. The Amana Society is now a producing and marketing cooperative of about fifteen hundred members.

This early era of sects and cults in the United States opened the way for unconventional movements and leaders to take hold in our society. Once the lid was lifted off this cauldron of new and sometimes bizarre beliefs, gurus of every stripe could stir the pot and come up with a new potion. A precedent was set for criticizing the established religions, the dominant society, the traditional ways of doing things. Popping up in every corner were itinerant preachers and faith healers, seers and mediums, traveling medicine men and shamans offering magic elixirs, and a wave of idealists professing radical politics and social systems.

Some cultlike activities, along with the beginnings of a new counterculture, emerged again in the 1940s and 1950s after World War II and the Korean War. Then a new set of disturbances in U.S. culture welled up during the 1960s with the expansion of an unpopular war in Southeast Asia, massive upheavals over civil rights, and a profound crisis in values defined by unprecedented affluence on the one hand and potential thermonuclear holocaust on the other. These glaring contradictions aggravated an already disjointed society into an even more unsettled state.

The 1960s: Fertile Ground for Cults

By the late sixties the United States was experiencing the kind of setting out of which new cults have often arisen. As the nation went through massive social and political changes—the drug culture, protest marches, anti–Vietnam War demonstrations, civil disobedience, student rebellions, the sexual revolution, and breakdowns in family life—the social climate was ripe for cult leaders to appear.

As we've learned, past cults often appealed to the marginal groups in the society of their period. In the sixties, the disenchanted young people were not those from economically marginal families but were the disenfranchised and the critics of the mainstream culture. Many U.S. youth were caught up in at least one of three popular rebellions: against political and economic monopolies (the New Left); against racial injustice (the civil rights movement); and against materialism in all its manifestations (the counterculture).

Even though we don't think of the counterculture movement as religious, there was an enormous draw in it toward things spiritual and Eastern, a draw that can be attributed to a number of factors. There was, for example, a large element of spiritualism in the back-to-the-land movement: people were "getting in touch" with nature, the rhythms of life, and the cosmic and universal. At the same time, this spiritualism was reinforced by the way some of the well-known radical leaders took on new names and new personas.

Richard Alpert became Baba Ram Dass, exhorting youth to "Be Here Now," while Timothy Leary, the granddaddy of LSD, cried, "Tune in, turn on, and drop out." Tuning in meant going inside your head, and being here now meant reaching out to understand everything. Besides the Beatles and Creedence Clearwater Revival, many young adults were listening to Indian musicians Ravi Shankar and Ali Akbar Khan. A wide spectrum of the so-called youth movement listened to sitar music and took hallucinogenic drugs.

The sixties' alternative life-style included transcendence of the self and personal enlightenment, a belief in world peace, free love, a desire for social change, and rejection of the traditional. What hippie didn't dream of trekking to Nepal? Who didn't have a worn-out copy of *The Tibetan Book of the Dead* in her knapsack? Who wouldn't consider making a move without first throwing the three brown Chinese coins with square holes in the centers and consulting the *I Ching*? Who wasn't enthralled with Carlos Castaneda and the teachings of Don Juan or tarot cards or astrological charts? Or who wasn't dabbling in witchcraft and going to covens? The world became vast, mysterious, unpredictable, yet knowable—but only with the aid of mystical instruments and wise teachers.

This fascination with both the spiritual and the exotic was surely a reaction to an ugly, unpopular war in Vietnam and a discredited government, and an expression of boredom with traditional values and nuclear families that were supposed to look like the Cleavers of *Leave It to Beaver*. Young people faced the complexity and privileges of a world that was advancing so fast anything seemed possible—yet at the same time everything seemed out of control. Citizens and police were fighting in the streets. Those working for social change—from the Kennedys and Martin Luther King, Jr., to the more militant black power organizations—were being set up for slaughter. The so-called military-industrial complex was making the threat of nuclear war a real possibility. No wonder a soft-spoken, smiling, gentle man with flowing robes could be seen to have the answer.

And so, some of our youth were vulnerable to recruitment into the myriad active neo-Christian and Eastern-style cults that emerged in this period of social upheaval and discontent. Cults such as the Hare Krishnas, the Children of God, Transcendental Meditation, The Way International, the Tony and Susan Alamo

Foundation, The Love Family, the Divine Light Mission, and the Unification Church—became youth cults, targeting primarily the young who felt estranged from their families and the establishment. These cults offered father or divinelike figures to youth needing models and identification.

Each self-appointed messiah claimed to have The Truth, the answer, the solution, and called for commitment, sacrifice, and zeal. Terms such as meditation, yoga, transcendence, and enlightenment became practically household words in the late 1960s and early 1970s.

Eventually, drug abuse and violent predators took an awful toll among the counterculture's generation of hippies. Many fled to form colonies, sometimes called communes, characterized by their "hang loose" ways. Those communes that endured through the 1960s or appeared during the 1970s—perhaps two or three thousand in North America alone—can generally be differentiated from cults in three respects.

1.   Cults are established by strong or charismatic leaders who control power hierarchies and material resources. Communes, on the other hand, tend to minimize organizational structure and deflate or expel power seekers.

2.   Cults possess some revealed "word" in the form of a book, manifesto, or doctrine, whereas communes invoke general commitments to peace and libertarian freedoms and a distaste for the parent culture's establishments.

3.   Cults create fortified boundaries, confining their membership in various ways and attacking those who would leave as defectors, deserters, or traitors; they recruit new members with ruthless energy and raise enormous sums of money; and they tend to view the outside world with increasing hostility and distrust as the organization ossifies. In contrast, communes are like nodes in the far-flung reticulum of the counterculture. Their boundaries are permeable membranes through which people come and go relatively unim-

peded, either to continue their pilgrimages or to return to a society regarded by the communards with feelings ranging from indifference to amusement to pity. Most communes, thus defined, seem to pose relatively little threat to society. Many cults, on the other hand, are increasingly perceived as dangerous both to their own members and to others.

Many of the communes faded quickly, for they did not offer the security, hope, and structure youth were seeking. Those young people who did not join a commune, or who tried communal living and left disappointed, often sought other solutions. Many were skillfully recruited into the apparent security of paternalistic religious and secular cults, which have been multiplying at an astonishing rate ever since.

The 1970s: Cults to Expand Awareness

As we moved into the seventies, we witnessed an era in which psychological awareness, consciousness expansion, and the human potential movement were strong influences. Young adults were told that mind-expanding experiences, or "mind trips," would bring new nirvanas. Thus, the first wave of cults, which had drawn heavily on Eastern philosophies in which meditation, yoga, and exotic practices were prominent, was soon supplemented by neo-Christian, political, and psychology-based groups, with an occasional surprising combination of ideologies.

In order to convey the wide-ranging nature of the many groups that have emerged in the past several decades, I have named many types of groups under several broad categories in the following descriptions of the groups that first flourished in the 1970s and 1980s. However, no category and no group within it should be viewed rigidly. Also, not all the groups mentioned in a category necessarily fall within the definition of a cult; some have been included, as the reader will see, in order to provide a full sense of the emerging social history and because their *content* could, under the right circumstances, be adopted by a self-proclaimed leader as cult content.

Transformational

The notion that we could psychologize life in America was widespread in the 1970s. The psychologizing of our society was based on the hope that each of us would become sensitive to cultural, racial, and ethnic differences and help to create a more integrated, genuine melting-pot society. After World War II, sensitivity training programs were commonly found in colleges, business training seminars, and private institutions, but these were soon superseded by encounter groups, whose techniques focused on making people change faster through confrontations with their peers in small groups. The idea was to meet the inner other and the inner you.

It was a natural progression for cultic groups and others using thought-reform techniques to add the psychological techniques from the sensitivity, encounter, and group therapy movements into the behavioral change programs used for new members. Now gaining attention were groups like Charles Dederich's drug rehabilitation program, Synanon, and miscellaneous groups that provided the right mix of personal transformation and exotic undertones to attract followers.

Political

The political groups were less visible than the others, as they were for the most part surviving clandestinely, following strict revolutionary rules. Emerging out of this period are the National Caucus of Labor Committees (NCLC); Venceremos; the Symbionese Liberation Army (soon to make national headlines for the Patricia Hearst kidnapping); the Democratic Workers Party and all of its front organizations, such as the Rebel Workers Organization, the Grass Roots Alliance, and U.S. Out of Central America; the New

Alliance Party and its storefront affiliates; and the National Labor Federation (NATLFD) and its many guises, such as California Homemakers Association, Eastern Farm Workers, and Western Service Workers. These left-wing political groups grew out of the vestiges of the antiwar movement and attracted hardworking idealists who did not want to give up on the struggle for social change.

Some of the teachings of what scholars have labeled right-wing *identity groups*—for example, the Posse Comitatus, LaPorte Church of Christ, White Aryan Resistance (WAR), the Silent Brotherhood, United American Front, the Church of the Creator (COTC), Aryan Nation, and The Covenant, the Sword and the Arm of the Lord (CSA), and racist skinheads—were also incorporated by some small extremist cults throughout the country.

Large Group Awareness Training

Another new type of group that became popular in the early seventies revolved around large group awareness training, or LGAT. LGAT groups represented commercially sold New Age thinking and the mass marketing of powerful therapeutic strategies carried out in large groups by nonprofessionals. The draw of these groups was the idea that each person is able to create his or her own reality. They used encounter group and hypnotic techniques to destabilize participants' view of the world. Strong peer pressure was used to finish the job and produce conformity.

Between 1971 and 1985, in particular, a number of LGAT groups gained large followings and subsequent notoriety, and some are still active in the 1990s. LGAT groups included est and its offshoots, such as Transformation Technologies and the Forum (Werner Erhard); Lifespring (John Hanley); Silva Mind Control (José Silva); Direct Centering (Gavin Barnes, aka Bayard Hora); Actualizations (Stewart Emery); ONE (Oury Engolz); Life Training (W. R. Whitten and K. B. Brown); Movement of Spiritual Inner Awareness (MSIA) and Insight Seminars (John-Roger Hinkins); PSI World (Thomas D. Wilhite); and Arica Institute

(Oscar Ichazo). This particular brand of New Age group gained significant access into the business world, an event that will be addressed in greater detail in a later chapter.

Spiritual

Another successful grouping combined Eastern and Western religious elements with a strong dose of transpersonal psychology and mysticism. Personal spiritual experiences were promoted, aided by talismans and seers. Potions, oils, crystals, magic wands, fortune-telling cards, sacred ashes, visions and trances, meditation, yoga, massage, and bodywork—including in some cases sexual touching and sexual acts—became the tools of the breed of pied piper that led these groups. As is not the case in other categories, many female leaders flourish here. Beliefs in karma (the Eastern version of predestination) and in psychic phenomena, such as auras, astral projections, past lives, and rebirthing, were the founding ideologies of these groups.

Spiritual groups included the Bhagwan Shree Rajneesh community; devotees of Sathya Sai Baba; the Church Universal and Triumphant led by Elizabeth Clare Prophet; the California-based Fellowship of Friends and certain other "Fourth Way" groups whose teachings are based on the works of G. I. Gurdjieff and P. D. Ouspensky; and some but not all groups formed around the study of *A Course in Miracles*, a three-volume text supposedly spoken by Jesus Christ over a period of seven or eight years to Helen Schucman, a psychologist employed at the time in the psychiatry department at Columbia University.

The 1980s: Psychological, Occult, and Prosperity Cults

As social and economic climates have changed, so has the nature of some cultic organizations. In the early to mid 1980s, there was a burst of new cults, including psychological, or psychotherapy, cults, occult groups, and prosperity groups (sometimes also called commercial cults).

Psychological

More and more people began to be caught up in psychotherapy cults, in which either professionals go astray and have multiple relationships with clients and patients or nonprofessionals form "therapy" groups. In both instances, cultic relationships occur and the therapists or pseudotherapists become landlords, employers, financial advisors, and lovers, sometimes having "patients" move in and live with them, perform household chores, and turn in paychecks to the leader who directs their lives. (See Chapter Seven for a more detailed description of therapy cults.)

Occult

Occult groups multiplied in the 1980s as well, an extension of the dabbling in the occult that occurred in the 1960s and the spiritual feminism that grew out of the women's movement of that same period and later. Occult groups espouse an interest in topics that appear to them to be hidden, secret, and esoteric, including the search for secret techniques to alter consciousness and the development of secret doctrines to explain existence and experience.

Occultism covers far more groups than those that deal in Satanism, black magic, astrology, and fortune telling. The most recent occult groups revolve around a fascination with mysterious origins, magic books, and special formulas. Their beliefs often, but not always, include a spoken disdain for mainstream religion, especially Christianity.

Occult groups range from the well-known Anton LaVey's Church of Satan and Michael Aquino's Temple of Set to individual dabblers in Satanism and the occult. Teens taken with secret rituals and handshakes also emerged in this period and some have been known to carry out antisocial and criminal acts.

Channeling also became quite popular in the early to mid 1980s. A person who calls herself or himself a channeler supposedly is a voice vehicle, speaking for an entity or person who lived centuries ago but is giving modern-day advice about finances, lifestyles, and so forth. It is my impression that channeling is a reframing and renaming of the old activity of mediumship. Mediums communicated with the dead. They held their sessions in dimly lit or dark rooms and contacted the loved ones who had died during the lifetimes of those attending the sessions. The New Age version avoids mention of the dead, and the channeler is like a television antenna, receiving messages from "entities," not the dead. Channeling makes it all very jolly and upbeat to hear from a centuries-gone entity. Those using channelers are supposed to hear not a spirit, not a voice from beyond the grave, but the advice of a powerful entity who has retained magical power to communicate over, usually, thousands of years. Controversial channeler J. Z. Knight, for example, claims to speak for Ramtha, a 35,000-year-old entity.

Prosperity

With the tightening of the economy in the late 1980s, a number of pied pipers appeared who offered prosperity-minded schemes, often professing as part of their pitch that positive thinking coupled with psychological awareness will bring personal prosperity. Prosperity groups continue to flourish in the 1990s, and most are financial scams. For example, somewhat charismatic schemers using this approach entice young working adults to move into a group living situation run by a leader who usually "psychologizes" about trust, integrity, and other virtues, using the vocabulary and experiential exercises of the human potential movement and encounter groups. These techniques keep members dependent on the central figure for both relational and living arrangements.

Eventually the conditions resemble those in the well-known cults. Members lose contact with their families and old friends, put all free time and money into the group, drop their careers, and work at low-level jobs with hours that permit more time with the leader and the group and less with the outside world. The personality changes formerly seen in members of exotic groups have now become prevalent in those living in these smaller cultic groups.

Examples of New Cults

The following experiences of two women illustrate the new cults' undue influence, which both resembles and differs from the more widely recognized involvement individuals have with established and better known cults. We look at a prosperity cult and a self-improvement cult.

"Tricia" was forty-two, recently divorced, lonely, and facing a future she had not planned for. Her divorce settlement was sparse, and she had negligible personal savings. Now a clerk in a small cosmetics boutique, she felt the need to get a better job and more training and education. She saw a notice in a coffee shop, offering a seminar based on discoveries of new ways for humans to think, enabling each person to prosper no matter what was going on politically or economically. Each person would learn how to "gather money, power and love," promised the ad. "Learn to think from a place of *having*, not from a basis of needing."

Tricia was puzzled by the ad but also intrigued. When she phoned, she was told she could begin that very night. The meeting was in a well-furnished home with about twenty women and five men present. "Glenda," the leader, was about fifty-five years old, expensively dressed; her partner, "Jonathan," was about forty, handsome, suave, seductive, and attentive to Tricia and the other attendees. Glenda lectured impressively about how "we are all gatherers—gatherers of money, power, and love." Those present were told that the reason they had not gathered all they wanted was because they made decisions "coming from poverty rather than from abundance."

Tricia soon caught on to the new jargon and felt some excitement about new possibilities in her life. Glenda outlined all the events those present were "committed to" in the coming weeks and included Tricia without hesitation. Each seminar cost fifteen dollars, with other meetings variously priced. Glenda preached that prosperity was a matter of the mind, that one could find a way to materialize money when it was needed. Members were admonished to break away from old friends who thought in terms of poverty, to spend their free time only with the group to keep their thinking right.

Tricia became completely involved and poorer than ever. She was expected to attend each of the many events, ranging from potluck suppers to special movie nights at which group members viewed Glenda's films of the big homes with swimming pools that had been "gathered" by other members. Soon Tricia was purchasing individual lessons from Glenda, sessions in which Glenda hypnotized her and taught relaxation and breathing exercises to produce "mental prosperity." Before long, Tricia was paying two hundred dollars a week to Glenda and was in debt, having borrowed from her mother and other relatives and having "maxed out" her credit cards. At this point, Glenda told Tricia to move into Our Big House, as it was called, with the group.

Tricia gave her furniture, her other valuables, and her car to Glenda. Glenda used such arrangements as proof that members were all thinking right, living better than ever, and being prosperity minded. It was only after about two years, when Tricia was again pressing her mother to give her some of what would be her inheritance, that her mother got Tricia to meet with some ex-cult members who helped Tricia see that the group was a prosperity cult that had actually increased her poverty. Tricia decided not to go back to the group.

In another case, "Mary Jo" was referred to me while she was being seen for treatment at a clinic following her return home from several months with a self-improvement life-style cult that focused on dieting.

Mary Jo had been asked by a casual acquaintance to participate in a "free, scientific, experimental weight control project." While vague, the description implied that scientists were providing new educational methods. Mary Jo was soon flattered by the male and female leaders into accepting their definition of her as a "natural clairvoyant healer" and their invitation "to go on course" with them. They induced her to leave her job and move into their small "weight control program." No longer earning a salary, she eventually turned over her car, savings, and property in return for the "courses in natural healing" that they urged her to pursue.

Growing more obese by the day, as were several other recruits, Mary Jo moved with the group to an isolated small town where they lived with the two leaders and were persuaded not to write or contact families and friends who would tend to "lower their consciousness" because outsiders were not privy to the "course." The course consisted of a twenty-hour daily routine filled with four to five hours of hypnosis and self-hypnosis exercises plus many periods of hyperventilation. Mary Jo spent additional hours "in group" and was taught to "speak in voices and to hear in voices."

Recruits were trained to link random nonsense syllables into rhythmic singsong patterns and to chant these aloud for interpretation by the female leader, who supposedly was "a natural knowing interpreter." After being given her interpretations for the day, Mary Jo was instructed to try to hallucinate what she had just heard as if it were coming from outside her head. In other words, her remembrances of the "interpretations" were now to be "heard in voices."

While attempting to accomplish this, Mary Jo was berated, humiliated, and alternately threatened with expulsion from the group or told she would have to "go on basic" again. During this process, she became psychotic. Her relationship with the group then ended and she was put on a bus with a ticket home to her parents.

Unfortunately, stories like Mary Jo's and Tricia's are all too common and are heard in the thousands by those mental health workers and other helping professionals who recognize and counsel individuals and families who have endured a cultic experience.

Cause for Concern

Not all the new religious, personal growth, self-help, or radical psychotherapy organizations are known to use mind control or other cultic techniques of deception and persuasion. Some organizations, however, have been centers of controversy for close to two decades, having given rise to grass-roots reactions and substantial media attention as early as the mid 1970s. Public concern has been focused on some groups' recruitment activities, the personality changes and emotional disorders developing in some members, and the culturally distinct life-styles associated with certain groups.

Over the years, besides the changes within the cults that have been with us for a quarter-century or more and the development of many new kinds of cults, there has also been a shift in the types of people who come out of cults. Formerly, young adults emerged from cults into which they had been recruited during or immediately after their college years. Now, children, teenagers, and young adults who were reared in cultic groups are emerging into the general society in need of special assistance because they know no other life than that of the cult in which they were raised. In addition to their limited experiences with the larger society, some have endured quite unusual experiences that ill equip them for life outside the group. Equally disturbing is that there are more older adult cult members coming out, people who have lost as much as fifteen to twenty-five years in a cult. These individuals are likely to have no social support, their families are often dead or completely estranged, and they have little idea how to cope. (I will examine this issue of escaping the cult environment and recovering from the cult experience in Part Three.)

What we see today is the continuing presence in society of either organized groups or individual persons who use intense influence on others in order to gain control and power—over money, people, and property. Besides being describable as cults or groups using thought-reform processes, instances of this process are also sometimes called scams, confidence games, hustles, undue influence, improper influence, deceptions, and frauds, among other labels. These names denote the reality behind the way the group or person induces others to go along with a plan that benefits the manipulator and exploits the manipulated, even though the latter may at first, or even for a long while, think that the venture is other than it really is.

Cult leaders and con artists are opportunists who read the times and the ever-changing culture and adapt their pitch to what will appeal at a given moment. These manipulators survive because they adapt and because they are chameleon-like. So, at some times we get cults based on health fads, business-training programs, get-rich-quick schemes, and relationship improvement seminars; at others we get fundamentalist religious cults, Eastern meditation groups, identity or hate groups, longevity groups, and so forth.

Ideas come and go. But the skillful word merchants know how to push people's buttons, how to get a responsive chord resonating in a listener. Thus the buzzwords also change across time. Ten years ago, the key words that would set off a responsive chord in people were community, communication, creativity, awareness, consciousness expansion, transcendental, transformational, holistic, peace, growth, stress, affirmations, and alternative. Today, the key words picked up by cults and manipulators are breakthrough, empowerment, spiritual awakening, paradigm, angels, self, identity, victim, guides, shamans, celebration, and source or sourcing.

Over the years, cults have shown themselves to be a variation on a theme, and their changing use of language is the way they modernize. But just as some sailors in Greek myth were lured to shipwreck by the Sirens' song, so some were saved when Odysseus stopped up their ears. We must constantly watch for the new buzz-words that might be used to entice the unsuspecting. We must know when the words that make us yearn to follow someone are a Sirens' song.

3

The Process of Brainwashing, Psychological Coercion, and Thought Reform

Leaders of cults and groups using thought-reform processes have taken in and controlled millions of persons to the detriment of their welfare. Sometimes such influence is called coercive persuasion or extraordinary influence, to distinguish it from everyday persuasion by friends, family, and other influences in our lives, including the media and advertising.

The key to successful thought reform is to keep the subjects unaware that they are being manipulated and controlled—and especially to keep them unaware that they are being moved along a path of change that will lead them to serve interests that are to their disadvantage. The usual outcome of thought-reform processes is that a person or group gains almost limitless control over the subjects for varying periods of time.

When cultic groups using this level of undue influence are seen in the cold light of day, uninformed observers often cannot grasp how the group worked. They wonder how a rational person would ever get involved. Recently, because of the media attention garnered by the actions of certain groups, the world has become somewhat more aware of thought reform, but most people still don't know how to deal with situations of extraordinary influence.

A number of terms have been used to describe this process, including *brainwashing, thought reform, coercive persuasion, mind control, coordinated programs of coercive influence and behavior control,* and *exploitative persuasion* (see Table 3.1). Perhaps the first and last terms convey something of the crux of what I will be describing in this chapter.

When I ask ordinary people what they think brainwashing is, they correctly grasp that it refers to the exploitative manipulation of one person by another. They usually describe a situation in which a person or group has conned others into going along with a plan put in place by the instigator. *Conned* has a widely understood meaning in our informal conversation and our streets, which

Table 3.1. Terms Used to Identify Thought Reform.

Term	Originator/Date
Thought struggle (*ssu-hsiang tou-cheng*)	Mao Tse-tung (1929)
Brainwashing (*hse nao*)	Hunter (1951)
Thought reform (*ssu-hsiang kai-tsao*)	Lifton (1956)
Debility, dependency, and dread (DDD syndrome)	Farber, Harlow, and West (1957)
Coercive persuasion	Schein (1961)
Mind control	Unknown (about 1980)
Systematic manipulation of psychological and social influence	Singer (1982)
Coordinated programs of coercive influence and behavioral control	Ofshe and Singer (1986)
Exploitative persuasion	Singer and Addis (1992)

is why it is generally difficult to manipulate street-smart kids. They already know to look for a double agenda, calling it a con game, snow job, scam, jiving someone, putting someone on, and many other names.

A certain type of psychological con game is exactly what goes on in a thought-reform environment. A complex set of interlocking factors is put into place, and these factors, either quickly or slowly depending on the situation and the subject, bring about deep changes in the mind-set and attitudes of the targeted individual. Through the manipulation of psychological *and* social factors, people's attitudes can indeed be changed, and their thinking and behavior radically altered.

Historical Examples of Brainwashing

The myth of the invulnerable mind discussed in Chapter One needs to be exposed over and over if we are to prevent Orwell's vision of 1984 from coming true at any time. In just the last sixty years, the world has seen numerous examples of how easily human conduct can be manipulated under certain circumstances.

During the 1930s purge trials in the former Soviet Union, men and women accused of committing crimes against the state were maneuvered into both falsely confessing to and falsely accusing others of these crimes. The world press expressed bewilderment and amazement at the phenomenon but, with few exceptions, soon lapsed into silence.

Then in the late 1940s and early 1950s, the world witnessed personnel at Chinese revolutionary universities implement a thought-reform program that changed the beliefs and behaviors of the citizens of the largest nation in the world. This program, which Mao Tse-tung wrote about as early as the 1920s, was put into place when the Communist regime took power in China on October 1, 1949. Chairman Mao had long planned how to change people's political selves—to achieve "ideological remolding," as he called it—through the use of a coordinated program of psychological, social, and political coercion. As a result, millions of Chinese citizens were induced to espouse new philosophies and exhibit new conduct.

The term *brainwashing* was first introduced into the Western world in 1951, when American foreign correspondent Edward Hunter, published a book titled *Brainwashing in Red China*. Hunter was the first to write about the phenomenon, based on his interviews of both Chinese and non-Chinese coming across the border from China into Hong Kong. His translator explained to him that the Communist process of ridding people of the vestiges of their old belief system was called colloquially *hse nao*, which literally means "wash brain," or "cleansing the mind."

The 1950s also brought the Korean War. North Korea's intensive indoctrination of United Nations' prisoners of war showed the world the extent to which captors would go to win converts to their political cause. The Korean program was based on methods used by the Chinese, combined with other social and psychological influence techniques.

Later in the same decade, Cardinal Mindszenty, the head of the Roman Catholic Church in Hungary and a man of tremendous personal forcefulness, strength of convictions, and faith in God, ended up being so manipulated and processed by his Russian captors that he—like the earlier purge trial victims—both falsely confessed and falsely accused his colleagues.

These extremes of social and psychological manipulations of thought and conduct were, and sometimes still are, disregarded by Americans because the events occurred far away and could be dismissed as merely foreign propaganda and political acts. Such reasoning is a variation of the "not me" myth: not in our land could such a thing happen. But later, certain events occurred in California that forced many to see that extremes of influence and manipulation were possible in the United States, too.

In 1969, Charles Manson manipulated a band of middle-class youths into believing his mad version of *Helter Skelter*. Under his influence and control, his followers carried out multiple vicious murders. Not long after, the Symbionese Liberation Army (SLA), a ragtag revolutionary group, kidnapped newspaper heiress Patricia Hearst and abused her psychologically and otherwise. The SLA used mind manipulations as well as gun-at-the-head methods to coerce Patty into compliance. They manipulated and controlled her behavior to the extent that she appeared with them in a bank robbery and feared returning to society, having been convinced by the SLA that the police and the FBI would shoot her.

This series of events from the 1930s to the present demonstrates that individual autonomy and personal identity are much more fragile than was once commonly believed. And that certain venal types have gotten hold of and perfected techniques of persuasion that are wreaking havoc in our society. Were George Orwell alive, he might be intrigued with the variety of situations in which mind-bending and thought-manipulating techniques are applied today.

Interestingly enough, Orwell was perhaps the first to note that language, not physical force, is key to manipulating minds. In fact, growing evidence in the behavioral sciences reveals that a smiling Big Brother has greater power to influence an individual's thought and decision making than does a visibly threatening person. As Orwell says of his brainwashed hero, at the close of his prophetic book: "He loved Big Brother."

Packaged Persuasion

Several years ago, a colleague and I interviewed a young couple at the request of their attorneys. The couple, who had once been good citizens and loving parents, had been accused of a spanking that allegedly led to their son's death. While they were members of a cult in West Virginia with a female leader, their twenty-three-month-old son allegedly had either hit or pushed the leader's grandchild during play. The parents were ordered to get the child to apologize; otherwise, according to the irate leader, no one would go to heaven. The boy was beaten with a wooden board by his father, with his mother in the room, for more than two and a half hours. The boy's blood pooled in the bruises in his buttocks and legs, and he died. In court, I described how the leader had slowly gained control of the members of her group and how the beating evolved from her teaching and control.

In another case, Ron Luff, a former Navy career petty officer with a series of recommendations for excellent conduct and performance, was convinced by his cult leader to follow that leader's orders. These orders were to help the leader kill an Ohio family of five, including three young daughters, dump the bodies into a lime pit in a barn, then go off on a long wilderness trek with the leader and his two dozen followers. Ron Luff was found guilty of aggravated murder and kidnapping and sentenced to 170 years in prison. The cult leader, Jeffrey Lundgren, was sentenced to die in Ohio's electric chair. Both cases are on appeal at the time of this book's writing.

People repeatedly ask me how cult leaders get their followers to do such things as give their wives to a child-molesting cult leader, drop out of medical school to follow a martial arts guru, give several million dollars to a self-appointed messiah who wears a wig and has his favorite women dress like Jezebel, or practice sexual abstinence while following a blatantly promiscuous guru. Because of the great discrepancies between individuals' conduct before cult membership and the behavior exhibited while in the cult, families, friends, and the public wonder how these changes in attitude and behavior are induced.

How cult leaders and other clever operators get people to do their bidding seems arcane and mysterious to most persons, but I find there is nothing esoteric about it at all. There are no secret drugs or potions. It is just words and group pressures, put together in packaged forms. Modern-day manipulators use methods of persuasion employed since the days of the cavemen, but the masterful con artists of today have hit upon a way to put the techniques together in packages that are especially successful. As a result, thought reform, as a form of influence and persuasion, falls on the extreme end of a continuum that also includes education as we typically see it, advertising, propaganda, and indoctrination (see Table 3.2).

Table 3.2. Continuum of Influence and Persuasion.

	Education	Advertising	Propaganda	Indoctrination	Thought Reform
Focus of body of knowledge	Many bodies of knowledge, based on scientific findings in various fields.	Body of knowledge concerns product, competitors, how to sell and influence via legal persuasion.	Body of knowledge centers on political persuasion of masses of people.	Body of knowledge is explicitly designed to inculcate organizational values.	Body of knowledge centers on changing people without their knowledge.
Direction & degree of exchange	Two-way pupil-teacher exchange encouraged.	Exchange can occur, but communication generally one-sided.	Some exchange occurs, but communication generally one-sided.	Limited exchange occurs; communication is one-sided.	No exchange occurs; communication is one-sided.
Ability to change	Change occurs as science advances; as students & other scholars offer criticism; as students & citizens evaluate programs.	Change made by those who pay for it, based upon the success of ad programs; by consumer law; & in response to consumer complaints.	Change based on changing tides in world politics and on political need to promote the group, nation, or international organization.	Change made through formal channels, via written suggestions to higher-ups.	Change occurs rarely; organization remains fairly rigid; change occurs primarily to improve thought-reform effectiveness.

Table 3.2. Continuum of Influence and Persuasion. (Cont.)

	Education	Advertising	Propaganda	Indoctrination	Thought Reform
Structure of persuasion	Uses teacher-pupil structure; logical thinking encouraged.	Uses an instructional mode to persuade consumer/buyer.	Takes authoritarian stance to persuade masses.	Takes authoritarian & hierarchical stance.	Takes authoritarian & hierarchical stance; no full awareness on part of learner.
Type of relationship	Instruction is time-limited; consensual.	Consumer/buyer can accept or ignore communication.	Learner support & engrossment expected.	Instruction is contractual; consensual.	Group attempts to retain people forever.
Deceptiveness	Is not deceptive.	Can be deceptive, selecting only positive views.	Can be deceptive; often exaggerated.	Is not deceptive.	Is deceptive.
Breadth of learning	Focuses on learning to learn & learning about reality; broad goal is rounded knowledge for development of the individual.	Has a narrow goal of swaying opinion to promote and sell an idea, object, or program; another goal is to enhance seller & possibly buyer.	Targets large political masses to make them believe a specific view or circumstance is good.	Stresses narrow learning for a specific goal: to become something or to train for performance of duties.	Individualized target; hidden agenda (you will be changed one step at a time to become deployable to serve leaders).
Tolerance	Respects differences.	Puts down competition.	Wants to lessen opposition.	Aware of differences.	No respect for differences.
Methods	Instructional techniques.	Mild to heavy persuasion.	Overt persuasion; sometimes unethical.	Disciplinary techniques.	Improper and unethical techniques.

There is a mistaken notion that thought reform can only be carried out in confined places and under threat of physical torture or death. But it is important to remember that the brainwashing programs of the forties and fifties were applied not only to military or civilian prisoners of war but also to the general population. In all our research, I and others who study these programs emphasize over and over that imprisonment and overt violence are not necessary and are actually counterproductive when influencing people to change their attitudes and behaviors. If one really wants to influence others, various coordinated soft-sell programs are cheaper, less obvious, and highly effective. The old maxim "Honey gathers more flies than vinegar" remains true today.

Attacking the Self

There is, however, an important distinction to be made between the version of thought reform prevalent in the 1940s and 1950s and the version used by a number of contemporary groups, including cults, large group awareness training programs, and assorted other groups. These latter-day efforts have built upon the age-old influence techniques to perfect amazingly successful programs of persuasion and change. What's new—and crucial—is that these programs change attitudes by attacking essential aspects of a person's sense of self, unlike the earlier brainwashing programs that primarily confronted a person's political beliefs.

Today's programs are designed to destabilize an individual's sense of self by undermining his or her basic consciousness, reality awareness, beliefs and worldview, emotional control, and defense mechanisms. This attack on a person's central stability, or self-concept, and on a person's capacity for self-evaluation is the principal technique that makes the newer programs work. Moreover, this attack is carried out under a variety of guises and conditions—and rarely does it include forced confinement or direct physical coercion. Rather, it is a subtle and powerful psychological process of destabilization and induced dependency.

Thankfully, these programs do not change people permanently. Nor are they 100 percent effective. Cults are not all alike, thought-reform programs are not all alike, and not everyone exposed to specific intense influence processes succumbs and follows the group. Some cults try to defend themselves by saying, in effect, "See, not everyone joins or stays, so we must not be using brainwashing techniques." Many recruits do succumb, however, and the better organized the influence processes used, the more people will succumb.

What is of concern, then, is that certain groups and training programs that have emerged in the last half century represent well-organized, highly orchestrated influence efforts that are widely successful in recruiting and converting people under certain conditions for certain ends. My interest has been in how these processes work, in the psychological and social techniques that produce these behavioral and attitudinal changes. I am less interested in whether the content of the group centers around religion, psychology, self-improvement, politics, life-style, or flying saucers. I am more interested in the widespread use of brainwashing techniques by crooks, swindlers, psychopaths, and egomaniacs of every sort.

How Thought Reform Works

Brainwashing is not experienced as a fever or a pain might be; it is an invisible social adaptation. When you are the subject of it, you are not aware of the intent of the influence processes that are going on, and especially, you are not aware of the changes taking place within you.

In his memoirs, Cardinal Mindszenty wrote, "Without knowing what had happened to me, I had become a different person." And when asked about being brainwashed, Patty Hearst said, "The strangest part of all this, however, as the SLA delighted in informing me later, was that they themselves were surprised at how docile and trusting I had become. . . . It was also true, I must admit, that the thought of escaping from them later simply never entered my mind. I had become convinced that there was no possibility of escape. . . . I suppose I could have walked out of the apartment and away from it all, but I didn't. It simply never occurred to me."

A thought-reform program is not a one-shot event but a gradual process of breaking down and transformation. It can be likened to gaining weight, a few ounces, a half pound, a pound at a time. Before long, without even noticing the initial changes—we are confronted with a new physique. So, too, with brainwashing. A twist here, a tweak there—and there it is: a new psychic attitude, a new mental outlook. These systematic manipulations of social and psychological influences under particular conditions are called *programs* because the means by which change is brought about is coordinated. And it is because the changes cause the learning and adoption of a certain set of attitudes, usually accompanied by a certain set of behaviors, that the effort and the result are called *thought reform*.

Thus, thought reform is a concerted effort to change a person's way of looking at the world, which will change his or her behavior. It is distinguished from other forms of social learning by the conditions under which it is conducted and by the techniques of environmental and interpersonal manipulation that are meant to suppress certain behavior and to elicit and train other behavior. And it does not consist of only one program—there are many ways and methods to accomplish it.

The tactics of a thought-reform program are organized to

- Destabilize a person's sense of self
- Get the person to drastically reinterpret his or her life's history and radically alter his or her worldview and accept a new version of reality and causality
- Develop in the person a dependence on the organization, and thereby turn the person into a deployable agent of the organization

Thought reform can be profitably looked at in at least three ways (summarized in Table 3.3). Robert Lifton has recognized eight

Table 3.3. Criteria for Thought Reform.

Conditions (Singer)	Themes (Lifton)	Stages (Schein)
1. Keep the person unaware of what is going on and the changes taking place.		1. Unfreezing.
2. Control the person's time and, if possible, physical environment. 3. Create a sense of powerlessness, covert fear, and dependency. 4. Suppress much of the person's old behavior and attitudes.	1. Milieu control. 2. Loading the language. 3. Demand for purity. 4. Confession.	
5. Instill new behavior and attitudes.	5. Mystical manipulation. 6. Doctrine over person.	2. Changing.
6. Put forth a closed system of logic; allow no real input or criticism.	7. Sacred science. 8. Dispensing of existence.	3. Refreezing.

themes of thought reform, I have identified six conditions, and Edgar Schein has named three stages. The themes and stages outlined by Lifton and Schein focus on the *sequence of the process*, while the circumstances I have outlined suggest the *conditions needed* in the surrounding environment if the process is to work.

Singer's Six Conditions

The following conditions create the atmosphere needed to put thought-reform processes into place. The degree to which these conditions are present increases the level of restrictiveness enforced by the cult and the overall effectiveness of the program.

1. Keep the person unaware that there is an agenda to control or change the person
2. Control time and physical environment (contacts, information)
3. Create a sense of powerlessness, fear, and dependency
4. Suppress old behavior and attitudes
5. Instill new behavior and attitudes
6. Put forth a closed system of logic

The trick is to proceed with the thought-reform process one step at a time so that the person does not notice that she or he is changing. I will explain more fully how each step works.

1. *Keep the person unaware of what is going on and how she or he is being changed a step at a time.* Imagine you are the person being influenced. You find yourself in an environment to which you are forced to adapt *in a series of steps*, each sufficiently minor so that you don't notice the changes in yourself and do not become aware of the goals of the program until late in the process (if ever). You are kept unaware of the orchestration of psychological and social forces meant to change your thinking and your behavior. The cult leaders make it seem as though what is going on is normal, that

everything is the way it's supposed to be. This atmosphere is reinforced by peer pressure and peer-modeled behavior, so that you
adapt to the environment without even realizing it.

For example, a young man was invited to a lecture. When he
arrived, he noticed many pairs of shoes lined against the wall and
people in their stocking feet. A woman nodded at his shoes, so he
took them off and set them with the others. Everyone was speaking in a soft voice, so he lowered his voice. The evening proceeded
with some ritual ceremonies, meditation, and a lecture by a robed
leader. Everything was paced slowly and led by this man, with the
rest quietly watching and listening. The young man also sat
docilely, even though he wanted to ask questions. He conformed
to what the group was doing. In this case, however, at the end of
the evening when he was asked to come back to another lecture,
he said, "Thanks, but no thanks," at which two men quickly ush-
ered him out a back door, so others wouldn't hear his displeasure.

The process of keeping people unaware is key to a cult's double
agenda: the leader slowly takes you through a series of events that
on the surface look like one agenda, while on another level, the
real agenda is to get you, the recruit or member, to obey and to give
up your autonomy, your past affiliations, and your belief systems.
The existence of the double agenda makes this process one of *non-
informed consent*.

2. *Control the person's social and/or physical environment; especially control the person's time*. Cults don't need to have you move
into the commune, farm, headquarters, or ashram and live within
the cult environment twenty-four hours a day in order to have control over you. They can control you just as effectively by having
you go to work every day with instructions that when not working—on your lunch hour, for example—you must do continuous
mind-occupying chanting or some other cult-related activity. Then,
after work, you must put all your time in with the organization.

3.   *Systematically create a sense of powerlessness in the person*.
Cults create this sense of powerlessness by stripping you of your support system and your ability to act independently. Former friends

and kinship networks are taken away. You, the recruit or follower, are isolated from your ordinary environments and sometimes removed to remote locations. Another way cults create a sense of powerlessness is by stripping people of their main occupation and sources of wealth. It is to achieve this condition that so many cultic organizations have members drop out of school, quit their jobs or give up their careers, and turn over their property, inheritances, and other resources to the organization. It is one of the steps in creating a sense of dependency on the organization and a continuing sense of individual powerlessness.

Once stripped of your usual support network and, in some cases, means of income, your confidence in your own perceptions erodes. As your sense of powerlessness increases, your good judgment and understanding of the world are diminished. At the same time as you are destabilized in relation to your ordinary reality and worldview, the cult confronts you with a new, unanimously (group-) approved worldview. As the group attacks your previous worldview, causing you distress and inner confusion, you are not allowed to speak about this confusion, nor can you object to it, because leadership constantly suppresses questions and counters any resistance. Through this process, your inner confidence is eroded. Moreover, the effectiveness of this approach can be speeded up if you are physically tired, which is why cult leaders see to it that followers are kept overly busy.

4.   *Manipulate a system of rewards, punishments, and experiences in such a way as to inhibit behavior that reflects the person's former social identity.* The expression of your beliefs, values, activities, and characteristic demeanor prior to contact with the group is suppressed, and you are manipulated into taking on a social identity preferred by the leadership. Old beliefs and old patterns of behavior are defined as irrelevant, if not evil. You quickly learn that leadership wants old ideas and old patterns eliminated, so you suppress them. For example, the public admission of sexual feelings in certain groups is met with overt disapproval by peers and superiors, accompanied by a directive to take a cold shower. An individual can

avoid public rebuke on this topic by no longer speaking on the entire topic of sexuality, warmth, or interest in another human being. The vacuum left is then filled with the group's ways of thinking and doing.

5. *Manipulate a system of rewards, punishments, and experiences in order to promote learning of the group's ideology or belief system and group-approved behaviors.* Once immersed in an environment in which you are totally dependent on the rewards given by those who control the setting, you can be confronted with massive demands to learn varying amounts of new information and behaviors. You are rewarded for proper performance with social and sometimes material reinforcement; if slow to learn or noncompliant, you are threatened with shunning, banning, and punishment which includes loss of esteem from others, loss of privileges, loss of status, and inner anxiety and guilt. In certain groups, physical punishment is meted out.

The more complicated and filled with contradictions the new system is and the more difficult it is to learn, the more effective the conversion process will be. For example, a recruit may constantly fail at mastering a complicated theology but can succeed and be rewarded for going out to solicit funds. In one cultic organization, the leadership introduces the new recruits to a complicated dodge-ball game. Only long-term members know the complex and ever-changing rules, and they end up literally leading and pushing the new recruits through the game. This, then, is followed by a very simple exercise in which members get together to "share." Older members stand up and share (that is, confess) some past bad deed. The new members, who failed so badly at the bewildering dodge-ball game, now can feel capable of succeeding by simply getting up and confessing something about their past that was, by group standards, bad.

Since esteem and affection from peers is so important to new recruits, any negative response is very meaningful. Approval comes from having your behaviors and thought patterns conform to the models put forth by the group. Your relationship with peers is threatened whenever you fail to learn or display new behaviors. Over time, an easy solution to the insecurity generated by the difficulties of learning the new system is to inhibit any display of doubt and, even if you don't understand the content, to merely acquiesce, affirm, and act as if you do understand and accept the new philosophy or content.

6. *Put forth a closed system of logic and an authoritarian structure that permits no feedback and refuses to be modified except by leadership approval or executive order.* If you criticize or complain, the leader or peers allege that *you* are defective, not the organization. In this closed system of logic, you are not allowed to question or doubt a tenet or rule or to call attention to factual information that suggests some internal contradiction within the belief system or a contradiction with what you've been told. If you do make such observations, they may be turned around and argued to mean the opposite of what you intended. You are made to feel that you are wrong. In cultic groups, the individual member is always wrong, and the system is always right.

For example, one cult member complained privately to his immediate leadership that he doubted he'd be able to kill his father if so instructed by the cult, even though that act was to signify true adherence to the cult's system. In response, he was told he needed more courses to overcome his obvious weakness because by now he should be more committed to the group.

In another case, a woman objected to her fund-raising team leader that it would be lying to people to say cult members were collecting money for a children's home when they knew the money went to the leader's headquarters. She was told, "That's evidence of your degraded mentality. You are restoring to our leader what's rightfully his, that's all!"

Another woman who wanted to go home to see her dying grandmother was refused her request. "We're strengthening you here," she was told. "This request is a sign of your selfishness. We're your new family, and we're right to not let you go."

The goal of all this is your conversion or remolding. As you learn to modify your former behaviors in order to be accepted in this closed and controlled environment, you change. You affirm that you accept and understand the ideology by beginning to talk in the simple catchphrases particular to the group. This "communication" has no foundation since, in reality, you have little understanding of the system beyond the catchphrases. But once you begin to express your seeming verbal acceptance of the group's ideology, then that ideology becomes the rule book for the subsequent direction and evaluation of your behavior.

Also, using the new language fosters your separation from your old conscience and belief system. Your new language allows you to justify activities that are clearly not in your interests, perhaps not even in the interests of humankind. Precisely those behaviors that lead to criticism from the outside world because they violate the norms and rules of the society as a whole are rationalized within the cult community through use of this new terminology, this new language.

For example, "heavenly deception" and "transcendental trickery" (terms used by two of the large cultic groups) are not called what they are—lying and deceptive fund-raising. Nor is the rule "do not talk to the systemites" called what it is—a way to isolate members from the rest of the world.

Lifton's Eight Themes

Paralleling Singer's six conditions are the eight psychological themes that psychiatrist Robert Lifton has identified as central to totalistic environments, including the Communist Chinese and Korean programs of the 1950s and today's cults. Cults invoke these themes for the purpose of promoting behavioral and attitudinal changes.

1. *Milieu control.* This is total control of communication in the group. In many groups, there is a "no gossip" or "no nattering"

rule that keeps people from expressing their doubts or misgivings about what is going on. This rule is usually rationalized by saying that gossip will tear apart the fabric of the group or destroy unity, when in reality the rule is a mechanism to keep members from communicating anything other than positive endorsements. Members are taught to report those who break the rule, a practice that also keeps members isolated from each other and increases dependence on the leadership.

Milieu control also often involves discouraging members from contacting relatives or friends outside the group and from reading anything not approved by the organization. They are sometimes told not to believe anything they see or hear reported by the media. One left-wing political cult, for example, maintains that the Berlin Wall is still standing and that the "bourgeois capitalist" press wants people to think otherwise in order to discredit communism.

2.   *Loading the language.* As members continue to formulate their ideas in the group's jargon, this language serves the purpose of constricting members' thinking and shutting down critical thinking abilities. At first, translating from their native tongue into "groupspeak" forces members to censor, edit, and slow down spontaneous bursts of criticism or oppositional ideas. That helps them to cut off and contain negative or resistive feelings. Eventually, speaking in cult jargon is second nature, and talking with outsiders becomes energy-consuming and awkward. Soon enough, members find it most comfortable to talk only among themselves in the new vocabulary. To reinforce this, all kinds of derogatory names are given to outsiders: wogs, systemites, reactionaries, unclean, of Satan.

One large international group, for example, has dictionaries for members to use. In one of these dictionaries, *criticism* is defined as "justification for having done an overt." Then one looks up *overt* and the dictionary states: "overt act: an overt act is not just injuring someone or something; an overt act is an act of omission or commission which does the least good for the least number of dynamics or the most harm to the greatest number of dynamics." Then the definition of *dynamics* says: "There could be said to be eight urges in life. . . ." And so, one can search from term to term trying to learn this new language. One researcher noted that the group's founder has stated that "new followers or potential converts should not be exposed to [the language and cosmology of the group] at too early a stage. 'Talking whole track to raw meat' is frowned upon."

When cults use such internal meanings, how is an outsider to know that *the devil disguise, just flesh relationships*, and *polluting* are terms for parents? That an *edu* is a lecture by the cult leader or that a *mislocation* is a mistake? A former cult member comments, "I was always being told, 'You are being too horizontal.'" Translated, this meant she was being reprimanded for listening to and being sympathetic to peers.

A dwindling group in Seattle, the Love Family, had a "rite of breathing." This sounds ordinary, but in fact for some members it turned out to be a lethal euphemism. The leader, a former California salesman, initiated this rite, in which members sat in a circle, passing around and sniffing a plastic bag containing a rag soaked with toluene, an industrial solvent. The group called the chemical "tell-u-all."

3. *Demand for purity.* An us-versus-them orientation is promoted by the all-or-nothing belief system of the group: we are right; they (outsiders, nonmembers) are wrong, evil, unenlightened, and so forth. Each idea or act is good or bad, pure or evil. Recruits gradually take in, or internalize, the critical, shaming essence of the cult environment, which builds up lots of guilt and shame. Most groups put forth that there is only one way to think, respond, or act in any given situation. There is no in between, and members are expected to judge themselves and others by this all-or-nothing standard. Anything can be done in the name of this purity; it is the justification for the group's internal moral and ethical code. In many groups, it is literally taught that the end justifies the means—and because the end (that is, the group) is pure, the means are simply tools to reach purity.

If you are a recruit, this ubiquitous guilt and shame creates and magnifies your dependence on the group. The group says in essence, "We love you because you are transforming yourself," which means that any moment you are not transforming yourself, you are slipping back. Thus you easily feel inadequate, as though you need "fixing" all the time, just as the outside world is being denounced all the time.

4. *Confession.* Confession is used to lead members to reveal past and present behavior, contacts with others, and undesirable feelings, seemingly in order to unburden themselves and become free. However, whatever you reveal is subsequently used to further mold you and to make you feel close to the group and estranged from nonmembers. (I sometimes call this technique *purge and merge.*) The information gained about you can be used against you to make you feel more guilty, powerless, fearful, and ultimately in need of the cult and the leader's goodness. And it can be used to get you to rewrite your personal history so as to denigrate your past life, making it seem illogical for you to want to return to that former life, family, and friends. Each group will have its own confession ritual, which may be carried out either one-on-one with a person in leadership or in group sessions. Members may also write reports on themselves and others.

Through the confession process and by instruction in the group's teachings, members learn that everything about their former lives, including friends, family, and nonmembers, is wrong and to be avoided. Outsiders will put you at risk of not attaining the purported goal: they will lessen your psychological awareness, hinder the group's political advancement, obstruct your path toward ultimate knowledge, or allow you to become stuck in your past life and incorrect thinking.

5. *Mystical manipulation.* The group manipulates members to think that their new feelings and behavior have arisen spontaneously in this new atmosphere. The leader implies that this is a chosen, select group with a higher purpose. Members become adept at watching to see what particular behavior is wanted, learning to be sensitive to all kinds of cues by which they are to judge and alter their own behavior. Cult leaders tell their followers, "You have chosen to be here. No one has told you to come here. No one has influenced you," when in fact the followers are in a situation they can't

leave owing to social pressure and their fear. Thus they come to believe that they are actually choosing this life. If outsiders hint that the devotees have been brainwashed or tricked, the members say, "Oh, no, I chose voluntarily." Cults thrive on this myth of voluntarism, insisting time and again that no member is being held against his or her will.

6. *Doctrine over person.* As members retrospectively alter their accounts of personal history, having been instructed either to rewrite that history or simply to ignore it, they are simultaneously taught to interpret reality through the group concepts and to ignore their own experiences and feelings as they occur. In many groups, from the days of early membership on, you will be told to stop paying attention to your own perceptions, since you are "uninstructed," and simply to go along with and accept the "instructed" view, the party line.

The rewriting of personal history more often than not becomes a re-creating, so that you learn to fit yourself into the group's interpretation of life. For example, one young man recently out of a cult reported to me that he was "a drug addict, violent, and irresponsible." It soon became clear from our discussions that none of this was true. His drug addiction amounted to three puffs of marijuana a number of years ago; his violence stemmed from his participation on a high school wrestling team; and his irresponsibility was based on his not having saved any money from his very small allowance as a teenager. However, the group he had been in had convinced him that these things represented terrible flaws.

7. *Sacred science.* The leader's wisdom is given a patina of science, adding a credible layer to his central philosophical, psychological, or political notion. He can then profess that the group's philosophy should be applied to all humankind and that anyone who disagrees or has alternative ideas is not only immoral and irreverent but also unscientific. Many leaders, for example, inflate their curricula vitae to make it look as though they are connected to higher powers, respected historical leaders, and so forth. Many a cult leader has said that he follows in the tradition of the great-

est—Sigmund Freud, Karl Marx, the Buddha, Martin Luther, or Jesus Christ.

8. *Dispensing of existence*. The cult's totalistic environment clearly emphasizes that the members are part of an elitist movement and are the select of the world. Nonmembers are unworthy, lesser beings. Most cults teach their members that "we are the best and only one," saying, in one way or another, "We are the governors of enlightenment and all outsiders are lower beings." This kind of thinking lays the foundation for dampening the good consciences members brought in with them and allows members, as agents or representatives of a "superior" group, to manipulate nonmembers for the good of the group. Besides reinforcing the us-versus-them mentality, this thinking means that your whole existence centers on being in the group. If you leave, you join nothingness. This is the final step in creating members' dependence on the group.

Numerous former cult members report that, when they look back at what they did or would have done at the command of the group, they are appalled and stricken. Many have said they would have killed their own parents if so ordered. Hundreds have told me of countless deceptions and lies, such as shortchanging donors on the street, using ruses to keep members from leaving, and urging persons who could ill afford it to run their credit cards up to their limit in order to sign up for further courses.

Schein's Three Stages

Next, we consider the stages people go through as their attitudes are changed by the group environment and the thought-reform processes. These were labeled by psychologist Edgar Schein as the stages of "unfreezing, changing, and refreezing."

1. *Unfreezing*. In this first stage, your past attitudes and choices—your whole sense of self and notion of how the world works—are destabilized by group lectures, personal counseling, rewards, punishments, and other exchanges in the group. This

destabilization is designed to produce what psychologists call an identity crisis. While you are looking back at your own world and behavior and values (that is, unfreezing them), you are simultaneously bombarded with the new system, which implies that you have been wrong in the past. This process makes you uncertain about what is right, what to do, and which choices to make.

As described earlier, successful behavioral change programs are designed to upset you to the point that your self-confidence is undermined. This makes you more open to suggestion and also more dependent on the environment for cues about "right thinking" and "right conduct." Your resistance to the new ideas lessens when you feel yourself teetering on an edge with massive anxiety about the right choices in life on the one side, and the group ideas that offer the way out of this distress on the other side.

Many groups use a "hot seat" technique or some other form of criticism to attain the goal of undercutting, destabilizing, and diminishing. For example, "Harry" had been in the Army, was approaching his late twenties, and was always very sure of himself. But when he joined a Bible cult, the leaders said he wasn't learning fast enough to speak in tongues. He was told that he was resistant, that this was a sign of his evil past. He was told this over and over, no matter how hard he tried. Before long, Harry seemed to lose confidence in himself, even in his memories of his Army successes. His own attitude about himself as well as his actual behavior was unfreezing.

2. *Changing.* During this second stage, you sense that the solutions offered by the group provide a path to follow. You feel that anxiety, uncertainty, and self-doubt can be reduced by adopting the concepts put forth by the group or leader. Additionally, you observe the behavior of the longer-term members, and you begin to emulate their ways. As social psychology experiments and observations have found for decades, once a person makes an open commitment before others to an idea, his or her subsequent behavior generally supports and reinforces the stated commitment. That is, if you say in front of others that you are making a commitment to be "pure,"

then you will feel pressured to follow what others define as the path of purity.

If you spend enough time in any environment, you will develop a personal history of experience and interaction in it. When that environment is constructed and managed in a certain way, then the experiences, interactions, and peer relations will be consistent with whatever public identity is fostered by the environment and will incorporate the values and opinions promulgated in that environment.

Now, when you engage in cooperative activity with peers in an environment that you do not realize is artificially constructed, you do not perceive your interactions to be coerced. And when you are encouraged but not forced to make verbal claims to "truly understanding the ideology and having been transformed," these interactions with your peers will tend to lead you to conclude that you hold beliefs consistent with your actions. In other words, you will think that you came upon the belief and behaviors yourself.

Peer pressure is very important to this process:

- If you say it in front of others, you'll do it.
- Once you do it, you'll think it.
- Once you think it (in an environment you do not perceive to be coercive), you'll believe that you thought it yourself.

Remember Harry? Convinced that he was not able to speak in tongues correctly because he was an evil person, Harry then started confessing his bad past, saying that his parents were alcoholics and his sister a prostitute, none of which was true. He left his job and took one that he was sent on by the group. He began to do whatever he was told in order to prove himself to the leadership. He even engaged in some illegal activities that would have been abhorrent to him prior to his cult involvement. Harry had been unfrozen and now he was changing.

3.   *Refreezing.* In this final phase, the group reinforces you in the desired behavior with social and psychological rewards, and pun-

ishes unwanted attitudes and behaviors with harsh criticism, group disapproval, social ostracism, and loss of status. Most of the modern-day thought-reform groups seek to produce smiling, non-resistant, hardworking persons who do not complain about group practices and do not question the authority of the guru, leader, or trainer. The more you display the group-approved attitudes and behavior, the more your compliance is interpreted by the leadership as showing that you now know that your life before you belonged to the group was wrong and that your new life is "the way."

As for Harry, when he became proficient in obeying, he was sent around to other chapters of his cult and touted as a very special and effective person. He was greatly rewarded. He stayed with the group for more than five years.

The degree to which a group or situation is structured according to these conditions, themes, and stages will determine the degree to which it is manipulative. Not all cults or groups that use thought-reform processes implement their mind-bending techniques in the same way or to the same extent. The implementation varies both within individual groups and across groups. Often, the peripheral members will have no awareness of the kinds of manipulations that go on in the upper or inner levels of a particular group or teaching. Thought reform is subtle, fluid, and insidious—and sometimes hard to identify, particularly for the novice or the overly idealistic. But when it is present, it has powerful repercussions.

Producing a New Identity

As part of the intense influence and change process in many cults, people take on a new social identity, which may or may not be obvious to an outsider. When groups refer to this new identity, they speak of members who are transformed, reborn, enlightened, empowered, rebirthed, or cleared. The group-approved behavior is reinforced and reinterpreted as demonstrating the emergence of "the new person." Members are expected to display this new social identity.

However, the vast majority of those who leave such groups drop the cult content, and the cult behavior and attitudes, and painstakingly take up where they left off prior to joining. Those who had been subjected to thought-reform processes in the Far East, for example, gradually dropped the adopted attitudes and behaviors and returned to their former selves as soon as they were away from the environment. We see from years of research with prisoners of war, hostages, battered wives, former cult members, and other recipients of intense influence that changes made under this influence are not stable and not permanent. The beliefs a person may adopt about the world, about a particular philosophy, and even about himself or herself are reversible when the person is out of the environment that induced those beliefs.

We might ask ourselves—and surely many former cult members have—how a person can display reprehensible conduct under some conditions, then turn around and resume normal activities under other conditions. The phenomenon has been variously described as doubling or as the formation of a pseudopersonality (or pseudoidentity), a superimposed identity, a cult self, or a cult personality. What is important about these labels is that they call attention to an important psychological and social phenomenon that needs to be studied more carefully—namely, that ordinary persons, with their own ideas and attitudes, can be rapidly turned around in their social identity but later can recover their old selves and move forward.

By this, I am not saying that people in cults or groups that use thought-reform processes are just faking it by role-playing, pretending, or acting. Anyone who has met a former friend who's been transformed into a recruiting zealot for a New Age transformational program, for example, knows that something more profound than role-playing is operating as that old friend defends her or his new self and new group, speaking single-mindedly, spouting intense, firmly stated dogma. This is not play-acting. It is far more instinctive and experienced as real.

Doubling, or the formation of a pseudopersonality, has become a key issue. It is a factor that ultimately allows cult members to leave their groups and permits us to understand why exit counseling works as a means of reawakening a person who has been exposed to thought-reform processes. The central fact is this: the social identity learned while a person is in a thought-reform system fades, much as a summer tan does when a person is no longer at the beach. The process is far more complicated than this analogy, of course, but I want to emphasize that cult thinking and behaviors are adaptive and not stable.

It is the cult environment that produces and keeps in place the cult identity. Some persons stay forever in the group, but the vast majority leave at some point, either walking away or being lured out by family and friends. An understanding of thought-reforming phenomena is vital to learning more about the role that group social support or pressure plays for all of us. It is important not only for families with relatives in cultic groups but also for ex-members wondering if there are psychological and social theories to explain what happened to them, and for everyone who wants to learn something about how we all operate.

Impermissible Experiments

Cults are carrying out impermissible experiments. What is an impermissible experiment? Professionals engaged in legitimate supervised medical and psychological research are held to certain standards that have been in place since the end of World War II and the establishment of the Nuremberg code of ethics, which states that in any setting where any type of human experimentation is done, the experiment cannot be performed without the informed consent of those who are to be participants. In getting this consent, the experimenters are to explain everything that will or may happen as a consequence of the person's coming into the experimental program, and the person must be fully capable of understanding those consequences. In the modern civilized world, those experimented upon must give their consent—whether the experiment is medical or psychological. If any scientist or researcher accepting federal and state money were to carry out the kinds of social experiments in behavioral control practiced by many of today's cults and groups that use thought-reform processes, they would surely be in deep trouble. Thus, when I'm asked why there aren't more published studies on thought reform, the answer is that it would be an impermissible experiment.

Many former cult members have said to me, "If I had known ahead of time each of the things that I eventually, one step at a time, was going to be led into doing, I never would have joined." Of course, the reason they are not told is that for thought reform to work, a cultic group needs the key factor of a hidden agenda. If these groups were to explain to people what they are doing, they would no longer have a thought-reform environment.

Imagine a cult recruiter approaching a person on the street and saying: "If you come to dinner and a lecture on stress at the place where I live, you'll end up being led to buy more and more expensive courses, to meditate and hyperventilate eight hours a day for thirty days in very expensive courses, and eventually to work for the organization to pay for the courses. You will leave your family and friends and put your time in almost exclusively with us." How may new members would she get to join?

Or how likely would anyone be to get consent for this proposal: "If you join my Bible study group, you will leave your family, be sent to faraway parts of the world, often to use your body as a lure to get men to join, and all the money you get by begging will be sent to the head of our cult back here in the United States, where he lives in luxury. And, oh, by the way, we are going to brainwash you into doing all the things we want done for his benefit"?

How would a recruiter explain and obtain consent if he had to say: "I will have you take this personality test that we always interpret as showing that your personality is a wreck. You'll be led to buy very expensive courses and pay thousands of dollars to explore your past lives, then to explore the past lives of countless little men you can't see who we claim cover your body"? How successful do you think that gimmick would be?

Many modern-day cultic groups are exposing their members to very intense psychological exploitation, stress, and social pressures in order to produce desired attitudinal changes. At the point of joining, and even for sometime thereafter, members have little idea of what they will ultimately be led to do. Not all, but many, of these groups are deceptive during the recruitment phase. And all, across the board, are deceptive about the bottom line. If those using thought-reform processes were providing the truth about their techniques, they would have to inform people in ways like those I have just illustrated. But it is because these cultic groups do not conform to the ethics and laws governing human participation in experiments that they continue to ply their trade as they do. One cult leader would even talk about her group to her inner circle as her "human experiment"!

There are people in all societies who are adept at reading others in order to know how best to work their own personal charm and their influence and persuasion techniques. They skillfully modify their approaches—some of which may be designed ahead of time, while others appear to evolve as leaders try out various patterns of persuasion. Certain groups have even consulted social psychologists who have helped them sequence and perfect their programs to make them more effective. But for the most part, leaders of cults and groups that use thought-reform processes draw upon traditional methods of influence, then use their own observations to perfect their recruiting and retain members once they have joined. What is crucial is that these programs are coordinated and packaged and, in most instances, involve a cadre of second-level helpers who carry out assigned roles in recruiting, modeling approved behavior, convincing individuals to stay, and perpetuating the behavior the leader wants.

We realize how fragile human social identity is when we see people caught up in today's cults and thought-reform groups and when we see cult leaders and other manipulators formulate their brainwashing programs around almost any theme. What makes the recent programs so effective in producing attitudinal and behavioral change is that persuasive techniques have been taken to a new level of sophistication. And through their new method of attacking the self, cults and other groups using thought-reform processes are pushing people to the brink of madness. In some cases, they push them over that edge. There are no controls on these snatchers of the minds and souls of our children, our friends, our relatives, our loved ones. Currently, the cults are without restraints and without consciences.

4

What's Wrong with Cults?

The growth of cults and their effects on individuals and family life have taken on new meaning in the past two decades. Cults are now an international phenomenon. There are millions of families in the United States, Canada, Europe, Australia, Japan, and elsewhere whose worlds have been drastically changed by a cult involvement. The influence of the cults in our midst also reaches into the political and economic realms, with repercussions for all of us.

The concerns that I share with others include the following:

- Cults are causing considerable damage to countless individuals and families in our society.
- Cults are using sophisticated psychological and social persuasion techniques to recruit and retain members. These techniques should be studied and revealed so that citizens can be taught countermeasures in order to avoid being exploited by such groups.
- Cults are using their wealth to curb fair criticism and comment through their threats of legal action and other intimidating actions.
- Cults represent encroachments of authoritarianism into our society under various guises, and this should be studied not only by behavioral scientists but also by ordinary citizens who care about their freedom.

The most cogent analysis of the problems and impact of cults in our society has arisen out of viewing their effects on individuals, families, and society as a public health issue, that is, a concern about the effect of certain practices on the health of the general population. Practices such as smoking, drinking alcohol, using illegal drugs, overeating, breathing polluted air, failing to get vaccinations, and eating in unclean restaurants can have deleterious effects. Those who study the impact of cult life find that its effects on individuals and families are in many ways also public health and safety issues.

Cults affect our lives in a number of ways, which I outline in the remainder of this chapter.

Cults Threaten Legitimate Institutions

Some cults in the United States have grown so large and wealthy that they have dominated surrounding communities. One well-known example is what happened in Antelope, Oregon, in the early 1980s. Under the guidance of Indian guru Bhagwan Shree Rajneesh and his top lieutenant, Ma Anand Sheela, a flock of disciples bought 125 square miles of undeveloped land and proceeded to build a city. They imported thirty-five hundred homeless people from around the country to vote in Antelope's local elections, in essence taking over the local government. They even changed the name of the town from Antelope to Rajneeshpuram. They also brought numerous unemployed street people into the area to serve as guards for the commune. When these recruits grew restive, they left the commune and became indigent welfare clients of various Oregon agencies. They were not taken care of by the cult but were left to the mercy of the local citizens.

Many other problems have arisen in various locales in relation to other cultic groups. Land and property purchases have affected local tax rates in certain cities and counties when cults registered as religious organizations have bought great chunks of property that then become tax-exempt. Withholding tax dollars is a common allegation against cultic groups. Over the years numerous legal clashes between cultic groups and local, state, and federal agencies have occurred; however, a history of these many cases, their charges, defenses, appeals, and resolutions, is beyond the scope of this book.

In recent years, some groups have also found new ways to recruit by gaining access to commercial businesses and government agencies. A series of cultic groups has begun selling business management programs that rely heavily on intense influence techniques rather than skills training and, in many instances, serve as avenues to increase the membership of the parent organizations. Professional offices—especially dental, chiropractic, and veterinarian—and a variety of industries have been targeted as candidates for purchasing workshops and seminars for their staff. Some of these cultic groups use large group awareness training (LGAT) techniques (see Chapter Eight).

Most managers are not aware of the true nature of these training sessions because often the courses are sold by cult affiliates, with a variety of names. In some cases, however, managers or bosses are cult followers or sympathizers, acting on cult orders. LGAT leaders scan the application forms of those who attend their workshops, and specific individuals are then approached and encouraged to convince their companies to buy the training program.

As mentioned, these programs, which are supposed to "transform" employees, usually are not skill-training courses but ways for the cult to get money and find new members. In some instances, the material used in the training programs is practically identical to material used by the parent group in in-house sessions or is adapted directly from group teachings. In February 1988, the Equal Employment Opportunity Commission issued a statement about "new age" business programs, alerting employers to the dangers of sending staff to such programs.

Many members of a variety of cults work for little or no pay in businesses owned and operated by their cults. Their earnings are siphoned off, directly or indirectly, to cult headquarters, along with company profits. This puts cults in a strategic position to place very low bids for jobs, which private industry cannot match. In this way, these cult businesses can secure many contracts. For example, using free or underpaid labor, these groups can run boats more cheaply or provide field hands at lower rates than other employers and so they compete unfairly in the marketplace. For example, one large group operated a cleaning firm. According to ex-members of the group, cleaning company employees turned over their paychecks to the organization. Because of this low cost of labor, the company was able to underbid its competitors and win a government contract to clean all carpets in federal offices in two California counties. Similarly, a small West Coast political cult had owned a full-service printing plant and could provide low-cost, high-quality, quick-turnaround jobs for such customers as banks, local magazines and publishers, catalogue companies, and advertising agencies, with cult members providing an endless supply of unpaid labor, often working round-the-clock double shifts to meet promised deadlines.

Occasionally, but unfortunately not very often, there is redress. In 1992, evangelist Tony Alamo settled a government suit against him by agreeing to pay $5 million to reimburse followers who worked long hours for less than the minimum wage. At one time the Tony and Susan Alamo Foundation operated in Arkansas, Tennessee, and California and ran a number of lucrative enterprises, including a restaurant, a service station, a cement company, a ranch, and a Nashville couturier for country-and-western entertainers. In fashion boutiques around the country, Alamo Designs sold extravagantly decorated designer jackets, with price tags ranging from $600 to $1,000.

By means of exploiting underpaid or unpaid labor, evading taxes, and taking advantage of a curious public and an open-minded business world eager for self-improvement, cults are able to expand their wealth, create new sources of potential recruits, and take work and income away from private businesses.

Cults Harm Our Children and
Tear Apart Our Families

In many ways, children are the most powerless victims of the harsh and arbitrary rule that characterizes life for many cult members. The following examples bring to light the indecencies that abound.

- In 1986, William A. Lewis, sixty-three-year-old leader of the Black Hebrew House of Judah in Michigan, was convicted of conspiracy to enslave children and causing the 1983 beating death of twelve-year-old John Yarbough in an act of discipline.

- In 1988, fifty-three children were removed by law enforcement officials from a group called Ecclesia Athletic Association, following the beating death of eight-year-old Dayna Lorae Broussard. The children raised in the group could not read and write but knew the Book of Romans by heart. Children aged three to eighteen were forced to run long distances and perform drills and exercises to earn money. The dead girl's father, who was the group's leader, and several of his followers were charged with slavery and violating the civil rights of more than two dozen children. The father died before his trial, but as part of a plea bargain, seven other members pleaded guilty to a federal charge of a conspiracy to deny civil rights. Earlier, four Ecclesia followers were convicted of manslaughter in the case of the dead young girl.

- In 1991, Tony Alamo, leader of the Holy Alamo Christian Church Consecrated, was arrested by the FBI after a two-year manhunt. He was charged with ordering four men to strike a ten-year-old boy with a wooden paddle 140 times. His criminal case is still pending.

A further concern for our society is that cults are diverting some of society's best minds away from education and rational thought. Numerous individuals are being prevented from contributing to humankind's welfare through science, medicine, teaching, ecology, and other careers. Instead, they are being lured into cults, where they may end up spending years contributing only to the power and comfort of the cult leader. They lose some of the most important years of their lives, and when they emerge they may be unable to use their former abilities and talents because they will be behind in so many ways.

Cults also turn members against their families, using a plethora of rationales made to fit the group's ideology. One political cult, for example, "tests" young recruits by having them deliberately lie to their parents while someone in leadership stands next to them when they make the call. This is a first step in both separating recruits from their families and teaching them to follow irrational orders. Psychotherapy and self-improvement cults are particularly known for getting members to produce revised personal histories and, especially, to view their parents as evil and no longer trustworthy. Similarly, as I have mentioned, the religious cults train members to regard outsiders, even blood relatives, as of Satan and to be avoided at all costs.

Some cults have begun to recruit the elderly or the infirm. I receive more and more requests for help in dealing with parents and grandparents who have been taken in by cults. As you can see, cults have indeed influenced all types of people and infiltrated all walks of life.

Cults Are Violent

Cults are abusive and destructive to varying degrees. Some abuse only their own members; others project the violence outward. Still others have it both ways. Cult members, at the direction of their leaders, have shot at law enforcement officers, engaged in drug dealing and prostitution, stockpiled illegal weapons, practiced repeated sexual abuse, beaten child members to death, enforced a variety of punishments against their own, and murdered dissident members. The following examples are a mere sampling of what we've witnessed in the past twenty-five years.

• In 1969, the Charles Manson "family" terrified the country with brutal murders committed in Hollywood.

- In 1977, a polygamy sect murdered a number of opponents and later murdered five persons who had left the group. Law enforcement authorities believe the cult is responsible for more than twenty murders since 1972. The leader, Ervil LeBaron, who fathered fifty-four children, died in 1981 while imprisoned for directing the killing of another polygamy group leader. Several cult members have been sentenced on a variety of federal charges.

- In 1982, members of a faith-healing cult in Miracle Valley, Arizona, attempted to bomb a sheriff's department. Later, when police tried to serve arrest warrants for traffic violations, the group opened fire, seriously wounding two police officers. Two cult members died in the shoot-out.

- In 1986, Keith Ham, also known as Swami Kirtanananda Bhaktipada, the leader of a Hare Krishna splinter group, and some of his followers were targets of a federal investigation into multiple murders, drug dealing, and child sexual abuse. Thomas Drescher, Ham's lieutenant, was convicted in 1987 of one murder and faces charges for another. Allegations against Ham included fraud, racketeering, and murder conspiracy to protect a multimillion-dollar business. In 1993, he won a new trial.

- In 1992, Yahweh Ben Yahweh, leader of a Miami-based group, was convicted of a murder conspiracy charge in the deaths of fourteen people. He was sentenced to eighteen years in federal prison.

Cults Engage in Conspiracy and Fraud

Not only have cultic groups engaged in openly violent behavior, but they have also engaged in other activities that have led to members' being convicted of crimes ranging from conspiracy to tax evasion, spying on governments, and fraud.

- In 1981, a federal appeals court upheld the convictions of nine Scientologists involved in a conspiracy to steal government documents about their group.

• In 1984, Unification Church leader Sun Myung Moon was convicted of conspiracy to obstruct justice and conspiracy to file false tax returns and sentenced to federal prison.

• In 1985, Bhagwan Shree Rajneesh was deported after pleading guilty to immigration fraud and to arranging sham marriages so that his foreign followers could stay in the United States. Later, a never-implemented plot to murder a government official critical of the group was revealed.

• In 1988, Lyndon LaRouche, Jr., and six members of his political organization were convicted of tax evasion, mail fraud, and conspiracy for allegedly bilking political supporters of $25 million. He was sentenced to fifteen years in federal prison and was released on parole in early 1994.

• In 1989, Ed Francis, husband of Elizabeth Clare Prophet of the Church Universal and Triumphant, based in Montana, pleaded guilty to conspiring with another group member to illegally purchase $130,000 worth of weapons. The cache included armor-piercing bullets, seven machine guns, military assault rifles, and 120,000 rounds of ammunition.

• In 1992, for the first time in Canada's history, a church was put on trial for criminal offenses. The Church of Scientology and three of its members were found guilty of breach of trust, and the court levied a fine of $250,000. The case stemmed from charges of infiltration of the Ontario government and three police forces in the 1970s. The Toronto Church of Scientology filed a $19 million countersuit against the Ontario Provincial Police and the attorney general's ministry, alleging illegal and unconstitutional search and seizure during the case-related raid of the church's Toronto headquarters.

Small Cults Can Be Just as Harmful as Large

A cult does not have to be large to wreak havoc upon individuals or society. Just consider the following:

- Circle of Friends leader George Jurcsek, seventy-three, was convicted of masterminding a student loan scam. Prior to his imprisonment he lived lavishly, relying on his followers' donated paychecks to pay for his mansions and limousines. According to former members, Jurcsek told them that if they left the group they would be stricken with AIDS or cancer.

- Maryland officials suspended the license of a doctor who allegedly had sex with patients, smoked illegal drugs with them, and portrayed himself as the "embodiment of God." Some former patients reported that he told them he was on a secret spiritual mission, part of which was to father his patients' children. One couple allowed the doctor to visit their home as often as five times a week for seven years, whereupon he would have sex with the wife while the husband remained downstairs. The doctor convinced the husband that this was part of the treatment for the wife, who was supposedly cutting her husband off spiritually.

This last example, which may appear more idiosyncratic than cultic, is in fact a prime example of the varieties of intense influence that exist both in cults and in ordinary life in every part of the country. Around us every day, people are experiencing psychological, spiritual, physical, and/or financial harm caused by cults large and small and by intense coordinated persuasion efforts. And some of these instances of coercive influence are not carried out by a group; instead, they occur in one-on-one situations where a nurse, a conservator, a lawyer, a doctor, or a mate has used *undue influence*, the legal term for cases of coercive persuasion, typically to gain a financial advantage—for example, in someone's will. Additional abuses of power include fraud or extortion, which, again, can occur one-on-one or in a group setting.

Other harmful situations may come about from trendy scams or get-rich-quick schemes that have adopted some of the well-publicized methods people have learned by observing the success of the LGATs. Recently, for example, a class action suit was brought against a man who was giving five-day seminars costing $15,000 and up for prospective real-estate entrepreneurs. Complainants said the course was a "boot camp from hell." Among other claims, they said they were made to sit through hours of motivational lectures in a chilly room with no breaks for meals, sometimes from dawn to midnight.

Cults Take Away Our Freedom

Because of the total commitment required of members and the severity of the demands made upon them, cults do very real harm to our democratic way of life. They intentionally disrupt educational and career goals, break up families, stifle personal relationships, and coerce followers into turning over savings, property, and other assets. In many instances, the effects of membership are traumatic, long lasting, and sometimes irreversible. The following illustrations of a few former cult members I've met with over the years provide evidence of the long-term harm caused by cults, yet barely scratch the surface of the enormity and severity of the problem.

> "Julia" joined a small Bible-based cult at age twenty-seven, after nearly completing a doctorate in education. The leader spoke highly of marriage, children, and serving mankind— the first step to achieving world peace and ending hunger was to become vegetarian and live in his group, he said. Although promising Julia a "blessed marriage," the leader banished any man who showed interest in her or she in him. Over the next seventeen years, Julia saw others being "matched" for marriage while the leader repeatedly assured Julia of the same. In her mid forties, finally seeing the leader for what he was—a user of her and others—and feeling totally betrayed and hopeless, Julia attempted suicide. After hospitalization she left the cult. She has never been able to "really trust anyone again [and] is philosophically shattered." She leads a reclusive life as a night clerk in a tiny motel.

"Cathy" had been a high school and college cheerleader, lively and full of fun, and planning to go to nursing school. During her two-year membership in a live-in psychology cult, everything about her was questioned by the leader, a woman claiming to have "the only therapy that evolves humans."

"I lost myself," said Cathy. "They told me I had to surrender my fake self, and they would remake me. I tried to do what they said, but I felt more and more empty, became more and more depressed. There just wasn't any 'me' anymore. When I couldn't even help in the kitchen, they called my parents to come and get me."

Now in her early thirties, Cathy has been out of the cult for nearly eight years, has not dated, lives at home with her parents, and works at part-time jobs. Neither medications nor psychotherapy has helped restore her to her once lively and spirited self.

Some cult members end up in psychiatric hospitals; others sometimes drift for years after a cult experience, never quite getting it together. People who have had such intense experiences, particularly when combined with a concerted breaking down of their selves, require special care afterward (see Chapter Twelve). Even those who may not experience severe psychological difficulties often will have considerable problems adjusting to normal life after leaving a cult.

Cults Take Away Our Possessions

Cult leaders have been able to get wealthy followers to turn over amazingly large amounts of money, just as they have been able to get the less well off to turn over everything they have, as in the following examples.

"Joseph" was a senior at a prestigious East Coast university and planned on a career in the diplomatic service. While alone in Washington, D.C., during a summer break, he was taken by a casual acquaintance to meet people in what turned out to be a cult. Initially, he was told that the group was students, families, and single adults living together to demonstrate harmonious communal living, and he was invited to stay with the group in the Maryland countryside. He was surprised to learn later that they in fact were teaching beliefs about astral projection. Joseph said he first felt they had pretty bizarre ideas; but since he also felt that everyone treated him "so special," he felt flattered and stayed to check them out further. Gradually, the group took over his life. Convinced that he had to stay away from his family and former friends, he abandoned his education and, before long, gave the group his inheritance. After seven years he had a mental breakdown and was thrown out of the cult. When I met Joseph, he was depressed, disheveled, and unemployable, living in a homeless men's shelter, and seeking legal assistance to see if he could get any of his inheritance back from the group.

"Ed" was in his early thirties when he gave $13 million to the self-appointed leader of an East Coast life-style cult that was based on an amalgam of health food and meditation and that had taken total control of the man's life. The cult leader had a military background and claimed knowledge of brainwashing and thought reform from his tour of duty in the Far East. Legal assistance over a period of time helped Ed recover a goodly portion of his inheritance.

Some students alleged that a retired university political science professor used his knowledge and charisma to turn a study group at a large university into a cult. The students claimed that houses and money were given to a supposed lodge dedicated to theosophy and to the professor's "retirement fund." The students also alleged that work for the professor's lodge and mountain-top retreat was done by students on university time. These followers were supposed to call the professor "the teacher," as he claimed to be "the most brilliant mind since Einstein" and stressed total obedience.

Helen Overington, age eighty-two, and her husband, of Baltimore, had lived a frugal life and had raised five children and educated them well. When her husband died, he left her $1 million. Disciples of Lyndon LaRouche, Jr., three-time candidate for U.S. President, allegedly induced the aged Mrs. Overington to give them more than $741,000 within a year's time. By the time her children caught on to what was happening, she could no longer afford health insurance or her Baltimore apartment and had to move in with a daughter. Away from the insistent pounding on her door and incessant phone calls, Mrs. Overington now can scarcely believe she gave so much money to the LaRoucheites. At the time she gave the money, LaRouche was still serving his fifteen-year prison term for mail fraud and tax evasion. At least sixteen of his associates have been indicted for fraudulent fund-raising, often from elderly women.

Luther Dulaney, at age twenty-six and with an inheritance from his grandfather, was induced by a small California cult of thirty members, the Church of Unlimited Devotion, to loan the group his $108,000 with no interest for a real-estate investment. The leader had referred to Luther as a "trust fund baby" on several occasions and anticipated convincing Luther not to collect on the loan. The group combined Krishna-Consciousness (ISKCON), Catholicism, and Sufism (one order of which is known in the West as the whirling dervishes). The church would follow the Grateful Dead road tours, attend the concerts, and sell handmade clothing in the venues' parking lots. According to former members, the group regarded Jerry Garcia's guitar as a channel for God's voice. They "meditated in motion" by dancing to the music of the Dead, and thus becoming known popularly as the Spinners. Luther has begun foreclosure proceedings to gain title to the now-defunct group's property.

Betsy Dovydenas was able to recover $6.6 million that she had given to The Bible Speaks when a Springfield, Massachusetts, Federal District Court judge ruled that fraud and deception were used by The Bible Speaks. The judge ruled that Mrs. Dovydenas had been lied to and manipulated to get her to donate the money.

Although there has been some litigation favorable to plaintiffs to remedy some devastating losses, in most cases cult victims have not pursued legal action.

Cults Escape Scrutiny

Despite a rather grim record of atrocious behavior, time and again cults escape the scrutiny and controls bestowed upon other organizations and activities.

Why is that? I ask myself. Is it because so many of them hide behind our country's Constitution by filing for religious status, which not only frees them from paying taxes but also avails them of certain privileges they surely have never earned? Is it because, as a society, we are wont to look the other way, to give the other guy the benefit of the doubt?

What is wrong with cults, besides their objectionable behavior, is that they are so little understood, so rarely given a hard look. If they were, many more of us would surely protest. Currently, most people remain relatively unaware of the existence of cults until startled by media coverage of a cult's bizarre or illegal behavior. When the subject does come up, people may have difficulty pinpointing the problem with cults. They may even say that what goes on in cults is no different from the behavior of their boss, who has all the say at work, or their authoritarian father or their dysfunctional family or the values imposed by the Judeo-Christian ethic.

But a cult is not benign simply because it may have one or two traits in common with other kinds of social groupings. The fact that cults are authoritarian and your father is also authoritarian does not make them the same. I like to call this way of thinking *the fallacy of one similarity*. For example, elephants, lions, and sheep all breathe oxygen. However, elephants are herbivores with no natural predators, lions are carnivores with no natural predators, and sheep are herbivores who get preyed on a lot. It is their differences that are paramount in explaining these animals' conduct. Their differences tell more about their specific activities than the fact that all breathe oxygen.

From time to time I will also hear someone compare cults to an organization like Alcoholics Anonymous (AA) or to some other group with a charismatic leader. Again, it is not the one feature—namely, a charismatic leader or adherence to a particular belief system—that cults may share with another group that is crucial; rather, it is the differences that are important. AA does not recruit deceptively, AA does not hide what membership eventually will entail, and members can leave at any point. AA focuses on helping people grow, while cults use their members to promote the growth of the cult and increase the cult leader's power and wealth. Cults are complex structures, and by taking any one point out of context, we can lose sight of the whole.

One former cult member was told by a current member of the group he had been in, "Everything is a cult. The biggest is the breathing cult, because we all breathe air. There is the Jerry Garcia cult, the Ben & Jerry Ice Cream cult, the *Rocky Horror* movie cult." He went on to disparage the ex-member for having written a critique of the group, saying, "You were just too weak. You just had a bad trip, couldn't cut the mustard. You probably had a bad time in the Boy Scouts. You are just a toad and an asshole." To equate cults with everything else and not see the inherent dangers and exploitative nature of cults ultimately provides ammunition to cult leaders who chastise defectors as snivelers, complainers, and weaklings.

The most frequent question I am asked in casual conversations, in classrooms, and in courtroom testimony is, "Well, aren't the Jesuits and the United States Marine Corps cults? Don't they do they same thing?" No, these groups are not cults, and they do not brainwash people. They are established albeit authoritarian groups with clear-cut training programs and work missions. They differ in a multitude of ways from cults.

In particular, neither of these groups deceptively recruits. Marine recruiters do not pretend to be florists or recruiters for children's clubs. Nor do Jesuits go afield claiming they are "just an international living group teaching breathing exercises to clear the mind of stress." In addition, neither group deceives members about the reality of membership, the bottom-line commitment, and the acts that will be expected.

I have had to point out why the United States Marine Corps is not a cult so many times that I carry a list to lectures and court appearances (Exhibit 4.1). It cites nineteen ways in which the practices of the Marine Corps differ from those found in most modern cults. Clearly, the Marine Corps is a military training program authorized by our society. It is based upon a known chain of command in a hierarchical, authoritarian system. But it is not a cult, it is not a brainwashing outfit, and it is controlled by the laws of our land.

Cults clearly differ from such purely authoritarian groups as the military, some types of sects and communes, and centuries-old Roman Catholic and Greek and Russian Orthodox orders. These groups, though rigid and controlling, lack a double agenda and are not manipulative or leader-centered. The differences become apparent when we examine the intensity and pervasiveness with which mind-manipulating techniques and deceptions are or are not applied.

Jesuit seminaries may isolate the seminarian from the rest of the world for periods of time, but the candidate is not deliberately deceived about the obligations and burdens of the priesthood. In fact, he is warned in advance about what is expected, and what he can and cannot do. He is also given every opportunity to withdraw. Some religious groups even impose a waiting or cooling-off period.

Mainstream religious organizations do not concentrate their search on the lonely and vulnerable; in fact, many orders use psychiatric screening to eliminate those whose motivations to join are expressions of emotional instability. Nor do mainstream religions focus recruitment on wealthy believers who are seen as pots of gold for the church, as is the case with those cults who target rich individuals.

Military training and legitimate executive training programs may use the dictates of authority as well as peer pressure to encourage the adoption of new patterns of thought and behavior. They do not seek, however, to accelerate the process by prolonged or intense physiological depletion or by stirring up feelings of dread, guilt, and sinfulness. While strenuous, military training is aimed at strengthening performance, whereas cults try to weaken the person. Few if any social institutions claiming First Amendment protection use conditioning techniques as intense, deceptive, or pervasive as those used by many contemporary cults.

And what is wrong with cults is not just that cults are secret societies. In our culture, there are openly recognized, social secret societies, such as the Masons, in which new members know up front that they will gradually learn the shared rituals of the group even though they do not know everything about the group right away. This is different from cultic groups and others that use thought-reform techniques. In these latter groups, there is deliberate deception about what the group is and what some of the rituals might be, and primarily, there is deception about what the ultimate goal will be for a member, what will ultimately be demanded and expected, and what the damages resulting from some of the practices might be. A secret handshake is not equivalent to mind control.

Today, the recruiting practices and programmatic activities of many cults have caused clear and tangible social concerns. How can society best protect individuals from physical and psychologi-

Exhibit 4.1. How the United States
Marine Corps Differs from Cults.

1. The Marine recruit clearly knows what the organization is that he or she is joining. What will be expected of him or her and what will transpire are laid out clearly before joining. There are no secret stages such as people come upon in cults. Cult recruits often attend a cult activity, are lured into "staying for a while," and soon find that they have joined the cult for life, or as one group requires, members sign up for a "billion year contract." The United States Marine Corps (USMC) program is set and outlined from the start.

2. The Marine recruit retains freedom of religion, politics, friends, family association, selection of spouse, and information access to television, radio, reading material, telephone, and mail.

3. The Marine serves a term of enlistment and departs freely. The Marine can reenlist if he or she desires but is not forced to remain.

4. Medical and dental care are available, encouraged, and permitted in the Marines. This is not true in the many cults that discourage and sometimes forbid medical care.

5. Training and education received in the Marines are usable later in life. Cults do not necessarily train a person in anything that has any value in the greater society.

6. In the USMC, public records are kept and are available. Cult records, if they exist, are confidential, hidden from members, and not shared.

7. USMC Inspector General procedures protect each Marine. Nothing protects cult members.

8. A military legal system is provided within the USMC; a Marine can also utilize off-base legal and law enforcement agencies and other representatives if needed. In cults, there is only the closed, internal system of justice, and no appeal, no recourse to outside support.

9. Families of military personnel talk and deal directly with schools. Children may attend public or private schools. In cults, children, child rearing, and education are often controlled by the whims and idiosyncracies of the cult leader.

10. The USMC is not a sovereign entity above the laws of the land. Cults consider themselves above the law, with their own brand of morality and justice, accountable to no one, not even their members.

11. A Marine gets to keep her or his pay, property owned and acquired, presents from relatives, inheritances, and so on. In many cults, mem-

Exhibit 4.1. How the United States
Marine Corps Differs from Cults. (Cont.)

bers are expected to turn over to the cult all monies and worldly possessions.

12. Rational behavior is valued in the USMC. Cults stultify members' critical thinking abilities and capacity for rational, independent thinking; normal thought processes are stifled and broken.

13. In the USMC, suggestions and criticism can be made to leadership and upper echelons through advocated, proper channels. There are no suggestion boxes in cults. The cult is always right, and the members (and outsiders) are always wrong.

14. Marines cannot be used for medical or psychological experiments without their informed consent. Cults essentially perform psychological experiments on their members through implementing thought-reform processes without members' knowledge or consent.

15. Reading, education, and knowledge are encouraged and provided through such agencies as Armed Services Radio and *Stars and Stripes*, and through books, post libraries, and so on. If cults do any education, it is only in their own teachings. Members come to know less and less about the outside world; contact with or information about life outside the cult is sometimes openly frowned upon, if not forbidden.

16. In the USMC, physical fitness is encouraged for all. Cults rarely encourage fitness or good health, except perhaps for members who serve as security guards or thugs.

17. Adequate and properly balanced nourishment is provided and advocated in the USMC. Many cults encourage or require unhealthy and bizarre diets. Typically, because of intense work schedules, lack of funds, and other cult demands, members are not able to maintain healthy eating habits.

18. Authorized review by outsiders, such as the U.S. Congress, is made of the practices of the USMC. Cults are accountable to no one and are rarely investigated, unless some gross criminal activity arouses the attention of the authorities or the public.

19. In the USMC, the methods of instruction are military training and education, even indoctrination into the traditions of the USMC, but brainwashing, or thought reform, is not used. Cults influence members by means of a coordinated program of psychological and social influence techniques, or brainwashing.

cal harm, from stultification of their ability to act autonomously, from loss of vital years of their life, and from dehumanizing exploitation—all without interfering with their freedom of choice in regard to religious practices and group association? And while protecting religious freedom, how can society protect the family as a social institution from the menace of the cult as a competing superfamily?

What Is to Be Done?

Even a brief review of cult casualties and consequences illustrates why we need to be concerned about cults. But our concern must focus on conduct, not beliefs. People are free to believe whatever they choose. Nevertheless, even in a democracy, after inspecting and evaluating the conduct of particular groups, citizens may have cause for concern when they see the effects on individuals subjugated to the will of cult leaders. Cults, as we've seen, are elitist and feel they have the right to determine who thrives or even survives. As citizens of a humane and free-thinking society, we should become concerned about the health, welfare, and safety of our fellow citizens, especially the children, who are in cults.

Great numbers of people have regarded cults as momentary fads that would soon fade. That is not the situation. We have to overcome the massive denial of those who have not bothered to learn about cults and of those who hide behind the myths. Some people tend to think that if they ignore a problem, it will go away. There are cult apologists who have looked at cults only superficially, who in their defense of the cults are feeding the myths and hindering public education about an issue that cries out for attention.

The psychotechnology of thought reform is not going to go away. It is also not harmless, as the apologists and cult spokespeople would have us believe. We have, in fact, seen cult techniques of persuasion and control become more skillful, more subtle, and more damaging during the past two decades. Education, information, and vigilance are constantly needed to keep us, and our minds, free.

PART TWO
How Do They Work?

5

Recruiting New Members

All of us are vulnerable to cult recruitment. So many cults, using so many guises and ploys, are actively looking for members at any given moment that surely there may be a cult for you. Whatever your age, whatever your interests, whatever your life-style, succumbing to the lure of a cult recruiter is as easy as getting a library card. There are as many ways to become involved with a cult as there are cults.

Each group develops its own recruitment methods—ranging from personal contacts to advertisements on kiosks, in newspapers and magazines, and on television and radio. The original point of recruitment may vary, but one constant factor is that rampant deceptions are involved. These deceptions extend from concealment of exactly what the group is at "the point of pick up" to concealment of the ultimate purpose of membership.

Someone may try to get you into a cult by contacting you on your computer bulletin board. You may sign up for a college class only to find that the instructor is a dedicated cultist, bent on surreptitiously recruiting students. You may visit your veterinarian, your chiropractor, your dentist, your optometrist, or your next-door neighbor, only to have her or him attempt to recruit you. In a recent survey of 381 former members of 101 different cultic groups, 66 percent stated that their initial contact with their group came through a friend or relative. The rest were recruited by strangers.

Cult recruitment occurs in four main stages: the first approach by a cult recruiter; the invitation to a wonderful place or special event or an important, alluring meeting; the first contact with the cult, where you are made to feel loved and wanted; and the follow-up, using psychologically persuasive techniques to ensure your quick return or greater commitment.

First Approach

Cult members are trained in persuasive methods of approaching potential recruits. Because we are all social creatures, most of us are prone to listen to nice-looking people who approach us in a friendly or helping manner and speak enthusiastically about what they believe in.

I have had a few persons tell me that when they were "down and out" on the streets of Los Angeles or San Francisco, they were recruited by sincere-sounding, street-preaching types, using heavy guilt and fear tactics related to the homeless person's drug and alcohol use. But what actually got them to check the group out was the personal offer of a place to stay, food, and companions who were not also on the streets. Both the sugar-and-honey and the "you must leave this sordid life" approaches are appealing because the solicitor offers something that the person feels would be good for her or him.

By and large, cult members did not seek out the group they joined but were personally approached in some way. A few persons get into cults by responding to advertisements, but even then, what ties the knot is the personal interaction with recruiters—individuals zealously focused on getting more members into the group.

Whom Do Cults Recruit?

In Chapter One, I noted that the key vulnerability factors are, first, being in between important affiliations, between commitments to work, school, or life in general, and second, being even slightly depressed or a bit lonely. Cults aim their recruitment at vulnerable people because these individuals are less likely to see through the layers of deceit. Cults target friendly, obedient, altruistic, and malleable persons because such individuals are easy to persuade and manage. Cults prefer not to deal with recalcitrant, disobedient, self-centered types, for they are simply too difficult to mold and control.

Another important factor is that the person approached by a cult recruiter must see that there is time available to check out the recruiter's proposal. Also, he or she must resonate to the offering. This means the recruiter must manipulate the first conversation, getting enough information about the person to shape the discussion and make the group seem like something the person would want to know about or experience.

Where Do Cults Recruit?

Cults recruit everywhere. They hold lectures, seminars, retreats, revivals, and meetings of all sorts, and they go door to door. They run schools, universities, health clinics, and businesses. They advertise in New Age magazines, in alternative newspapers, and in business journals. They have tables at professional and trade meetings, computer expositions, publishing exhibitions, and street fairs. One large cult has a rock band that tours the country and serves as an attraction in malls and large assembly areas. Of course, cult members also recruit among their own family circles, friendship networks, co-workers, and vocational or hobby associations.

Although cults are active everywhere, schools and university campuses have been a fertile field for recruitment for all types of cults since the sixties. Some cults assign members to recruit on junior and senior high school grounds, in college dormitories and at freshmen activities days, and at all sorts of campus events and locales.

In the survey mentioned earlier, of the 381 former members, 43 percent were students when they were recruited (10 percent in high school, 27 percent in college, and 6 percent in graduate school), and 38 percent of these students dropped out of school once they'd joined the group.

Here, for example, is the experience of one college student.

"Charles," a university senior active in a number of social and political causes, felt he could handle any verbal challenges that came his way. He was bright, educated, articulate, and before this experience, would never have dreamed he could get caught up in a cult.

"Barnabas," the leader of a small cult, had written to a university official saying that he operated an international foundation and was looking for an outstanding student to include on his team. Without any exploration into the validity of this claim, an administrator sent the letter to a department head who gave Charles's name to the cult leader. Barnabas sought out Charles and introduced himself, stating that he headed a peace foundation and wanted to put students in charge of segments of the new world order.

Tall, demanding, articulate, and energetic, Barnabas managed to impress Charles and several other students who agreed to work with him. Barnabas soon wore them down through long, haranguing, sleep-depriving sessions conducted in their residence hall. He showed up at Charles's classes, sat beside him, and did not let him out of his sight. Soon, Charles left school to trek up and down the West Coast with Barnabas, stopping at automatic teller machines for Charles to withdraw cash for bus tickets and meals. Barnabas also got other students to leave school.

Cults use a variety of strategies and change them as needed in order to increase their possibilities for success. Former members have told me how, from time to time, their leaders changed tactics, announcing that certain ploys would work better.

For example, an interesting change of methods was described by a woman who had been trained by her Bible cult leader to go to college dorms and eating areas, approach women students who were alone, and start conversations with them to get them to attend "study groups." One day, her cult leader abruptly changed procedures. Up to that point, individual members had gone out seeking people of the same sex. "Now," the leader proclaimed, "we will have team gathering and reaping. From now on, two sisters or two brothers will go out as pairs to gather and reap, and that way they can approach both men and women." The leader said it was "too sexual" for a man to be approached by a lone woman, or a woman to be approached by a lone man, but two women or two men made such an approach "friendship," and the teams would be able to recruit both male and female students faster. The woman said the new method worked.

Each cult develops its own methods. Some have manuals on how to recruit and provide special training for those members assigned to recruitment. One group sends recruiters out to "look for raw meat"; some have recruitment quotas for each member. Other cults tell members to write up lists of everyone they know and then approach those people to join. Cult leadership helps members refine their recruitment approaches and identify weak spots in the prospective members, based on descriptions in written reports. There is no limit to the ingenuity and also the trickery used. Former cult members often tell me that they didn't even notice their first fatal step toward joining because so much deception was involved.

I have also had people say to me, "No one could argue me into one of those weird groups!" to which I usually respond, "That's right. Arguing is not very seductive. Charm and flattery are." Then I ask, "Did someone ever induce you to go to something, to do something, to believe something that you later found out was a 'line'?" Most people have had such an experience and when they think of the recruitment process that way can understand it a little better.

Invitation

Once contact with a prospective member is made, the pursuit may go something like this:

First, the recruiter, appearing nonthreatening, learns something about the potential recruit in order to put into play the idea that the recruiter and the recruit are alike, that they share commonalities and are in sync.

Second, through this process, the recruiter gets the potential recruit to feel that he or she is resonating with this nice person who is showing such personal care and interest.

Third, the recruiter mirrors the interests and attitudes of the potential recruit, whether these interests are spirituality, nursing, political change, music, or any other area. The recruiter then demonstrates that he has something to offer the potential recruit by extending a verbal invitation to an event, a class, or a dinner.

A *front group* is an organization that serves as a false front for another operation that remains behind the scenes. Most cults have front groups, sometimes a variety of them, set up specifically to appeal to a range of interests. Among these front groups are instructional classes, study groups, Bible groups, social clubs, hobby organizations, management- or job-related training seminars, grass-roots activities, neighborhood associations, political committees, sales schemes, meditation or yoga classes, travel clubs, workers' groups, weight-loss programs, medical offices, psychotherapy clinics, and printing and publishing collectives.

Generally, when a person goes to the first event, he or she sees no indication of a connection to a cult or some background organization. Often even the leader's name doesn't come up until some time after the recruit is drawn further into the recruitment web.

Street Recruitment

On several occasions I have gone out on the streets of Berkeley near the University of California campus with a former cult member who had been a very successful street recruiter. I would be present as she did her old pitch, just as she did in the cult, to get a stranger on the street to promise to come that night or sometime soon to a lecture, a dinner, a meeting for a political cause, or an event focused on ecology issues, self-improvement, or the UFO phenomenon. We targeted nonstudent types, making test cases of the over-thirty crowd—businesspeople and professors, both men and women—to assess how a sophisticated and well-educated audience would respond. Marveling, I would watch my friend work the technique she had learned in the cult. She would talk with a person on the street for a short time; then after the person agreed to come to an event, my friend would introduce me, saying that I was a professor studying cults and that, since she had been in a certain cult and spent much time recruiting, she was showing me exactly how it worked. The people who had been approached were astonished. "But I believed you!" they would exclaim. "You seem like such a nice person. You couldn't have been in a cult."

Often the person who had been approached would ask, "But how did you know I would be interested in a peace group?" or whichever lure had worked. My friend would then repeat her questions and the person's answers, showing how she had capitalized on clues to get a bit more information, and then had made her offer match what the person had unwittingly indicated an interest in. She would explain that she had done the pitch exactly as she had when she recruited for the cult and that it was the standard pitch taught in that group. We would then thank the person and say we hoped he or she had profited from seeing how easily anyone can be tricked and persuaded with soft talk, charm, and an interesting, appealing topic, all of which could be a fabrication—or step one to joining a cult. Almost without fail, each person remarked, "Is that how it's done? It was so smooth. Seemed so honest. I thought cults harangued people with sin, or enlightenment, or something, and argued with them to join."

That First Fatal Step

Many former cult members have referred to "that first fatal step." As they look back, they realize that, for a combination of reasons, their first step of acquiescing to an invitation or a request was the start of weeks, months, or years in a cult. In most cases, potential recruits are pressed to attend an event right away. The recruiter says the event is perfect for them, and gives them no time to reflect on whether they really want to go. Here's a specific example of the way this first step can work.

"Mike" was in his thirties when he came to Berkeley to study for the California Bar Exam. One day, he was approached by two charming women who said they lived in an "international communal living group" that had a place near the snow country. The women were "so personal, so personable, so charming, so clean-looking, so sincere," and their pitch was so seductive, so urgent, and so singularly appealing, that within three hours he had taken them to his apartment, gotten his camera, his ski equipment, some of his study materials, and his certificate of ownership for his car. He said later that, at the time, he did not even question why they wanted him to bring the deed to his car.

They had convinced him that he could study at their retreat. They promised him that he would have his own cabin and good food and that other law students would be there. They said there would be some lectures about their group but assured him he could spend time studying.

Mike spent nearly ten days in the country. His stay ended only when he threatened that if his car was not produced and he was not allowed to leave he would file legal charges against the group. All the visible telephones were broken, and "visitors" were not permitted into the leaders' building to use the working phones. He never had one moment alone the entire time. When, after three days, he realized the group was really a religious cult, he said he wanted to leave. But suddenly, they couldn't locate his car or his ski equipment and camera. When he finally got his car, which they claimed had been moved some miles across the property to a safe place, he drove off leaving behind his other valuables. He was simply relieved to get away.

Former cult members have told me that what they were told, what they read, and what they experienced on first meeting the recruiter had enough appeal at that point in their lives that it hooked them—in more ways than one. The hook was a combination of their own needs at the time and the personality and approach of the recruiter, plus the fact that the topic the recruiter mentioned clicked with them. The recruiter also convinced them they had the time to check it out, and they were convinced that they needed what was being offered.

First Cult Contact

Cults are not like most groups we know in our society. On the surface they may seem like mundane groups, but they differ in many ways. Joining a cult is not like joining the local country club, the Baptist Church, or a Rotary Club, or like taking employment with a commercial enterprise or legitimate nonprofit organization. These latter groups want you to know just who they are and what their program is; they want full capacity, informed consent from you before you join or take the job.

Cults are also reminiscent of a jack-in-the-box—a pretty, innocuous-looking container that, when opened, surprises you with a pop-out figure, often a scary one. Similarly, surprising and frightening things pop out over the course of membership in a cult. What you first see is not what's inside.

Some groups invite you to a meal, claiming to be campus peace organizations when in fact they are fronts for an international cult. They invite you to the country for a three-day seminar. Then, once you're there, they ask you to stay for a one-week program, then another one for twenty-one days. After that amount of time, you'll be so inculcated with their ideas that they'll be able to send you out on the streets to collect money and enlist new members. Within a month or so of their first involvement, thanks to the techniques described in Chapter Three, most recruits are caught.

Recruits are brought to camps in the country, weekend retreats, clandestine cult facilities, workshops in the desert, and a host of other places to isolate them from access to their usual social life. Cult leaders and heads of other groups using thought-reform processes know that this change of place is a practical and effective means of quickly changing behavior and conduct. When cut off from social support, social background, families, familiar surroundings, friends, jobs, schoolmates, and classes and brought into new environs with a new ambience, few can resist the pull to fit in.

Most cults have specific plans for drawing in each recruit. As soon as any interest is shown by the recruits, they may be *love bombed* by the recruiter or other cult members. This process of feigning friendship and interest in the recruit was initially associated with one of the early youth cults, but soon it was taken up by a number of groups as part of their program for luring people in. Love bombing is a coordinated effort, usually under the direction of leadership, that involves long-term members' flooding recruits and newer members with flattery, verbal seduction, affectionate but usually nonsexual touching, and lots of attention to their every remark. Love bombing—or the offer of instant companionship—is a deceptive ploy accounting for many successful recruitment drives.

In addition, the newcomer is surrounded by long-term members. Not only are these more experienced members trained to love bomb the potential recruit, but they are on their best behavior, proudly proclaiming the joys of membership, the advantages of the new belief system, and the uniqueness of the leader. Consciously or unconsciously, these members always speak and make their presentations in cult jargon, which they all seem to understand but which tends to make the newcomer feel out of sorts, a bit alienated, and undereducated by cult standards. The lonely visitor or seminar attendee begins to want some sense of connection to the rest of the group. With all the surrounding reinforcement, soon enough the newcomer realizes that, in order to be accepted and part of the group, she or he simply needs to mirror the behavior of other members and imitate their language.

Because many groups use this tactic of having older members train and watch over recruits and newer members, recruits are never alone and cannot talk freely with other recruits. Immediately, the cult's training program and the thought-reform atmosphere (as described in Chapter Three), reinforced by the modeling behavior of older members, prevents recruits and new members from challenging the system. There is no opportunity for doubts or negative feelings to be supported, corroborated, or validated. In one way or another, in every kind of cult, recruits are told that negativity is never to be expressed. Should they have any questions, hesitations, or bad feelings, they are told to consult with an upper-level person, or their trainer, helper, or guide. Isolated from others who have doubts and questions, recruits are left with the impression that everyone else agrees with what is going on.

The complete attention of the newcomers is engaged through a heavy schedule of such activities as playing games, attending lectures, group singing, doing collective work, studying basic texts, joining picket lines, going on fund-raising drives, or completing various assigned tasks, such as writing a personal autobiography for examination by the group. In this way, recruits are kept occupied to such a degree that they don't get around to thinking about what they are doing or what is being done to them.

Follow-Up: Gaining Greater Commitment

When some people think of cult recruitment, they picture a rant-ing, wild-eyed zealot. This image is a far cry from the sophistica-tion of the actual recruitment process. Effective cult leaders and recruiters verbally seduce, charm, manipulate, and trick people into taking that first fatal step and then into making increasing commitments to the group. The selling of the cult's program pro-ceeds by means of calculated persuasion procedures. And these recruitment and conversion practices belie the cults' claim that people freely join them. Most recruits have little real knowledge of what will eventually happen to them, and it's rare for a new member to exercise anything like fully informed consent in mak-ing the decision to join. More likely, he or she makes an emo-tionally based acquiescence to complex, powerful, and organized persuasion tactics.

As new members are gradually exposed to the series of classes, events, and/or experiences that will, one step at a time, cut them off from their pasts and the world as they knew it and change them so gradually that they won't notice, they are also often kept awake for long periods doing their work assignments, studying, listening to lectures, meditating, chanting, and so on. Soon they become sleep-deficient, which further disturbs their critical faculties. Lack of food or sudden changes in diet cause yet other incapacities and confusion. Before long, recruits immersed in this new environment are, without realizing it, beginning to think in a new way.

In addition, cults control the information flow for all members. They may control ingoing and outgoing correspondence, telephone calls, radio or television use, unauthorized reading matter, visits by outsiders, and trips to the outside. In some cults, the telephones just happen to be broken; in others, especially in the political cults, use of phones is restricted as a "security" precaution. In the end, members' contacts with former ties are either completely cut off or strongly discouraged by both leadership and peers. To avoid disfavor and conflict, recruits go along with the program.

Manipulation and Deception

Manipulation of thoughts and feelings is central to the success of the cult recruitment process. Cults play upon normal feelings of ambivalence, and this is especially successful with young people, who have less life experience. For example, it is almost impossible for adolescents and young adults not to have mixed feelings about their parents. Even the most beloved mothers and fathers have had encounters with their children that leave memories of anger or disappointment, and most parents have at least a few irritating habits or peculiarities. Many cults make a point of tapping into these unresolved feelings and exploiting them to bind members to the group.

Some cults also use dress or other external features as visible symbols in converting newcomers to the cult's ways. If you really want to change people, change their appearance. Thus cult members can be asked or told to cut their hair or wear it in a particular style, wear different clothes, take on new names, and assume certain gestures or mannerisms. One large cult, for example, has its members adopt vegetarianism, wear light-colored clothing, and chant. New members are taught to regard their mothers and fathers as "flesh-eating parents who wear ungodly clothing, intellectualize, and are unenlightened." Cult members soon cut off ties with flesh-eaters; wear light-colored clothes; avoid reflective, critical thinking about anything, much less the group; and occupy their time with almost continuous internal chanting.

Some groups also take advantage of certain coincidences, exploiting them as divine happenings to bolster faith in the group ideology and convince recruits that a meeting or simple happenstance was a predestined event. For example, some cult members on very poorly balanced diets appear pink-cheeked and youthful, until one notices their faces seem chapped and covered with tiny pinhead lesions, which some dermatologists tell me suggest a vitamin A deficiency. The cult, however, interprets this skin discomfort as an indication that the members have become "children of

Father," "children of God," and are now "Baby Christians." In another example, a woman's brother, who lived out of town, came to the cult house to visit her while she was working her shift in a cult-owned factory. For this reason she missed seeing him, but cult officials told her, "See, the Divine Plan willed it that you must not see your brother."

On occasion, recruits are even put into brief trance states. Most people don't realize that a person can be hypnotized in simple and subtle ways, without the spectacular commands used by hypnotists who perform onstage. Someone can get you to totally concentrate on something such as an imaginary scene while he or she softly repeats subtle suggestions. Soon you will pretty much eliminate critical thinking and fall into a mild temporary trance. (This technique is discussed further in Chapter Seven.) Through a specific, deliberate program, cult recruits and members at times can be put or fall into changed states of consciousness, which contribute to their gradually becoming restricted in their thinking.

Reflective, critical, evaluative thought, especially that critical of the cult, becomes aversive and avoided. The member will appear as you or I do, and will function well in ordinary tasks, but the cult lectures and procedures tend to gradually induce members to experience anxiety whenever they critically evaluate the cult. Soon they are conditioned to avoid critical thinking, especially about the cult, because doing so becomes associated with pangs of anxiety and guilt.

Inducing Guilt

As part of the process of inducing guilt, all the recruit's former personal connections are deemed satanic or evil by the cult and are shown to be "against the chosen way." Since nonbelievers are bad, all relations with parents, friends, and other nonmembers are supposed to be halted. Any weakness in this area is considered very bad. The ultimate effect is that recruits assume a deep feeling of guilt about their pasts. Besides having their families and personal relationships condemned, recruits are also led to believe that they themselves were "bad people" before joining the group. Guilt feelings are produced en masse in cults.

Even more guilt is induced as recruits are set up to believe that if they ever leave the group all their ancestors and descendants will be damned or they themselves will die a pitiful death or become losers or lost souls. In this way, anxiety is heaped upon the guilt. Just as the initial love bombing awakened feelings of warmth, acceptance, and worthiness, now group condemnation leaves recruits full of self-doubt, guilt, and anxiety. Through this kind of manipulation, they are convinced that they can be saved only if they stay within the group.

Eventually, they no longer call or write to their families and friends. They may drop out of school or subordinate school to cult activities and end up unable to attend classes because cult activities occupy so much time. They may quit their jobs or go about them in a humdrum, distracted manner, losing all interest in prior careers or life goals. If elderly, they drop contact with family, friends, and neighbors and exhibit sudden changes of interest. It should be noted, however, that some of the more recent cults, in particular those espousing self-improvement or prosperity philosophies, tend to keep members busy working at their regular jobs and even taking on more than one job, so that they can earn more money to buy courses of various kinds from the cult.

Young and Old Alike Are Vulnerable

In recent years, we have witnessed an infiltration of cult recruitment into all walks of life. In addition to the average citizen, they go after movie stars and other celebrities, as well as respected medical professionals and business leaders. But cult leaders also seem to have decided that "gold is with the old," so lately, the elderly, particularly widowed women, have become targets of a number of cults that hope to inherit wealth and possessions from these trusting followers. A person who educates others about cults writes, "I liken it to a compass suddenly shifting when the magnetic pole changes—where the money goes, there go the cults." Widowed middle-aged and older women may have clear titles to houses, cars, and other property, and easy access to savings accounts, retirement funds, and social security checks.

In addition to having money, these women are often lonely and vulnerable, another quality that makes them prime targets. Their children and grandchildren are usually busy with their own lives, and many widows are fearful of managing their affairs alone and want security and companionship. Cult leaders' promises can easily attract these women, tempting them to check out the group. Some of the agencies and organizations that educate the public about cults and serve as networking resources report that nearly half of their clients are young adults trying to extricate their mothers from cults.

Female gurus are particularly successful in recruiting older women. Channelers J. Z. Knight in Washington state and Penny Torres-Rubin in Oregon, and the leader of the Church Universal and Triumphant, Elizabeth Clare Prophet, have had large followings of older women. Bible cults and groups that offer eternal life also appeal to older persons. A few cults have gone directly into nursing and retirement homes, offering the residents entertainment and friendly, youthful visitors in order to access potential followers. Some cults have centered their recruitment drives in states like Arizona and Florida, where many elderly retire. Other cults instruct members to offer to go shopping for the elderly, mow their lawns, and visit them regularly to get them into the group.

Once recruited, the elderly can be urged to sell property and give the proceeds to the cult and to turn over their incomes and investments, as some of the examples in Chapter Four illustrated. Sometimes adult children and grandchildren of these elderly members cannot locate them because the cult moves them out of their homes and because, like younger recruits, the elderly are urged to drop all contact with family, friends, and neighbors.

Targeting the Elderly

Not long ago, someone came to see me because his recently widowed mother was intensely involved with a new group. After she had moved to Arizona, she met a woman in her condominium who was devoted to CBJ (Charles, BernaDeane, and James, also known as Chuck, Bernie, and Jim), aka The Flame Foundation, aka The Eternal Flame, now called People Forever International, Inc.

Once, Chuck performed in a nightclub, Bernie modeled, and Jim studied yoga and sold real estate. Today, these leaders, who live together, claim to be the first humans to have gone through a cellular biological transformation (in their words, a "cellular awakening") and to have achieved physical immortality.

The group appears to recruit in at least three ways: members bring in friends locally; the leaders give seminars at various locations where CBJ is recruiting heavily; and associates in centers around the country recruit people they meet to go with them to large events at the Scottsdale, Arizona, headquarters. During testimonial periods at these events, each attendee is under great social pressure, amidst the excitement of the contrived atmosphere, to testify about what good things have come into her or his life by participating. Event videotapes portray persons of all ages dancing, clapping, and shouting, giving tearfully grateful testimonials, with CBJ hovering over and proudly proclaiming their love. CBJ also exhort attendees to buy CBJ products, give donations, and produce money for the organization.

Families and friends report that after a person returns home to pack his or her belongings in order to move to be with CBJ for eternal life, the newly recruited CBJer is accompanied by an escort. Families—even spouses—are not able to talk or be with their loved one alone at any time.

A book put out by CBJ states that as physical immortals "we have the ability to continuously renew, regenerate, restructure, and recreate our physical bodies so that we can remain here forever. As immortals, we have the ability to acclimate ourselves to any situation, to prevent ourselves from being subject to aging and death. . . . We're talking about our physical body being able to constantly rejuvenate itself, renew itself and not go into the grave." The authors go on to tell readers that by fusing with one another the energy produced can spare them from any type of death, including deaths caused by accidents.

CBJ provides an example of the wide age range of people now being recruited to cults, the many approaches used, and another interesting feature—the multiple names such groups may use across time.

Targeting the Young

Another group that uses many names and has garnered attention in recent years is led by a "guru" who targets younger people. Known by a number of "heavenly" names, the group advertises classes sponsored by a variety of front organizations in the form of institutes, societies, forums, seminars, dinners, series, and discussions. The guru's name is never mentioned in the ads, which are geared toward individuals in their twenties and women.

Followers display posters on college campuses and surrounding areas and take out ads in New Age publications, offering their free seminars on such subjects as meditation, metaphysics, career advances, financial success, and empowerment. Once someone responds to an ad or personal invitation, the recruitment process goes something like this, as reported by former members and relatives of members: first, during the free seminar, certain attendees are selected as prospective recruits. They are individually contacted by the seminar leader or an assigned follower, who cultivates a personal friendship. The assigned devotee tells each recruit about the devotee's powerful spiritual leader, and at some point it is revealed who that leader is. Next, the recruit is invited to attend an all-expense-paid trip to a lecture by the leader in another city. And finally, after hearing one or more lectures, active recruits are invited to attend a formal dinner with the leader. At the same time, the recruiter, who is now both a personal friend and teacher, urges the recruit to become a student of the leader. A lot of pressure is put on recruits to submit; simultaneously, they are subjected to love bombing and made to feel very special and liked.

The leader reportedly uses a variety of techniques to sway recruits. He uses voice and hand manipulations and controlled heat, light, and sound to produce a form of mass hypnosis. He creates an illusion of changing form, levitating, and emitting an aura. Recruits are told that they are special people who have gained wisdom and power in past incarnations and that he can help them reclaim and reinforce that power.

He is purported to preach a combination of Buddhism and capitalism that is supposed to result in both spiritual and temporal affluence. Former followers state that they and others paid anywhere from $3,000 to $6,000 per month to attend his seminars, saying that he convinces them that he is responsible for their successes, for which they must pay him. Special fees paid to him reportedly can be as high as $10,000.

Former followers say they were given instruction in technical jobs and job hunting, and they allege that sometimes they were told to fudge their résumés so they could get high-paying jobs as supposed technical wizards. Some had as little as six months of training before being instructed to seek high-power consulting positions. The larger their salaries, the greater the share to the leader, they stated. According to reports, this guru manipulates a couple of hundred people into giving him millions of dollars each year.

The Double Agenda

Not all cults are live-in groups, and not all execute the quick, intense thought-reform processes that some are known for. However, when a large portion of members live separately, the cult simply moves more slowly in changing members' behavior. The double agenda is still present, and it is through concerted efforts and programs of manipulation that live-out cults, too, successfully accomplish their goal of binding new members to the group.

Although different in content, most cults resemble each other in many ways. They are especially similar in their use of powerful social and psychological pressures that include isolating individuals from their pasts, denigrating their current sense of self, and making them give up and forget their former lives in order to stay with the group. In the process, their behavior and attitudes are changed. Most of this change, if not all, occurs without the new member's awareness. One man writing of his two years with Sathya Sai Baba said, "We were being deculturized on a fast-track growth curve . . . in our own cosmic training camp. . . . What had at first looked like the gates of Heaven, when I first entered Baba's kingdom, had suddenly one day become the gates of Hell."

Whether it includes blatant deception at the point of recruitment or a lot of little deceptions along the way, the double agenda clearly differentiates cults from other groups who attract members, such as legitimate schools and institutionalized religions, the military, and a variety of volunteer organizations. Cults know that if you knew from the get go what you were in for and why, you would never join. It's as simple as that.

6

Physiological Persuasion Techniques

Generally cults and groups using thought-reform processes do not have a visible product, such as a computer or a book or a car, to sell. They have an invisible product. Therefore, those who offer psychological, political, or spiritual transformations and enlightenment have learned that either they need to prove that they have special knowledge of some kind and that a follower will gain something unusual by participating in their group, or they need to use specific persuasion techniques that will convince followers to stay with them.

We know that people can be led to buy almost anything, from the Brooklyn Bridge to ointments that stop aging. They also have been willing to pay hundreds of dollars to sit in ballrooms and be harangued by New Age trainers promising them "breakthroughs" and "transformations." But it is helpful to the sellers if they can find ways of actually showing or convincing you, the buyer, that there is something going on that they are causing and that you can be changed by that something.

In addition to buying almost anything, people can apparently be led to believe almost anything. If cult leaders can't give you "proof," then they can manipulate you into believing. Through a variety of skillful manipulations and deceptions, they will persuade you that they have the ultimate solution.

In general, cult leaders combine two methods of persuasion:

- Inducing predictable physiological responses by subjecting followers to certain planned experiences and exercises, and then interpreting those responses in ways favorable to the leaders' interests

- Eliciting certain behavioral and emotional responses by subjecting followers to psychological pressures and manipulations, then exploiting those responses to induce further dependence on the cult

This chapter will focus on the physiological techniques, and the next chapter will focus on the psychological techniques. However, although I discuss each type of persuasion separately, *no cult or cultic group uses just one type.* The power of the thought-reform processes in today's cultic groups is based precisely on the fact that cults use a variety of sophisticated techniques to recruit, convert, control, and retain members.

Mass Marketing of Experiential Exercises

Even though the United States has always been considered a melting pot of various nationalities, until the mid sixties a large portion of those coming to this country were non-Asians of Judeo-Christian backgrounds.

Neither Judaism nor Christianity as known in the Western world makes use of the types of experiential exercises that permeate Eastern religions, such exercises as mantra meditation, spin dancing, and other, from the Western point of view, exotic rituals and procedures. Many groups among the first wave of youth cults in the United States in the 1960s, however, were based on Eastern experiential rituals. Soon, not just the Eastern-style groups but many other cults and groups using thought-reform techniques began to incorporate these and other experiential exercises to manipulate and control devotees.

The literature from the Far East indicates that Eastern religious teachers always supervised individual students, carefully watching for deleterious effects from prescribed exercises and tailoring practices to prevent damage to the students. This supervision is lacking in modern-day applications. Various persons have taken these ancient experiential exercises and applied them in a group context, not necessarily to benefit their followers but to convince and control them. Not only have these exercises been adopted by cultic groups of all kinds but some of the larger cults and organizations using thought-reform processes have also begun mass marketing experiential techniques, again to the detriment of the purchaser and consumer.

The courses begin with inexpensive, seemingly innocuous procedures that have a certain appeal and that are highly promoted by members acting on behalf of the leaders. These introductory programs are followed by offers of increasingly expensive, longer, and more intense courses. Many groups refer to the later courses as *intensives*, and tout them as a means to help the neophyte achieve perfection faster.

Goods such as tennis shoes, breakfast cereal, and radios and computers are mass marketed with the understanding that if something doesn't suit you it can be taken back and exchanged and that the buyer-seller relationship is shaped by contracts, warranties, and consumer protection laws. But in the area of mind and emotion manipulation, we have no consumer laws. In fact, the persons misusing and abusing these experiential exercises often do not inform buyers or followers that not everyone benefits from or feels comfortable doing these exercises, which tend to produce both mental and physiological effects.

Thus the potential for harm is doublefold. First, there is no informed consent obtained from the consumers before the vendors begin to apply their wares. And second, the consumers are not told that some of these exercises may cause negative side effects or unpleasant responses or conditions and may change a person's life for the worse for some time to come. In fact, most people do not have a full, clear picture of what is going to come with membership in the manipulative group.

The mass marketing of experiential exercises was pervasive in the eighties, and remains prominent in the nineties. Negative publicity and the harrowing experiences of some program participants have not seemed to deter the program sellers. Although some groups have disappeared or gone out of business, others simply changed their names or reformulated their approaches and carry on to this day.

Techniques Producing Predictable Physiological Responses

Following are some of the more frequent physiological methods of producing various mental and physical feelings taught to members as group activities. Members' responses to these activities are reinterpreted in desirable ways by group leaders or trainers, so as to convince both neophytes and devotees that the processes are good for them. The process of positive reinterpretation, sometimes called *proof through reframing,* is a persuasion technique commonly used by cults.

Hyperventilation

Hyperventilation is an overall label for the effects caused by overbreathing and repetitive sighing. The condition is easily induced by having people do continuous loud shouting and chanting. For example, the effect can be produced by having individuals stand and repeatedly thrust their clenched fists outward while simultaneously shouting in a loud voice with heavy exhalation, "Love our Leader! Love our Leader! Love our Leader!" Overbreathing can also be produced through intense heavy expelling of air in more private, quiet ritualized chants.

A former Rajneesh follower demonstrated for me what he termed Hoo meditation, a frequent exercise in that group. He stood with his feet wide apart, his arms above his head, and began to bow at the waist, rapidly with stiff arms, blowing out air as sharply, force-fully, and as fast as he could, turning the heavy puffs into the sound "hoo" while bowing. This was done, he said, until most members fell to the mats on the floor.

I asked several medical doctors to give me a brief explanation of hyperventilation, or overbreathing, so I could help former cult members understand the effect. The physicians explained that con-tinuous overbreathing, by causing large volumes of air to pass in and out of the lungs, produces a drop in the carbon dioxide level in the bloodstream, which in turn causes the blood to become more alkaline. This is called respiratory alkalosis.

A mild degree of respiratory alkalosis produces dizziness or light-headedness; people feel "high" and experience loss of critical thought and judgment. More prolonged or vigorous overbreathing produces numbness and tingling of the fingers, toes, and lips; sweat-ing; pounding of the heart; ringing in the ears; tremulousness; and feelings of fear, panic, and, unreality. Even more vigorous and pro-longed overbreathing can cause muscle cramps, including clawlike rigidity of the hands and feet, body cramps, and severe chest pain and tightness. Heart irregularities can develop, and convulsive ten-dencies can be exaggerated.

Respiratory alkalosis also causes fainting. People often drop to the floor and are briefly unconscious. While they are unconscious, underbreathing occurs to compensate for the period of over-breathing and to restore the normal acid-base balance of the blood. People awaken limp, exhausted, and aware that they have been through a dramatic and frightening experience.

Cults, quacks, and manipulators have become aware of the pre-dictable outcomes of hyperventilation—the giddiness, the out-of-control feeling, the possible loss of consciousness, the tingling, and the clenching of fingers and toes. Similarly, they have recog-nized the impact of immediately reframing the experience. By consciously reframing, or relabeling, the effects, thus confounding individuals' gut-level reactions that something unpleasant has hap-pened, leaders turn a frightening state into a supposedly positive one, telling neophytes, for example, that they are "becoming blissed out, . . . getting or receiving the spirit, . . . on the path." In private, the leaders of some groups have names such as *lobstering* or *tuna-ing,* for the clawlike clenching and the falling to the floor produced by hyperventilation practices.

I have observed several groups that have members sit on the floor in a darkened room and rapidly and repeatedly yell such phrases as "fear, fear, fear" or "out Satan out." After a number of minutes, when the leaders assess that many in the room feel giddy and tingling, the leaders turn up the lights and reframe the physical condition: "See, as we told you, you are going to be transformed!" Although many in the room appeared to be educated, no one spoke about recognizing the effects of hyperventilation, effects most of us have heard about in high school or college science courses. Because of peer pressure and social constraints built in by group procedures, no one asked, "Are you sure this isn't really the effect of hyperventilation rather than out-of-this-world ecstacy and enlightenment?"

Former group members who have been taught to speak in tongues have described to me how they felt after prolonged peri-ods of chanting the "tongues." They felt spacey and dizzy; some felt elated. They realized something had happened to them, and they were told that this feeling was related to their becoming more fully members of the group. They were told this was how they were sup-posed to feel. They soon understood that they were not to com-plain about these odd feelings but to see them as progress. At the time, they made no connection between their physical state and the physiological exercises involved in speaking in tongues.

Within some cultic groups, older members demonstrate chant-ing techniques, urging the newer members to say the chant phrases along with them. The new members soon learn to imitate the tonal quality, patterns, and rhythms of their neighbors. Carried out for a prolonged period in a loud voice, sometimes accompanied with swaying, this exercise, too, produces the hyperventilation syn-drome, which is then relabeled as progress, closeness to God, or a new level of enlightenment.

A psychotherapy cult using various breathing techniques explains, as members feel odd sensations, "You are beginning to experience feelings. You have never felt feelings before. Up till now you were closed down; feel that birth of feelings." A political cult leader told her followers after each long session of chanting slogans and overbreathing that "you are feeling the fire of the revolution—first within you, then among us, then the world. You are growing with the movement."

Repetitive Motion

Constant swaying motions, clapping added to chanting, or almost any repeated motion helps to alter a person's general state of awareness. Often the repetitive movements are combined with forms of chanting to blend the effects of hyperventilation and dizziness. Dizziness can be produced by simple spinning or spin dancing (in which the person also whirls around and around), prolonged swaying, and trance dancing (often done kneeling and rocking from side to side and backward and forward, with rhythmic repetitive drumming and background music). Again, the effects of these motions are relabeled by group leaders as ecstacy or new levels of awareness.

I have observed a number of cultic performances and noted many physiological effects and accompanying reinterpretations. In Chapter Four, I described the Spinners, or the Church of Unlimited Devotion. Members spin (much in the manner of Sufi dancing) to rock music. Another group offering psychological expansion has taken aspects of North African desert tribes' traditional trance dances, applied them in classroom settings, and reframed the resultant giddiness and light-headedness as "getting out of your head and into your heart."

A cult offering a "live forever" formula uses spin dancing to demonstrate members' newfound joy that no one need die. The group tells members giddy from spin dancing, "you're coming into our world. Here we are. Spin, spin toward us . . . into your new self."

Change in Diet, Sleep, and Stress

Abrupt, radical, or prolonged dietary changes, prolonged sleep loss, and increased general stress also bring about predictable physiological responses.

Gastrointestinal Distress and Other Diet-Related Effects. Many groups encourage and/or institute vegetarianism as part of members' conduct. In some cases, this dietary requirement may come only at later stages of membership or within certain select circles. Other groups simply institute cheap diets to save money and to modify behavior.

Vegetarianism can be healthy when individuals study and select proper daily combinations of foods. In contrast, a number of cults abruptly put new members on low-protein, improperly balanced vegetarian diets. Suddenly eating only vegetables and fruit with no concern for securing the proper proteins and amino acids produces odd sensations in the lower digestive tract. The manipulators in certain cults label this "doing battle with Satan" and tell neophyte members that their lower intestinal pains and churning are evidence of their basic sinfulness and their need to learn the group's ways in order to battle Satan. Some of the neo-Hindu groups reframe the digestive upsets as the working off of past-life karma.

A number of former cult followers who had lived overseas with a cult told me that not only had they been vegetarians while in their group but that they also had been conditioned to feel revulsion when they smelled meat and fish being cooked. This ingrained attitude later proves to be a problem for those who leave the group and find themselves living in a home, going to restaurants, or attending picnics where meat is cooked and eaten.

People in the human manipulation business know that, after a time, the body adapts and the intestinal discomfort of a sudden change in diet decreases. When this occurs, the leaders tell the new member that it means he or she is properly submitting to the leader or is achieving a higher level of awareness. Neophytes quickly realize that to complain aloud is tantamount to admitting their "sinfulness," and the resultant guilt that this induces keeps them silent and looking to the leadership for ways to dispel the guilt. Ex-cult members who had served in leadership positions told me that they had experienced these bodily reactions and received these reinterpretations; then as they took on leadership and training responsibilities, they were instructed to look for, even suggest, the possible appearance of these predictable symptoms in new members and to give the newcomers the same explanations the older members had once heard.

There are twenty amino acids in complete protein: twelve are labeled as nonessential because the human body can produce them, but eight are essential amino acids that must be gotten from meat, fish, poultry, milk products, beans, and nuts. Thus, unbalanced vegetarian diets not only do not provide the needed protein but also can cause a vitamin B_{12} deficiency—a vitamin needed to produce red blood cells. One cult cookbook, available for the last twenty years, provides recipes approved by the group. Some feast dishes appear tempting. However, ex-members report that if one is not a fan of dried beans, the amino acids may not get into one's daily fare.

Many groups have also hit upon *sugar buzzing*, that is, loading a person with lots of sugar, a technique that helps overcome low feelings and makes people temporarily feel energized. One former cult member said that, in her particular temple, she was to buy two and a half pounds of sugar per member per week to mix into various mushes, milk drinks, and desserts. During long sessions in one of the political cults, leaders would often give someone twenty-five or fifty dollars to go out and buy an armload of candy bars to bring back to the members at the meeting to keep everyone going.

Hormonal Changes. Stress, poor diet, and inadequate rest can result in hormonal changes that cause menstruation to cease in women and beard growth to diminish or cease in men. Manipulators deliberately misattribute these conditions, citing them as evidence that the women are pregnant with God and the men have become children of the leader, avatar, or guru.

I have interviewed many young men in their mid twenties who after leaving their groups were as clean shaven as prepubescent boys and were concerned whether their beard growth would renew itself. After a period of rest, good diet, and less stress, all these men seemed to return to a normal appearance. Many women were both glad and surprised when menstruation returned after they left their groups. While in their cults, these persons had been on exhausting work routines, often going for months on three to five hours of rest a night, with occasional days of total collapse into sleep, for which they were berated because it was said to show that they were in "lower conditions," lazy, or sinful.

Members of groups with mobile fund-raising teams and of nomadic groups, such as the Garbage Eaters, suffer particular problems and stresses because they travel and live off food from dumpsters behind restaurants and supermarkets or eat poorly balanced fast-food diets. Among those who have experienced particular deprivations are cult members who toiled in fields or worked in cult-owned and -operated factories; members of a group that reportedly has detention facilities who were incarcerated in a jail-like situation for long periods for supposed misdemeanors; and members of one political cult who were guarded and confined under house arrest, made to sit in one position for days on end, and interrogated for "crimes against the party." These and other former members have reported extreme exhaustion from excessive work, sleep loss, poor food, and unusual stresses that were excessive even by their groups' standards. They too experienced bodily changes and illnesses.

Purgings, Colonics, and Sweating. Techniques involving purgings, colonics, and sweating are used in various cultic groups as symbolic cleansing rituals, but they actually serve the covert role of keeping members debilitated, docile, and dependent on the group for their well-being and care. Former participants in one cult reported they had participated in "colon-cleanse" programs in which they took a regimen of laxatives, detoxicants, cult-recommended vitamin tablets, and water and juice combined with colonics (enemas). When presented with details of this regime, medical doctors have commented that such activities could weaken already exhausted and malnourished members.

The leader of one cultic group introduced a procedure "to clean out and purify one's system" and produce "sparkling results." Promoted as a program "for anyone," it consists of a combination of running and sweating for five hours a day for two weeks, plus a regimen of oils and vitamins that included from two tablespoons to one-half cup of oils and rather large dosages of certain vitamins— for example, niacin "increased gradiently to as high as 5,000 mg." Massive doses, particularly of niacin, reportedly can cause extreme and uncomfortable reactions. Recent studies have shown that high-strength niacin dosages can cause such adverse effects as facial flush, rash, itching, fatigue, and a temporary wartlike skin disfigurement, as well as liver toxicity.

People undergoing the procedure are also instructed to run in a "rubberized or vinyl sweatsuit" and, after their circulation has been increased through the running, they are to spend the bulk of their time in a sauna. "Sweating in the sauna is done at temperatures ranging anywhere from 140 degrees to 180 degrees." In contrast, maintenance officials at a health club tell me the average temperature for saunas is between 115 and 120 degrees.

Reportedly, each of these procedures can produce visible body responses, which can then be reframed and reinterpreted as desired by the group leader according to his philosophy. Again, such reframing is meant to demonstrate that a visible effect is generated not as an expected physiological response but as evidence of whatever the leader says.

Body Manipulations

Unusual physiological effects can be produced by a person acting either alone or with others to perform body manipulations. Leaders of cults and thought-reform groups employ a number of these manipulations and interpret the experiences to mean what they want followers to think.

Pushing on Eyeballs. Former members report that in the Divine Light Mission the lights would be dimmed and the guru would pass among the followers bestowing "divine light" on individuals by pressing on their eyes until the pressure on the optic nerve caused them to see flashes of light. This was reframed as Divine Light.

Pressing on Ears. In this same group, members were instructed to plug their ears with their fingers, pushing until they heard a buzzing sound which was interpreted as hearing Divine Harmony.

Painful Manipulations. Some former members of a psychology-based cult have described a number of practices their leader instituted that were allegedly to balance members' inner and outer selves but were, in fact, painful physical manipulations used to punish people and to get them in line with the leader's plans. These manipulations were called *bodywork,* and the point was to elicit pain and "awareness." The motto was "No pain, no gain."

A group member would lie on a table and the administrator of the exercise would press his thumb into a sensitive area of the person's body, such as the diaphragm, the perineum, or the roof of the mouth. If this did not produce enough pain, the practitioner then used his elbow on major body areas. If he needed more leverage to produce pain, he would straddle the person on the table. One former member described just how pain applied in this way could achieve behavioral change:

> When I came into the group I had long hair and a beard. I was soon sent for bodywork. The man doing the bodywork started pressing on my hip with his elbow, and I curled up because it hurt so much. He told me I was going into a fetus, that I was going back into the womb. Then he gave me the awareness that I was afraid to come out of the womb. The

pain was from my mother. My mother was unhappy about me. She was unhappy that I had long hair and a beard. So the awareness was: you're not respecting your mom and you're reacting against your mom. So I lay there and told my mom I'd cut my hair, and when he let go the pain was gone.

In this technique, pain is inflicted by a person who is supposed to be able to discern what is actually causing the pain—in this instance, not the one person's elbow in the other person's hip but the other person's need to cut his hair in order to stop reacting against his mother. Followers in this group became very careful to obey the leaders' dictates in order to avoid these painful bodywork awareness sessions.

Relaxation-Induced Anxiety

It has been known in the professional literature for some time that not everyone responds well to closed-eye relaxation techniques or to mantra meditation, in which the meditator repeats an incantation. Some individuals find these procedures relaxing and welcome, but a noticeable number experience discomfort and distress. Even ancient literature on mantra meditation warns of the need for the teacher to monitor learners and help them avoid difficulties, and those teaching mantra meditation and other closed-eye techniques today have also learned from experience that many meditators experience some distressing responses. Instead of feeling relaxed, some feel increased tension, break out in perspiration, find their hearts racing, or become distressingly aware of many aspects of their body.

In recent years, it has been in vogue to speak of the stress of life and how to reduce it. Many different cultic groups have offered meditation as a cure-all for stress, and have done a real Madison Avenue packaging of the typical bodily responses found in a number of people when they close their eyes and attempt empty-mind meditation. The cult groups call this *unstressing* and reframe any distress it causes as a necessary and positive response. This strategy allows the leader to urge the meditator to keep on meditating and to blame her or him for having so much inner stress or for not doing the process correctly or often enough.

Only in the last few years have these uncomfortable responses been studied as a phenomenon, termed *relaxation-induced anxiety* (RIA) by researchers. Ethical instructors of meditation, such as licensed psychologists or psychiatrists who use it as a therapeutic technique or noncultic meditation instructors who teach meditation as a relaxation technique, will explain these uncomfortable responses to see if knowledge helps to alleviate the response, or they may drop the procedures producing the responses and substitute others that produce less discomfort.

RIA symptoms fall into three clusters. The first includes various distressing sensations. The meditator feels either lighter and floating or heavy and sinking. His or her body may seem to change size or orientation. Some people feel hot or cold; some report tingling and numbness; and others experience visual, auditory, taste, and smell sensations. Scientists think some of these symptoms reflect an increased dominance of the parasympathetic nervous system during relaxation, and result from blood vessel dilation and the feelings of warmth and heaviness that ensue.

The second cluster of responses contains physiological-behavioral activity that is either motoric, that is, stemming from the muscles—jerks, tics, spasms, twitches, and restlessness for example—or that arises from bursts of sympathetic nervous system activity—racing heart or sweaty palms for example.

The third cluster includes abrupt and disturbing ideas and emotional states that seem primitive (just as dream contents may for example) and that intrude into the alleged state of relaxation. Sadness, rage, joy, or sexual feelings burst into the meditator's awareness, much to his or her distress.

These predictable bodily responses are no doubt what are going on when meditators complain of odd and disconcerting effects. I have interviewed a number of former meditation cult members who supervised the meditation of newer members. When the newcomers complained about these distressing sensations, the supervisors were taught to assure the members that these were "unstressings" and that the cure was to meditate longer and more often. Many of these supervisors were themselves suffering from the same sensations.

These five major categories of activities—hyperventilation, repetitive motions, changes in diet and in sleep and stress levels, body manipulations, and relaxation-induced anxiety—are experiences that are known to produce certain physiological and psychological effects. An experienced mind manipulator can interpret these expected human responses to his benefit. He can say that he or his methods in fact produced the effects, and he can name (or reframe) these effects to fit into the philosophy he is promoting. In the reframing process, he can also blame the person who dares to complain if bothered by the induced states.

In the remainder of this chapter, I will illustrate the use of some of these techniques and their reframing by various meditation groups, and describe some meditators who suffered severe after effects.

Meditation May Not Always Be Good for You

There are many kinds of meditation being promoted by various individuals, groups, and cults. In a recent copy of a California free newspaper, I counted advertisements for at least forty different meditation groups and courses, a portion of which were recognizable cultic groups.

Like many cultic groups, meditation cults have varying degrees of membership and commitment, which become known to members only as time goes on. Those who sample only the beginning course may have little or no knowledge of what a long-term association may entail. They don't know that they will be approached to purchase courses in how to levitate and fly, to do astral self-projection, perhaps even to become celibate monks. Neither are they informed that a number of persons have had bad results from participation in the behaviors and exercises advocated by the group. Similarly, they are not told that the group is a religious movement. One former devotee of a large group was told by trainers at the start that what was being taught was a simple, effortless technique for releasing stress with no religious implications, but, says the ex-member, "I was effectively made into a Hindu believer by the time I was finished with my training nine and half years later."

By the mid 1970s, more than one million persons in the United States reportedly purchased one of the more popular introductory courses offered by one group. Since then, approximately another million in the United States and three to four million worldwide are reported to have taken this introductory course.

An entire volume could be written about the multitude of courses meditators may be urged to purchase, including seminars overseas and courses at universities and institutes around the country. Those who buy advanced courses are expected to meditate for much longer periods than novices. Each day, hours of meditation combined with prolonged hyperventilation are followed by the viewing of repetitive soporific videotapes, usually of the guru or swami lecturing, while the meditators are isolated from outside contacts and from variety in their experiences. In some groups, courses can cost from $3,000 to $4,000 each. Some former members of one group stated that they worked for the organization full-time for a year with no pay in return for the "flying course."

Individuals who purchase a group's initial course usually have no idea what may come into their lives in the way of financial costs or time commitments, nor any inkling of the changes to expect in their relationships with family and friends if they continue in the program. Neither do they know beforehand about the impacts on their thinking and emotions—not all for the better.

Many meditation cult adherents are urged by their leaders to move in with other meditators. In one group, they are told that if large enough numbers of meditators congregate, their meditating could influence the weather or reduce crime. In some groups, they are told that by becoming physically more distant from nonmeditators they'll be protected from those whose lower levels of consciousness awareness might rub off on the meditators. Outsiders are regarded as lower-status beings whose presence could threaten a meditator's condition, and therefore the meditator is encouraged to separate from family and nonmeditating friends.

By the mid 1970s, clinical reports of negative outcomes resulting from various mantra meditation programs began to dot the psychiatric literature. Clinicians reported that some meditators were finding themselves in self-induced altered states, wherein they felt unreal or found their surroundings unreal. Some persons became unemployable because they were unable to control these episodes. Other clinical reports indicated that indiscriminate use of mantra meditation could precipitate more serious psychiatric problems ranging from depression and agitation to psychotic decompensation.

Over the years, there has been a great deal of research on meditation practices. In a series of studies, Leon Otis, a psychologist at Stanford Research Institute, pointed out that despite the alleged benefits for all who take up the practice as advertised by one meditation organization, his research proved otherwise. Although we might expect that more dropouts than long-term meditators would claim adverse effects, according to Otis the reverse is true. In fact, the number and severity of complaints are positively related to duration of meditation. Also not supported by research is the notion that initial uncomfortable feelings are transient. Meditators reported continuing adverse effects: they had become "anxious, confused, frustrated, depressed, and/or withdrawn (or more so) since starting [meditation]." These findings are consistent with those of a variety of studies.

Another researcher, Canadian professor of psychology Michael Persinger, finds that for some individuals meditation techniques bring on such symptoms of complex partial epilepsy as having visual abnormalities, hearing voices, feeling vibrations, and experiencing automatic behaviors. Another concern, explored by researchers Michael Murphy and Steven Donovan, is that advanced practitioners rank high in suggestibility, meaning that their physical or mental state is easily influenced by the process of suggestion. Whether they become more suggestible because of participation in meditation practices or are highly suggestible to begin with, a state which might reinforce their continuation of the practice, has not been determined. Either way, this suggestibility puts them at risk of losing personal autonomy.

When meditators first reported experiencing depersonalization and derealization (feeling removed from one's body or as if one were watching oneself), it was believed that these altered states were connected to actual periods of meditation. Psychiatrists eventually recognized, however, that these were states of *involuntary meditation*, for want of a better name, that were intruding into the waking consciousness of meditators when they were not deliberately meditating. Unfortunately—and much to the distress of some meditators—"a depersonalized state can become an apparently permanent mode of functioning, [with] the apparent long-term loss of the ability to feel strong emotions, either negative or positive."

A number of persons in the United States have brought legal suits for damages allegedly suffered as a consequence of their participation in meditation programs. Settlements to the individuals were made by the organization offering the programs.

Meditation Casualties

The foregoing brief review of the work of several researchers supports my observations based on interviewing or providing therapy to more than seventy persons who had meditated from four to seventeen years in various groups.

These individuals sought help for major psychological symptoms that had emerged during their meditation practice. They wanted explanations for what had happened to them and felt they needed treatment in order to get their lives going again. Cognitive difficulties—that is, problems with thinking and attention—were rampant, and they were also experiencing major emotional afflictions. They felt these problems were linked to the practices of mantra meditation, overbreathing, and being encouraged to keep on meditating even after reporting negative experiences to group leaders. Some had begun legal cases alleging damages from their years in meditation groups.

Predominantly middle-class Caucasians, these former cult members were all over the age of thirty when I saw them. Some had joined a meditation group while in high school or soon after. One person had entered a group at age fourteen and left at thirty-one. None had a history of major mental disorders prior to participation in a meditation group. Some had had family and social trouble typical of their age group at the time, and some had experienced minor depression from disappointments, and so forth, but nothing remarkable. None had a family history of major mental disorders. Some of the former members' families had a few alcoholics or individuals who had suffered personal losses and a resultant depression.

A few examples will illustrate these former members' range of impairments, some of which remain after many years out of the cultic group.

Blackouts, lack of sensory filters, and anxiety attacks. "John," age thirty-six, meditated off and on for nine years; during the last two years of that time, he was encouraged to do intensives. Formerly a business executive, now, one year after leaving a meditation-based group, he is living on public funds, having been diagnosed as mentally disabled and incapable of working. He suffers from fainting, blackouts, severe and frequent anxiety attacks, and exhaustion. John feels he no longer has protective barriers for his senses. "There is no way to keep things out from the outside," he complains. "Everything gets in through my senses. They taught me to fear that my body was filled with odd, bizarre, scary things over which I had no control." Although he is in therapy, he is unable to function if there is any stress in his environment. He stays away from people, takes walks in the woods alone, and rests a lot.

Fog and space. "Lisa" was in a meditation group for thirteen years. During nine of those years, she suffered from unique dissociative experiences in which she would "space out." In looking across a room, Lisa would see a waist-high orange fog. In spite of finding herself in this peculiar state, with the interruptions and distractions it presented, she was able to carry on the simple, necessary tasks of daily living. Her level of functioning was poor, however, due to her preoccupation with the fog and to feeling detached and flat.

Altered states and memory difficulties. "Rick" joined a meditation group in 1975, at age seventeen, and meditated for eleven years. He experienced his first distressing symptoms at his first advanced course, when overbreathing and yogic exercises were added to his mantra meditation. He described states of euphoria; periods of dissociation, depersonalization, confusion, and irritability; and memory difficulties. When he eventually left the group, he had difficulties with reading, memory, concentration, and focusing; had involuntary body shaking; and experienced frequent episodes of dissociation.

Loss of boundaries. "Bruno," an architect in his early forties, went to his first extended meditation event at a hotel in another city after a year of doing the initial brief meditations. The out-of-town event was an intense program requiring many hours of meditation, overbreathing, and never being alone. He lost track of time and felt odd and not himself. He finally fled the course after an unsettling experience in his hotel room: "Suddenly I became one with the air conditioner. I just dissolved, and it seemed that when the air conditioner started up it just took me out of my body. There wasn't any me on the bed—I was 'at one' with the motor sounds. It was unspeakable terror. I had dissolved and melded with a motor sound!"

When he told the trainers how distressed he was, they told him "something good is happening" and instructed him to meditate more. After he returned home, he remained anxious, had trouble sleeping, and was very tired for some weeks. Temporary sedative medication prescribed by his physician aided his recovery.

Inappropriate and unrelated bursts of emotion. "Tom," age twenty-six, signed up for a course in which he engaged in his first extended meditating. During this meditating, he developed RIA symptoms that continued after the course was over. His worst symptom was feeling sudden surges of intense anger unrelated to anything that was going on. At other times— when he was on a bus, streetcar, elevator, escalator, or in a car—he experienced bursts of inappropriate aggressive sexual urges. He said motion was driving him crazy. He described the few minutes of monotony and motion just prior to the sudden bursts of emotion as having the same sensation as a waking dream. For several months, he feared he was losing his mind, and he was becoming phobic about going out alone to public places because he never knew when these episodes would occur.

Muscle jerking. "Josh" had spent more than a dozen years in a meditation group, wanting to be a teacher. His major symptom—marked head and neck jerking that he could not control—developed during and after the group's flying course. The condition was so severe that the organization wouldn't allow Josh to appear in public. After leaving the group, he sought training in a career in which he did not have to deal with the public and his co-workers could be told what caused the jerking. Currently, his physician has prescribed an anti-seizure medication which Josh reports is very helpful.

Long-term emotional flatness. "June" meditated and took courses for nine years. She had no complaints, but her husband, young adult children, parents, and siblings claimed she had become "depressed, spacey, unenthused, not careful or caring about things." June was emotionally flat—there was little variation in her facial expression, the pitch of her voice remained low and even, and her body and hand movements were minimal when she spoke, no matter what she was talking about. She reported to me that the only problems she had noted from the meditation were that she "lost a lot of time," her eyes "went out of focus," and she felt "stopped" quite often when alone. When asked about feeling stopped, she recalled numerous instances in which she lost an awareness of the passage of time and had a blank mind with no idea what she was supposed to do next. She would be released from that state when family members came home. According to her family, prior to her meditating, June had been a warm and compassionate person, responsive and involved with what was going on, even prone to temper blow-ups. Nothing in her history or responses indicated that she was a schizoid personality. Today, June appears impersonal in social situations and seems to have ceased experiencing and displaying strong emotional feelings, either positive or negative, as a consequence of her prolonged meditation.

Seizures. "Calvin," now forty, began meditation courses at age fifteen and soon wanted to be a teacher with the organization offering the courses. Early in college, he took his first prolonged meditation course, which consisted of yogic exercises followed first by slow overbreathing and then by increased meditation time. He also took a course that included overbreathing as fast as one could, alternately closing one then the other nostril, to be done after yoga exercises and prior to meditation. He suffered his first complex partial seizure (a form of epileptic seizure) in the fast-breathing program. He left the program, sought a medical diagnosis, and is still on antiseizure medication twenty-five years later. During his seizures (brief periods of loss of contact with what was going on around him) he made jerking, purposeless movements and loud sounds; afterward, he felt confused. His friends reported that during the seizures Calvin didn't seem to hear them and that he lurched and staggered while jerking and grunting loudly.

Visual hallucinations. "Caryn" meditated for seventeen years. "I saw little creatures with wings during intensive meditation periods," she reported. "They were like my pets. They'd tell me things. I began to not be able to tell who was a person and who was a deva [a Hindu nature spirit]." The leaders in the group praised her and, no matter how distressed these events made her feel, told her to meditate more and longer.

Caryn said she learned how to conceal her fear and confusion because she was terrified of being thrown out of the group. She had affiliated with it at age fourteen and was totally dependent on it. Having been encouraged long ago to break all contact with her family, she had felt she had no place else to go.

I am not saying that everyone who meditates has problems. I have spoken with many persons who find brief meditation relaxing and who are enthusiastic about their personal quiet time. These persons did not become members of cults, however, nor were they part of tight social groups of meditators in which, no matter how uncomfortable their reactions, they felt socially coerced into continuing the practices or were instructed to do even more meditating and hyperventilation.

The problem arises when, as we see happening today, a number of cultic groups use the rationale that their program of procedures is "good for mankind" and thus can be applied to everyone.

In this milieu, participants who complain that a certain procedure produces a negative effect on them are diverted and shushed. The group accomplishes this diversion by telling these individuals that they should do more, that they're not meditating correctly, and that their complaints are a sign of their "badness." By this time, those with the distressing symptoms are usually dependent on the organization, so they simply curb their expressions of distress for fear of being excluded.

In short, among other misdeeds, cultic groups ignore the importance of individual differences. History is replete with occasions on which persons or groups have tried to apply one panacea to all humankind's ills. In our era, we see cultic groups applying their brand of meditation to all takers, the assembly-line approach to meditation.

For centuries, meditation practices were taught within specific cosmologies of knowledge and beliefs. In contrast to these time-honored traditions, in which teachers watched and guided their pupils so that harmful outcomes could be avoided, meditation today is being sold by mass marketing. As the examples here have shown, there are dangers to individuals in the mass application of a process known to have a range of destabilizing emotional and mental effects. However, as is usual in cults, the cult leader thinks only of himself and his successes (how great it must be to say that millions are practicing "my" meditation technique!) and ignores the detrimental effects on specific followers.

Is Meditation Ever Beneficial?

Often at public lectures I am asked whether short-term meditation is ever beneficial to a person. And my answer goes something like this: if, without surrendering your life to a cult, you sit and do one of the two traditional methods of meditation, yes, that can be very helpful. Through the ages, the first method, empty-mind mantra meditation based on the Hindu tradition, has been useful to many people. The second method, reflective meditation, comes out of the Judeo-Christian tradition. Here, you sit and reflect as your way of focusing, and this too has brought moments of peace to thousands.

Meditation, in itself, is not good or bad. But when a venal person wants to sell you courses and persuade you to turn over your life to him, you must beware. If you end up a slave to a money-making power-seeking organization that pays no heed to the real difficulties you may experience as a result of certain practices, that is a bad use of those powerful practices.

Herbert Benson, author of the popular book, *The Relaxation Response,* says meditation doesn't have to be costly—and you don't need to buy a mantra. Just pick any word. For example, some meditators merely repeat the word "one" and, in so doing, find peace and quiet. Rather than give your life away, simply clear your mind by diverting your thoughts to some simple activity or idea for a moment or two, when you feel like it and free of charge. During any meditation or relaxation experiences, if you feel any mental or physical discomfort, I recommend that you stop and consult a professional.

7

Psychological Persuasion Techniques

Cult leaders do not have schools of persuasion to attend. They become masters of the folk art of human manipulation through testing and observing what works. They modify their approaches and techniques and use centuries-old manipulative devices to lead people to change. There is no school of persuasion, but there are many ways to learn how to manipulate people. You can go to the library and read how confidence games are run and how street scams and hustles are worked by bunco artists. You can learn from reading newspapers and the popular press and from watching how salespeople operate and how street-smart people lead and hustle others to do their bidding. If you want to study more academic sources, there are good books in social psychology spelling out how influence is manipulated and how group process affects behavior. You can read the classic works on thought reform and brainwashing and catch on to the use of "struggle groups" and the mobilization of peer pressure. Indeed, the folk art of human manipulation and persuasion can be learned and perfected.

There is no end to the ways a person can learn to manipulate others, especially if that person has no conscience, feels no guilt over living off the labors and money of others, and is determined to lead. As parents, teachers, clergy, and others who attempt to get people to change their behavior are painfully aware, however, simply suggesting or hinting to someone that he or she should do something, and even ordering or telling someone to do something, may not evoke that person's cooperation. Even threats may not gain compliance. So how do some cult leaders manage to manipulate people so successfully?

They use a combination of persuasion techniques: the physiological ones outlined in the previous chapter and the psychological ones described in this chapter. Here, we explore the use of trance and hypnosis, trickery, personal history revision, emotional manipulation, and the all-important peer pressure. No matter which techniques are used, the resultant behavioral change, as we saw in Chapter Three, continues to be accomplished in small incremental steps.

Trance and Hypnosis

Hypnosis is classed as a psychological rather than a physiological method because it is essentially a form of highly focused mental concentration in which one person allows another to structure the object of the concentration and simultaneously suspends critical judgment and peripheral awareness. When this method is used in a cultic environment, it becomes a form of psychological manipulation and coercion because the cult leader implants suggestions aimed at his own agenda while the person is in a vulnerable state.

A trance is a phenomenon in which our consciousness or awareness is modified. Our awareness seems to split as our active critical-evaluative thinking dims, and we slip from an active into a passive-receptive mode of mental processing. We listen or look without reflection or evaluation. We suspend rational analysis, independent judgment, and conscious decision making about what we are hearing or taking in. We lose the boundaries between what we wish were true and what is factual. Imagination and reality intertwine, and our self and the selves of others seem more like one self. Our mental gears shift into receptivity, leaving active mental processing in neutral.

Trancelike states can occur during hypnosis, during complete absorption in reading or hearing stories, and during marked concentration. They are sometimes referred to as *altered states of consciousness*. While in an altered state, for the most part we experience an absence of our usual generalized reality orientation (GRO)—that is, we are not actively noticing or aware of our environment and our part in it. In normal waking life, our GRO is our frame of reference, serving as background to our ongoing conscious experiences, our awareness. Our GRO shapes a context within which we interpret what is going on. This frame of reference can fade away under certain circumstances: hypnosis, meditation, guided imagery, drug use, fatigue, and sensory deprivation. When our GRO is weakened, we become both more suggestible to outside influences and more influenced by inner fantasies.

A number of cults use techniques that put people into an altered state of consciousness, making them more compliant. I am not saying that cult members walk around mesmerized, tranced out, and hypnotized for years on end. What I am saying is this: many cults and groups that use thought-reform techniques engage members in a fair amount of behavior that induces trances, as evidenced by the types and quality of the lectures and sermons and the required activities, such as prolonged chanting or meditation, and repetitive rote behavior. When transient trance states are induced, they may be inadvertent by-products of the group's exercises and methods of using language, or they may well be induced by design, although often not identified by the group as trance-inducing techniques. The most common procedure used is known as *naturalistic trance induction*, and many cults have relied on this technique.

One of the best explanations of how to go about inducing human cooperation and compliance in certain settings grows out of studies done of such naturalistic trance inductions. In the professional world of psychology, these indirect trance inductions were designed to bypass the usual resistance of patients who sought help but also resisted change when given direct instructions or suggestions. Naturalistic trance induction is also the model for some of the maneuvers used by cult leaders to change the attitudes and behaviors of their followers.

Naturalistic Trance Induction

The work of Milton Erickson, a renowned medical hypnotist, and his colleagues provides an excellent compilation of the methods and techniques that can be used to elicit cooperation and decrease resistance to change. A number of these techniques are among the processes we see used in cults.

Milton Erickson was interested in hypnosis and trance in a very special way. As both a researcher in hypnosis and an experienced psychiatrist, he knew how difficult it is to help people change, especially when they must change their habit patterns. Dedicated to helping people, Erickson devised a unique way of treating his patients, and his work offers one of the clearest explanations of how ordinary words, conversational style, and careful pacing and leading of an interaction can bring one person to the point of being able to secure the cooperation of another person without using pressure, high-demand announcements, or commands.

Until Erickson's work became known, most persons who employed trances—whether they were stage hypnotists, scientists studying hypnosis, or dentists and others using it to reduce pain and anxiety—relied on *formal trance inductions*, procedures clearly announced to the patient—"I am going to hypnotize you. Please close your eyes and relax." Erickson redefined hypnosis, seeing it as an interchange between two people in which the hypnotist gains the subject's cooperation, deals in various ways with resistance to cooperation, and promotes acknowledgment from the person that something is happening. Through this process, the hypnotherapist indirectly suggests the behavioral changes the patient comes to make.

During Erickson's *naturalistic inductions*, he did not announce, "We are now doing hypnosis." Nor did he even mention that "this is hypnosis." Instead, he "paced and led" the person he was work-ing with into whatever levels of trance the person could attain at a particular time. People who went to him knowing his fame as a medical hypnotist found themselves sitting talking with him, hear-ing him tell tales and chatting along disarmingly, unaware that what was transpiring between them was producing trances of vary-ing depths. As a result of these interactions, the patients' attitudes toward themselves and life were changing. Erickson's development of naturalistic trance induction was a major contribution to thera-peutic intervention.

A critical difference between Milton Erickson's work and cult leaders' methods is that Erickson kept the best interests of his patients foremost and did nothing self-serving with what he rec-ognized as a very powerful means of changing people. He used influ-ence techniques to help his patients change for their own betterment and based his treatment methods on decades of astute and careful observations of patients. Nevertheless, Erickson's care-fully noted observations on influence help us recognize and label the techniques put into play in cults and thought-reform groups. In Chapter Three, I outlined what thought reform is and the three stages of unfreezing, changing, and refreezing a person's attitudes and behavior. Erickson's work gives us a way to understand the con-text in which the moment-to-moment alterations take place and the methods used during the process of change induction.

It is the naturalistic trance induction that is likely to occur in cults, thought-reform groups, and some New Age groups. Most leaders of these groups probably do not consider what they are doing as trance induction. However, even when trances per se are not produced, the activities of skilled recruiters and cult leaders capitalize on the essential ingredients of pacing and leading, exploiting positive transference (discussed later in the chapter), and making indirect suggestions, all of which are central to the processes of hypnosis and trance.

It is my contention that a number of speeches given by certain cult leaders, and some group chants, fit the criteria for producing transient levels of trance. For example, one of my graduate students made a comparison of the taped speeches of charismatic cult leaders, television evangelists, and mainstream church leaders, looking for persuasive and trance-inducing qualities. Her findings, based on the evaluations of trained raters, showed that the speeches by cult leaders and fundamentalist evangelists had more hypnotic qualities than those of the mainstream church leaders.

Cult members are also trained and rehearsed in certain styles of presentation and taught to look for the desired effects in as many listeners as possible. For example, a man who had become an elder in a Bible cult was presented with typed-out lectures and instructions from his leader in how to repeat phrases over and over in specially cadenced singsongs. The leader taught him how to make a short one-page lecture with biblical quotes stretch out for an hour or longer. An informal survey of ministers and people familiar with giving public speeches shows that a similar page would take them about three minutes to present aloud, even a bit slowly. The man said he knew church members were being "tranced out" as he spoke, and he was given great prestige in the group because he followed the coaching well and could imitate the leader's ways of giving the sermons.

One widely used trance induction process, described in the work of Hillel Zeitlin, is to evoke universal experiences, as is done in these words: "Who among us has not stood on a hillside, looking out over a valley . . . and felt some mysterious emotion welling up in our heart?" Evoking a feeling of universality in a person helps the speaker solicit cooperation from that person.

Sometimes the induction method is speech filled with paradox and discrepancy—that is, the message is not logical and you are unable to follow it, but it is presented as though it were logical. Trying to follow what is being said can actually detach the listener from reality. A good example of this technique comes from cult leader Bhagwan Shree Rajneesh's comments at an initiation ceremony in which he gave each disciple a new name along with directives to wear first orange- and then plum-colored clothing and a necklace with his picture on it. Reading what Rajneesh said can give you a feeling for what words can do to cause a person to enter a light trance, or space out.

> First, the picture is not mine. The picture only appears to be mine. No picture of me is really possible. The moment one knows oneself, one knows something that cannot be depicted, described, framed. I exist as an emptiness that cannot be pictured, that cannot be photographed. That is why I could put the picture there. . . . The more you know the picture—the more you concentrate on it, the more you come in tune with it—the more you will feel what I am saying. The more you concentrate on it, the more there will not be a picture there.

Rajneesh perhaps was aware of the common human response to doing something repetitively: the repeated act can lose meaning. Children catch on, for example, to how they can say their names over and over until they have no meaning. In the quotation, Rajneesh is capitalizing on the way words commonly lose meaning through banal repetition. In relation to a trancelike state, he is also implanting the suggestion that "the more you concentrate on it, the more there will not be any picture there."

Guided Imagery

Indirect trance induction also grows out of storytelling and other verbal experiences. Cult leaders often speak repetitively, rhythmically, in hard-to-follow ways, and combine with these features the telling of tales and parables that are highly visualizable. They use words to create mental imagery, commonly called *guided imagery*.

In these guided-imagery exercises, the listener is urged to picture the story being told. The speaker may say, "Stop reflecting. Just go with the picture." Those who do stop reflecting on their nearby circumstances and go with the picture suddenly feel absorbed, relaxed, and very focused. And guided-imagery stories lead many people to experience altered states of consciousness.

A considerable number of different guided-imagery techniques are used by cult leaders and trainers to remove followers from their normal frames of reference. One technique is to tell long detailed stories that hold listeners' attention and get them absorbed, while lowering their awareness of the reality around them. As a result, they enter a trancelike state in which they are more likely to heed the suggestions and absorb the content of what is being said than if they were listening in an evaluative, rational way. The leaders who use guided imagery and other verbal techniques navigate through these exercises according to how much the listeners seem to be attaching to the words, how submerged and quiet they become.

For many persons, entering a trance state is pleasurable. It provides a respite from thought about the woes of everyday life. Thus, for example, about sixty years ago, people used to get together to read trance poetry. This poetry was an aspect of Romanticism, a nineteenth-century literary, philosophical, and artistic movement that was a reaction to an earlier neoclassical movement focused on intellectualism. Among the influences on Romantic poetry were mesmerism, the opium-induced hallucinations of British writer Thomas De Quincey, and Germanic authors' stress on imagination. When read aloud under suitable circumstances, a number of poems from this period have a decided trance-inducing effect. Poems such as Poe's "Annabel Lee," Gray's "Elegy," Tennyson's "Bugle Song," and Coleridge's "The Rime of the Ancient Mariner" are of this type. Early in this century, groups would gather to have a good reader read such poetry aloud in order to induce a condition of rapt attention and intense emotional responsivity in a sizable portion of the audience. Some reported the experience was intense enough to be called "sublime ecstasy." These group readings, as well as solitary silent readings of certain kinds of poems, produced what are best called trance-augmented aesthetic experiences.

Students of this phenomenon have listed six qualities of trance-inducing poetry: (1) freedom from abruptness, (2) marked regularity of soothing rhythm, (3) refrain and frequent repetition, (4) ornamented harmonious rhythm to fix attention, (5) vagueness of imagery, and (6) fatiguing obscurities. It is these very qualities that can be identified in analyzing the speech of many cult leaders, particularly when they are addressing groups of members and sympathizers.

Some leaders combine storytelling imagery with shouting, rhythmic clapping, and dancing to induce altered states. These processes, the reader will recognize, combine both overbreathing and trance induction in one event. So not all guided imagery is quiet, and surely not all cult leaders know the details of how trance induction through absorption works or the intricacies of hyperventilation. But from what has been described to me and others, I believe that the successful cult leaders monitor, observe, and learn from what they try and, as needed, revise and reformulate the folk art of persuasion.

One leader of a Bible cult repeated long, colorful tales of his childhood as the content for his guided imagery. The history he told was later found by ex-members to be mostly fictional. The main thrust of his tales was to point out how pure and clean and innocent he was as a child. He explained that these traits led him to his special mission as a leader. Ex-members recalled that they spaced out during his tales and left the meetings feeling subdued and obedient. Interestingly, they said his guided imagery often was about achieving a mind such as he had had as a child: "Get your mind as it once was, the mind of a child, free and innocent, not a thought in your mind. Let me think for you."

Some of the psychotherapy cults and thought-reform groups use guided imagery to regress members back to childhood. The purpose is to stir up recall of past pain and loneliness and, at the same time, induce members to blame their parents for allowing them to be alone and neglected when they were children. The following brief sample of a regression technique comes from a man who had been in a group that used a great deal of visualization. He was told:

Close your eyes and go back in time to your childhood. See yourself at about age six. It is like a dream. You see yourself in a woods. You are young and all alone. You walk between the trees to a clearing in the center. You see an old wall with a wooden gate that opens easily. You step inside, look around. You see some toys from when you were very young. The stuffed animal you loved, but it's cast aside, all alone and neglected. You look over across the way and see some clothes you wore when you were young. There they are all dusty and torn. You see the blanket you used to take to bed with you. You see your old bed across the way. You begin to feel as lonely now as you did as a little kid in bed, all alone. Who did you long for? Did they come? Why are you crying all alone in your bed? Think about all those lonely times and all those broken promises. Dad forgetting to come home to play, Mom not coming to put you to bed. All those broken promises. They are still deep inside, pulling at you, you are crying out alone and no one comes.

This guided imagery has the psychological goal of stirring up emotions, causing you, the group member, to return to childhood memories and recapture sadness. It also has the goal of implying that there are even more painful memories yet to be found, intimating that your parents caused all the miseries in your life. This allows the leader then to show you the way to happiness through learning his message and way of life: to come to find your new family and to feel loved here, blame those awful parents and don't go near them.

Guided imagery can have any content, and the group process of hearing others cry and sob as they recall past traumas has a powerful impact, for it induces a contagion of feeling and participation that can be heady for most persons.

Indirect Directives

Cult members often say to their families and friends, "No one orders me around. I choose to do what I do." Getting members to think that way is one of the manipulations mastered by cult leaders who have become skillful at getting acts carried out through indirection and implication. Accomplishing this task is easier when the member is in an altered state, fatigued, or otherwise anxious or under stress.

Indirect, or implied directives are not found only in cults but are commonplace throughout society. For example, recently the *Los Angeles Times* was about to enter a photo for a Pulitzer Prize but withdrew the picture as a "fabrication" after rumors circulated that the picture had been staged. The photo showed a firefighter dousing his head with water from a swimming pool while a luxurious home was consumed by flames. There was no longer water pressure to fight the fire, nothing to spray on the flames. The paper tracked down the firefighter, who said the photographer had suggested that he go to the pool and pour water on his head. The photographer defended himself by saying, "I deny categorically asking or telling any fireman to pose for me in front of a pool. I may have been guilty of saying this would make a nice shot, but to the best of my recollection, I did not directly ask him to do it." This photographer got cooperation in the same way that cult leaders do: namely, imply that something should happen, and it does. Especially if the person hearing the suggestion is generally cooperative, tired, and does not quite know what to do next. What a frustrating and worn-down state the firefighter must have been in—facing a raging inferno of flame and having no water with which to fight it. In such a suggestible and vulnerable frame of mind, the firefighter took the photographer's hint as a directive.

That is exactly how cult leaders get many of their wishes carried out. Few need to scream out commands. Here are several cult-related illustrations:

• After Synanon leader Chuck Dederich sat musing over his microphone about how greedy lawyers were and how he wanted some of their ears in a glass of alcohol, two young male followers, members of his Imperial Marines, took a rattlesnake and put it in a lawyer's mailbox. In a media interview, Synanon's resident PR man said, "No one is ordered or forced to do anything against their will. . . . Dederich may advocate it—yes, he's a great advocate. But he is very careful not to order it." (This infamous event is discussed further in Chapter Nine.)

• One former cult member told me, "I had never been directly told to kill my father, but I knew that if I should see the need to save the group, I would do it without any direction beyond what I knew I must do."

• Another former cult member said, "Our leader never told me to whip my son, but I knew that when he didn't smile when I told him to be quiet that I must spank and spank him until he smiled. I couldn't get him to, and he was bruised all over his legs and bottom before I stopped. I just knew I must do it."

• In another cult, the leader often said during lectures that people who don't obey must be punished. This was a repetitious theme backed up with many examples. Shortly after such a lecture, during a group work session, one woman began to shake and slap another woman who wasn't working hard enough. Later she said, "It was his words and how much I wanted him to like me. I saw myself doing as he would. He didn't have to be there, he did-n't have to tell me when or who or where. I wanted to do just what he wanted, so I began to shake and slap one woman. I realized I was flailing away at her. It was as if he and I were one at the moment."

Trickery

I don't want to convey the idea that cult leaders sit down and plan on a drawing board how they are going to proceed in great detail. But in studying certain cults, I have come to see that often the leader has sharpened his techniques as time goes on. Likewise, leaders of different groups may use the same technique.

The two examples that follow illustrate how cult leaders come upon identical tricks to create the impression they have supernormal power and knowledge. The first example was told to me by a survivor of Jim Jones's Peoples Temple and the second by a woman who had left a channeling cult.

Jim Jones instructed pairs of female members to visit the homes of persons who had signed cards the first time they attended a Peoples Temple event but who had not come back regularly. While one woman talked with the person, the other would ask to use the bathroom. She would then jot down notes on special clothing or features observed in the house, especially making careful notations about medicines in the bathroom cabinet, and getting names of doctors, pharmacies, and medications. Then she'd rejoin the conversation in the other room and invite the person to come again soon to the Temple.

At each Temple event, outsiders were asked to sign in. Before Jones went to the pulpit, one of his followers would match the sign-in cards with the information gleaned from the medicine cabinets and homes and place these behind a tall rim that topped the pulpit. Then Jones could close his eyes, look up, and proclaim he was having a vision or receiving a message that someone who owned a blue suit with gold buttons on it or who was a patient of Dr. Smith and took diabetes medicine was in the vicinity. This convinced the newcomer that Jones had supernormal powers and the ability to gain knowledge by means beyond the usual mortal ones.

A similar device was employed by the leader of a channeling cult who claimed to be in touch with an ancient "entity" who gave advice to the channeler to pass on to his followers. Those who attended a session at the channeler's salon, where crystals, exercise programs, and diet aids were also sold, wrote their names, addresses, and phone numbers in a "guest book" to be eligible for "door prizes." Shortly afterward, a visitor from the salon would drop by the homes of those who'd been to the salon to leave a small gift, usually colorful crystals or massage oils, saying the person's name had been picked in a drawing. The visitor was always a warm and disarming female. She would ask to use the bathroom and, while there, would quickly write down information from prescription medicines in the cabinet. Upon leaving, she would present a card listing times of future channeling sessions, inviting the person to attend again soon.

When someone who had been visited signed in at a session, a woman watching the guest book would go to the back room and pull out a 5 x 7 card with the information about the person. Then during the channeling, the long-gone entity might ask for "one of Dr. Smitherton's patients—the lady who takes Xanax." He gives her advice to "relax, take more time for herself, and to come again to visit here, it is so relaxing." This establishes the channeler's credibility since it appears that the entity knows things he could not know unless he truly were magical and had skills beyond those of ordinary mortals.

Other devices to convince followers of special powers are simply magician's tricks. Sathya Sai Baba, an Indian with a large following, is described as "a divine incarnation, an avatar, a god-man" by his devotees. He is most touted for his "miracles," which his followers interpret as "convincing symbols of his love." Baba's miracles include materializing objects, rings, pendants, and, most often, penis-shaped stones called *lingams*, which he either solemnly or jokingly presents to wondrous devotees. Another of Sai Baba's specialties is spewing *vibhuti*, sacred ash which is supposed to have healing powers, from his fingers.

Revision of Personal History

There is a widespread practice in cults of having the long-term members tell their tales, that is, stand before the group and recount their personal histories. Groups have different names for this exercise. For example, some former members have told me of "cereal drama," at-breakfast tales through which new members learn to embellish their pasts to make them sound like the ones they are hearing from older members. Another is called "running your own dirty story," meaning make your history sound the worst possible.

Such revision of history is used in both live-in and live-out cults, and the cults' general purpose in the exercise is "to let members see why being with us is the right place to be."

Former cult members tell me that they quickly learned how to tell their own histories by listening to those who had been in the organization longer. New members got the idea right away that they were to tell only sad, negative, unwholesome events, recount only disastrous relationships, and end with praise about the group. They were never to tell about good times, fine parents, loving siblings, hardworking relatives, or positive life experiences. Families had to be portrayed as abusive, alcoholic, uncaring, self-centered, bourgeois or capitalistic, and otherwise despicable. Since we are all prone to adapt to the environment in which we exist, it is not surprising that cult newcomers soon began to revise their personal histories according to what they heard from others around them. With each telling, they would embellish how awful their families had been; how meaningless their lives; how sinful, how drug-ridden, how selfish they were before joining the group.

There are several specific reasons why historical revision is important to cults. The group philosophy often rests on the idea that the cult is an elite organization, the new order, and made up of the most advanced beings. Therefore it is necessary for the leadership to make striking contrasts between group members and nonmembers in order to convince members that the outer world is bad and the group world is good. These tales of debauched pasts in an evil world, told by smiling, normal-looking people, are persuasive to newcomers. Revisions of personal histories provide useful propaganda against parents, friends, and those aspects of the world the leader wants to denigrate. They also reinforce the cult's repeated suggestions that the mainstream world is to be shunned and ridiculed. They prove that it's safer to stay in the protective good world of the group.

Demonstrating to potential members and newcomers that the group has really caused members' lives to change for the better also aids recruitment. Older members are conditioned to spin off horrendous tales about their past and to say how great things are now that they are with this group, and many ex-members have told me that, during their first few days or weeks in the group, they were particularly struck by other members' sad, sordid, brutal pasts. Only later, when bit by bit they gained some real information about others and the group, did they realize that the tales were exaggerated or totally fabricated, as were the ones they themselves ended up constructing. The more hideously they portrayed their pasts, the more approval the leader gave. Former Synanon members told me that they had learned to "run [their] dirty stories" by inventing drug-using, alcohol-abusing pasts based on the stories they heard. As they stayed longer in the group, they too learned to deliver tales of dramatic degradation to impress newcomers.

A number of persons coming out of Bible groups have told me that the practice of "witnessing"—both as an effort to recruit and as part of the initiatory program for a newcomer—consisted of the construction of tales that described how members had left lives of travail and now led lives of joy, camaraderie, and blessedness and that ended with urging the listener to come with the members into this happy family.

In some political cults, members repeatedly had to go over their backgrounds as part of examining their "class history." Each person's life was orally inspected and reviled. Members were told their thinking was totally determined by the bad class they had been reared in. Even working-class members had their thinking pulled apart and attacked as still reflecting "the training and education that is controlled by the ruling [bourgeois] class." Some leftist groups rebuke their members with Chairman Mao's words that "every kind of thinking is stamped with the brand of class." In some rightist groups, members have to "purify" their personal histories by not mentioning relatives, friends, or "connections" who are not of the right political persuasion in their outlook or who are, for example, of color or foreign born.

New Age and psychotherapy cults are well known for their use of history revision to get members or "patients" to develop and accept a personal history that fits with and justifies the teachings of the cult. A former member of the Sullivanians, a psychotherapy/political cult discussed later in this chapter, described her experience this way:

> My therapist often asked me about my childhood and encouraged me to talk about events that were painful. She said that it sounded like my parents didn't really want me or at best were simply unable to love me because their parents hadn't been able to love them. She said she thought it best for my therapy if I didn't see my parents for a while—just until I could understand my history better. She encouraged me to tell my personal history to my friends and to listen to theirs. My painful childhood memories were always validated, while the happy ones were disregarded. I became convinced that I had had a miserable childhood and it seemed like my new friends were the only ones who could understand since their family lives had been as miserable as mine.

Yet another kind of history revision occurs in groups that practice past-lives work. Various methods are used by the different groups, but at some point members learn they will be going back in time to "visualize and reexperience" their past lives.

An anthropologist studying one such group had an informant who told her of three past lives: one was a life as a young Arab boy, around 1784, whose tribe had assigned him to cut off the eyelids of a spy who had been caught by the tribe. Another past life had taken place in Italy around 343 A.D., when the informant was on the staff of torturers who used a hot poker to poke out the eyes of a young blond girl to get information from her. She said she poked out an eye only to discover the girl was innocent. Yet another past life had occurred around 440 B.C. In that year, she had been designated warrior of the day and was to kill an enemy. The group's success in instilling the belief that she had done these things left her having to live with the notion that she is a violent sadistic killer.

I have interviewed a number of former adherents of groups that have members create and relive past lives as part of the group practices. Almost every past life told to me was filled with either extreme tension and fear or considerable violence. One man who won a large legal suit against his former group had been led to think that in past lives he had been three murderous characters, identified by the group as Thorgon, Ultraviolence, and Tyrannical Ninja. These synthetic identities evolved from a combination of direct suggestion, learned trance induction, and the philosophy of the group.

People have told me of finding themselves in past lives in which they were individuals trapped in spaceships flying through space on their way to fiery crashes, killers in medieval villages who were burned at the stake, soldiers attacked by others and trampled by horses, and killers of babies. One story about a life as a respected priest in old Spain started out like a success story but ended with the priest's being stoned to death for an affair with a nobleman's wife. Some people also express enduring concern because they have been both males and females in their past lives.

Later, when I describe the problems individuals encounter after leaving cults and groups that use thought-reform processes, I'll discuss the psychological impact that history revision has on most persons (see Chapter Twelve).

Peer Pressure and Modeling

The old maxim "When in Rome do as the Romans do" underlies much of our adaptation to new social groups. It is both convenient and congenial to adapt. We look around and see models, and we comport ourselves to be like them. Most cults train new members, either through overtly stated policies or by more implicit shaping, to act in ways desired by the group. To increase members' recruiting potential, typically cults train members to smile, appear happy, be outgoing, and give attention to newcomers.

Peer pressure is an effective means to get people to fit their behavior to group norms. In cults, this works for new and old members alike, going far beyond what is generally seen in society at large. In an atmosphere that states or implies that there is only one way to be and this is it, it is most important to have models around to imitate. Robert Lifton speaks of the totalism of the person meeting the totalistic ideology of a group, an idea that suggests why adaptation filters down to the clothing, the smiles, the language— all the details of behavior that are either approved or shunned.

For example, a number of women, particularly those from religious and political cults, told me that without being aware of it and without ever being told to do so, they slipped from dressing in ordinary clothes into wearing dark colors, long skirts, flat heels, and no makeup. Those who had been in psychotherapy cults tell me they were chastised if they did not provide "deep" revelations from their past. In the section on historical revision earlier in this chapter, we saw the importance of peer pressure and modeling in getting members to conform. Other ex-members have told me of seeing peers write letters to parents and friends based on sample letters provided by leadership. Several cults label some of these model letters *disconnect letters*.

In these activities, there is no need for cult leaders to fuss and belabor followers, as parents and teachers are wont to do with children and students. The clever cult leader or mind manipulator manages to use the innate tendencies toward group conformity that we bring with us as a powerful tool for change. No one has to announce the rules to us. Most of us look around and discern what they are and how we should behave. And most cults weed out "bad actors" at the point of recruitment: the disobedient, the unruly, the delinquent, the hard to handle and difficult to influence are turned away. They take too much time and thus are not cost effective to change, and they break up the atmosphere the leader wants to keep in place, the ambience that by fitting in things will go better.

Emotional Manipulation

When leaders do not browbeat members into conformity but instead make use of the way people in groups learn through what

they see other group members doing, personal behavioral and attitudinal changes are less noticeable to individuals. As one former
cult member after another has told me, "I changed without being
aware of it." This unconscious change is partly due to the power of
the contagion of mood in groups. Cults induce feelings of guilt,
shame, and fear, and use sex and intimacy controls to keep members dependent on the group. Robert Cialdini, a social psychologist who studies automatic influence, mindless compliance, and
why people say yes without thinking, is interested in how
exploiters, cult leaders, con artists, salespeople, and other "compliance professionals" can get individuals to fall into blind patterns of
obedience. Some of our tendencies to engage in fixed-action patterns serve us well most of the time, but our propensity for patterned behavior can also be used by manipulators to dupe and
control us.

According to Cialdini, the majority of the thousands of different tactics that compliance professionals use fall into six categories,
and each category is based on a psychological principle that directs
human behavior. These six principles are:

1. *Consistency.* We try to justify our earlier behavior.

2. *Reciprocity.* If somebody gives us something, we try to repay
   in kind.

3. *Social proof.* We try to find out what other people think is
   correct.

4. *Authority.* We have a deep-seated sense of duty to authority
   figures.

5. *Liking.* We obey people we like.

6. *Scarcity.* If we come to want something, we can be made to
   fear that if we wait it will be gone. The opportunity to get it
   may pass. We want to take it now—whatever is being
   offered, from an object to cosmic consciousness.

Looking at this list and thinking about our own behavior makes
it easier to see how a manipulative person can move someone along
a given pathway—depending on his or her skills and the person's

state of being and circumstances. We can see how transformations occur when the six principles are skillfully put into play by cult leaders and cultic groups. For example:

1. *Consistency.* If you have made a commitment to the group and then break it, you can be made to feel guilty.
2. *Reciprocity.* If you accept the group's food and attention, you feel you should repay them.
3. *Social proof.* If you look around in the group, you will see people behaving in particular ways. You imitate what you see and assume that such behavior is proper, good, and expected.
4. *Authority.* If you tend to respect authority, and your cult leader claims superior knowledge, power, and special missions in life, you accept him as an authority.
5. *Liking.* If you are the object of love bombing and other tactics that surround you, make you feel wanted and loved, and make you like the people in the group, you feel you ought to obey these people.
6. *Scarcity.* If you are told that without the group you will miss out on living a life without stress; miss out on attaining cosmic awareness and bliss; miss out on changing the world instantly or gaining the ability to travel back in time; or miss out on whatever the group offers that is tailored to seem essential to you, you will feel you must buy in now.

Keep these six compliance principles in mind as you read this example of emotional manipulation:

Having graduated from high school in a small town, "Beth" wanted time before her college classes began to get acquainted with the area and the campus, and maybe make a friend or two, so she moved into the large state university dorm early. As she was leaving one morning to go exploring, a young woman sitting in the dorm lobby cheerfully jumped up and began talking with her. Before long, the woman invited Beth to accompany her to a country farm, supposedly sponsored by students in a group studying world hunger.

After a few days at the farm, Beth was tired. She felt bombarded with many ideas that were contrary to her own, ideas that made her feel all wrong and uncertain. Yet she liked the woman who had brought her and felt surrounded by happy, smiling people who kept hugging her, complimenting her, and begging her to stay. At one point, she began to cry over the conflict she felt between wanting to stay at the farm, where it seemed so secure and loving, and going back to the huge university.

The male leader of the group lectured vaguely but emphatically about the ecology of the mind, the restoration of true harmony versus artificiality, and how to be an activist. Beth did not know why, but she began to feel inadequate. The abstractions the leader spoke about were not ideas Beth was familiar with, but the other members, almost all women, nodded knowingly and adoringly as the leader lectured.

Before coming to college, Beth had been concerned about being from a small farming town in another state. Now, the vague philosophy of the lectures made her feel guilty that her parents could afford to send her to a large, expensive university while there was so much hunger on the planet. Finally, during a lecture on how "educational institutions, even your own families, throw out good food while little children around the world are starving," Beth began to cry uncontrollably.

At this emotional outburst, which she said she was later trained to watch for in newcomers, some of the other group members hugged her and told her her feelings were an indication of her great depth of sensitivity. She could become a leader of women, they said. She should spend her time with them and start college later. Beth felt relieved and stopped thinking about leaving. The group made parents sound slothful and cold, and all the new members soon stopped calling, writing, and accepting visits from families and old friends because they were not with "the movement."

Two years later, Beth finally ran away from the farm and called her parents. She had spent the time fund-raising and deceptively recruiting other young persons who worked to support a self-designated messiah who claimed he was appointed "The Guardian." Beth did not find out about the leader's sexual abuse of some of the women in the group, nor did she question where the money she and others raised in the name of "ecology studies" went until a few months before she finally was able to plan how she would get away from the group.

It takes vigilance, stamina, and unending internal fortitude to live life and use our minds. We must pay heed to what humankind has learned about how free minds and free humans build better worlds cooperatively—something that does not occur under the dominion of a self-appointed exploiter who does not really have our welfare or the welfare of humankind as his central aim but merely his own temporal security and comfort.

Psychotherapy Cults

Psychotherapy cults provide good examples of cult leaders' use of psychological persuasion techniques, in particular emotional manipulation and peer pressure. These cults tend to arise when legitimate individual or group psychotherapy becomes corrupted, or when opportunistic nonprofessionals simply deceive and prey upon the unwary.

Two colleagues and I studied twenty-two psychotherapy cults. We interviewed as many persons as were available from each group, read documents, and listened to tapes of the leaders and of group sessions. My colleague Maurice Temerlin interviewed thirty-eight former "patients," and I interviewed eighty-two.

The leaders of these groups ranged from college faculty members to a paroled felon with less than a high school education. The groups, located in six states, varied in size from 15 to more than 300 members. The largest had 350 live-in members and 400 peripheral members. The groups had been in existence for five to twenty-five years, and all but two are still in existence. Fifteen of the groups were led by trained professionals (psychiatrists, psychologists, social workers); the remaining seven were run by nonprofessionals (ranging from former clerks to convicted felons). These "therapists" were, with one exception, Caucasian. The patients were primarily middle-class to upper-middle-class Caucasians with some college or advanced degrees.

Some of these therapy cults formed when professionals deviated from ethically based, fee-for-service, confidential relationships with clients to form cohesive, psychologically incestuous groups. These professionals misused therapeutic techniques and manipulated the professional relationship to their own advantage. They also violated ethical prohibitions by forming exploitative relationships with clients who became their friends, lovers, relatives, employees, colleagues, and students. Simultaneously, patients became like siblings, bonded together to admire and support their common therapist.

A major deviance in psychotherapy cults revolves around the therapeutic phenomenon known as *transference*. Transference is an important aspect of insight-oriented psychotherapy. Normally, the client and therapist examine together the attitudes the client transfers from earlier life experiences onto the therapist as well as onto other authority persons. Often these are positive expectations, of a "good daddy" for example, but some clients transfer negative attitudes. Both the positive and negative attitudes come out of clients' own expectations and are not founded on the therapist's conduct and attitudes. In these cultic situations, however, rather than study and understand the transferences, the therapists/leaders promoted their idolization by their patients.

Instead of having their personal autonomy encouraged, patients were led into submissive, obedient, dependent relations with their therapists. The improprieties of the role violations were compounded by the therapists' use of indirect, deceptive, and coercive influence techniques, which led patients to comply with the therapists' wishes.

In addition, other cultlike behavior was noted in these therapy cults. In one case, two mental health professionals offered their clinic as a place in which students working on advanced degrees in psychology and counseling could perform required supervised work in the field. They induced the trainees to move in with the professionals, get money from their families for therapy, get siblings to join the group for therapy, and recruit other trainees at their schools. These professionals led their followers to believe that only this therapy could save them and the world. The group has grown and moved to a rural setting where it is running a residential treatment program. The followers maintain the property, care for the resident patients, and attempt to recruit other trainees and patients. They are also compiling and attempting to edit the taped ramblings of the leaders.

Here are some other prominent examples of the ways in which therapy cults work:

The Sullivanians

This group began in 1957 when a dissident group of therapists broke away from the William Alanson White Institute founded by Harry Stack Sullivan, a respected psychiatrist who was influential in the 1950s. What started out as a new therapy center evolved into a psychotherapy collective and finally into a cult that controlled almost all areas of the lives of approximately two hundred so-called patients. The basic philosophy of the group was that the nuclear family is the root of all evil, and that a child born or brought into the group shouldn't have a special relationship with her or his parents, just as adult Sullivanians weren't supposed to talk to their parents.

Many who left said the leaders dictated members' living arrangements, sexual practices, choice of profession, hobbies, and child-rearing practices. Members were required to go to thrice-weekly therapy sessions with a Sullivanian therapist. Group members, even married ones, lived in apartments with more than a dozen roommates of the same sex and were encouraged to sleep with a different member of the opposite sex each night. Much litigation between current and former members has taken place, particularly regarding child custody. When founder and leader Saul Newton died, the group more or less fell apart.

Center for Feeling Therapy

The Center for Feeling Therapy was based in Hollywood, California, and lasted for ten years. It had 350 patients living near one another and sharing homes. Hundreds more were nonresident outpatients, and still others communicated with "therapists" by letter.

Maximum benefits supposedly came only to residents, and patients were led to see themselves as the potential leaders of a therapy movement that would dominate the twenty-first century. Two of the psychologists billed themselves as "the Butch Cassidy and the Sundance Kid of psychology." The leaders claimed that patients could reach the next stage of human evolution by following the leaders' dictates.

I interviewed thirty-seven members of this group, studied ninety-two affidavits and countless legal documents, listened to tapes of so-called therapy sessions, and appeared as a witness for the State of California at license revocation hearings. Other witnesses also described the group as a cult. All twelve therapists associated with the center—one physician; five psychologists; five marriage, family, and child counselors; and one psychiatric technician—lost or surrendered their licenses. The ninety-four-day hearing before an administrative law judge was the "longest, costliest, and most complex psychotherapy malpractice case in California history." The therapists were found guilty of acts of gross negligence, incompetence, patient abuse, aiding and abetting the unlicensed practice of psychology, false advertising, fraud, and deception.

Former patients testified that they were seduced by the therapists, given sex assignments, publicly ridiculed and humiliated, and then charged high fees for such treatment. An ex-patient described witnessing a woman who was ordered to remove her blouse and crawl on the floor, mooing like a cow. Others told of being beaten during therapy. A male patient who wanted to return to college and stop working in a garage run by the therapists was made to wear diapers, sleep in a crib, and eat baby food for eight weeks because his therapist said the man wanted to live his life like a baby.

Although settlement figures were sealed, according to the *Los Angeles Times*, the civil cases were settled for more than $6 million. Witnesses described the group as a cult that brainwashed members and forced women to have abortions and to give children up for adoption, telling the women they were "too crazy" to care for children. Connections to families were broken, except to collect money for more therapy. Therapists had sexual intimacies with patients, forced them to stand naked before the group, beat them, and had patients beaten by other patients.

The therapists, who collected "fines" and "donations" running into the thousands of dollars from individuals, allegedly used the money to buy a ranch in Arizona. The group began to split apart when all the therapists went to the ranch, leaving the patients in Los Angeles, free to talk openly with one another. This information exchange, without fear of the therapists' hearing, was the turning point for many as they began to see what had happened to them.

The administrative law judge wrote in his decision that "the therapists preyed on young and credulous persons who were in a unique position to be misled" and that no patient who had testi-

fied at the hearing could be deemed "to have consented to or antic-
ipated the almost Gothic maelstrom that they were being drawn
into." The judge also wrote that the center purported to offer treatment "by all of the world's eight or ten premier psychotherapists"
in a set-up that allowed them to "solicit money, sex or free labor
from patients" and to coerce them into "obsessive devotion."

Dr. Tim

This cultic group has been operating since 1971, even though Dr.
"Tim" has been dead for several years. Dr. Tim started the group
when he was forty, divorced, and a clinical psychologist living in
the eastern United States. He had patients move into his home,
charging them a monthly therapy fee plus room and board. He and
his followers fled overseas when legal charges were filed against him,
alleging he had engaged in sex with minors. The group lived communally overseas for about seven years until, once again, similar
legal charges threatened the leader, and the group then fled to the
West Coast of the United States.

The group averaged about forty members, including a few children. There was a fair turnover in membership, even though Dr.
Tim warned that leaving him would cause individuals to lead lives
of mental suffering. Leaving was also literally difficult, because Dr.
Tim sent the largest men in the group to retrieve anyone who left
who could be located. Those who tried to leave openly were physically restrained.

Dr. Tim told his clients that he was "more enlightened than
Jesus, and had created the ultimate therapy, combining Freud, Zen,
Kundalini yoga, and LSD." The latter, he said, was to "override
their egos." No criticism or complaints were tolerated by Tim, who
said such complaining indicated "being in your head" rather than
"in your feelings." Anything other than feeling was labeled "being
in your stuff" and considered an indication of mental disorder. Dr.
Tim "diagnosed" each new member as showing signs of severe mental illness, telling each one that only he could cure the person.

All phone calls to family were surreptitiously taped and used by Tim in group sessions to demonstrate how harmful parents are. He had patients give up their careers when the group lived overseas; instead, members worked as hotel and restaurant staff and were told always to be near him so they could care for the large house and grounds he had purchased. He taught them to think of him and the group as "family." He also broke up and prevented marriages and had children raised by the group rather than their parents. A nine-year-old girl reportedly was kept in her room for the major portion of three years, with group members often forgetting her food because they were stoned on drugs.

He promoted group homosexual contacts by having the men in groups of four or five do a "yoga" exercise in which he had them lie on the floor with one middle finger in their mouth and the other middle finger in another man's anus while the same was done to them. While supervising these sessions, Dr. Tim would berate the men, who were bewildered because he had prescribed the practice.

After his death, a small segment of the followers continued to meet, and to this day these followers proclaim what a wonderful therapist was Dr. Tim.

Nonprofessional Therapy Cults

Parolees "Stanley" and "David" have each developed a psychological cult in East Coast states that have no laws regulating psychological practices. When these men returned to their communities, they drew upon their group therapy experiences during incarceration to develop restrictive, cultic groups. One group is based on primal scream techniques, the other on confrontational attack therapy.

A state prison parolee, Stanley operates out of an apartment in a busy metropolitan neighborhood. He recruits from nearby coffeehouses, bookstores, and diners by inviting single men and women to have coffee and talk with him about his "therapy." He sometimes posts notices offering free lectures on sex, psychology, and loneliness. His street smarts, con-artist skills, and jargon combine to convey intense attention and seductiveness. He secures detailed histories in private sessions, charging modest fees for initial meetings but, over time, develops costly intensive sessions with all fees to be paid in cash. Combining his knowledge of a person with techniques learned in prison group therapy, Stanley strips recruits of their defenses and gets them dependent on him, convincing them they are badly damaged.

About fifteen persons over the past dozen years have spent their free time with Stanley. They see him for individual therapy several times a week, participate in groups with him and other followers, rely on him for most major decisions in their lives, and have forsaken their families for him. There has been a turnover in followers, but a few have been present since Stanley began the group.

David learned confrontational attack therapy of a Synanon type while in a drug rehabilitation program in prison. Using high-confrontation techniques and his assured, smooth, aggressive, and controlling ways, David has controlled the lives of a group averaging sixty persons for more than ten years. Under his orders, "patients" have limited their friendships to others in the group, severed relationships with their families of origin, spent most of their free time with David, and structured their lives according to his dictates. He directs marathon confrontation groups; gives individual counseling; supervises the medical, financial, and social lives of his clients; and has his clients spend their vacations with him at a suburban home they have helped finance in his name.

"Ray," like David and Stanley, with no professional credentials, was able to start a cultic psychotherapy group about eight years ago and has maintained a group of about thirty persons since then. A major portion of his followers are psychologists and graduate trainees in psychology. Ray attracts them through widely publicized advertisements for seminars on empowerment. His ads say he will teach you to how to "merge, transform, and marry your own experience." He claims he is "totally free and if you want freedom badly enough, the universe just lays down at your feet."

Ray sells three-week basic training seminars, usually held at attractive vacation resorts. He selectively recruits certain seminar attendees to move to his home near a large city, where he claims they will "transform, loosen up, learn to surrender, be in service, and get off their holding positions, and will learn to trust." He has a "trust fund" to which followers are urged to contribute "cash only, no checks, no credit cards."

After recruits move in, they are told that they are "losers who should surrender their lives to him as he is the Master Guide." Since most are out-of-state professionals, they often have trouble securing licenses and jobs in the new area and must take menial jobs to support their work with Ray. Those I interviewed said they became depressed, demoralized, chronically anxious, and lost their self-esteem under Ray's barrage of psychological criticism. They said they looked to Ray for behavioral cues about how they should act.

An experienced clinician in her late thirties gave up her administrative career in a reputable clinic to be in the group for several years. She remarked, "Somehow when I was around him, I lost my sense of self. I lost all my knowledge, all my diagnostic skills. I failed to recognize a brilliant psychopath had control over me." The group continues to thrive, and Ray now has two large facilities to house followers.

These examples clearly demonstrate that cultic groups make use of psychological techniques. Also, although I have been focusing on specific psychotherapy cults, they are not the only ones using these techniques. Psychological techniques are used by all types of cults, and I emphasize once again that, although the content of cults may vary, the basic ways they secure members, the techniques they use to unfreeze, change, and refreeze members into doing what the leader wants, and their results are similar.

As I have suggested here, some of the most potent and common psychological techniques used by cult leaders are trance induction, guided imagery, and indirect suggestion. These methods use language, demeanor, and setting to decrease critical, reflective, evaluative thinking. Cult leaders also use just plain trickery to mystify followers and create an aura of superhuman skills. And they also draw upon the power of personal history revision, emotional manipulation, and peer pressure to produce behavioral and attitudinal changes.

Indeed, these techniques are so commonly used in cults that we all need to look for them when we hear about a group and wonder if it is cultic, deceptive, and manipulative. Being familiar with cults' techniques can also be useful when you are talking to a friend or relative who has become involved with something new and seems to be overly fascinated, bewitched, or infatuated with the group or person.

Also, as we are coming to see, there is no short, simple way to explain how thought reform works or how cult leaders "do it." There are a multitude of ways one person can use language, personal charm, and determination combined with lots of physiological tricks and coercive psychological maneuvers to win some degree of control over almost any other person at any time. And if a person does come under the spell or domination of a cult leader, the lessons in this book can help us all appreciate how much education will be needed to assist that person to understand and break free from what has happened.

8

Intruding into the Workplace

There are many advancement programs, workshops, seminars, and training sessions currently utilized by companies and corporations in the United States and elsewhere that are legitimate in their intentions and often effective in their outcomes. Some of these programs have incorporated new ideas and new ways of thinking, which is why, on occasion, they are referred to as New Age training programs. This in itself does not make them harmful or of evil intent. Yet, a small but significant portion of these programs are *not* what they appear to be. In some cases, they are fronts for cults or other organizations using thought-reform processes that can cause considerable psychological harm and turmoil and can even precipitate psychoses in some employees without delivering any increased skill, productivity, profit, or other purported benefit.

Several years ago, the executive vice president of the American Society for Training and Development estimated that $150 million was being spent annually by U.S. businesses on suspicious training programs. This may not seem like a lot compared to the billions of dollars spent overall in this country on motivational training, but when we consider the loss of time as well as money on programs that produce no positive job-related effect and merely seek to sell more and more seminars, when we realize the distress caused to employees who are unprepared for the emotional and psychological duress of some of the sessions, when we realize the intrusion into personal beliefs perpetrated by those programs that

misrepresent themselves, then we see a trend of impact on everyday life that cannot be ignored.

Certain programs introduced into industrial and office settings
have been causing particular criticism and alarm. Sold under the
guise of management and communication courses, these programs
are frequently purported in advertisements and word-of-mouth sales
to be able to "motivate" and even "transform" employees. The
details of what motivation and transformation involve are usually
left vague but cryptically promising.

There are three primary reasons for discussing such programs
in this book. The first is to reiterate the ever-present need to evaluate the premises beneath the various offerings that are made to us
daily. We must always ask ourselves, Who is this person offering me
some new cure-all—some religious, political, social, psychological,
health-related, or other life pathway that he wants me to purchase
and follow?

The second reason is to bring attention to the fact that certain
training programs use the same types of intense influence techniques that are identified with cults. Also, many of these programs
are actually recruiting venues for certain cults. Cults have put on
three-piece suits and come directly into the workplace, disguised
as self-improvement management courses.

The third reason is that the philosophy of life espoused in many
of these programs falls within the realm of religious issues and personal belief systems, an important matter for many people. Under-
neath some New Age offerings there sometimes lies a philosophical
and spiritual cosmology, a theory on the nature and principles of
the universe. New Age cosmology generally views reality as one
unitary organic whole with no independent parts, and this cosmology constitutes a belief system or religion that, at root, differs
from, say, Christianity or Judaism.

A 1992 Gallup Poll reveals that more and more Americans—
now 58 percent—consider religion to be "very important" in their
lives. According to the Gallup organization's 1992–93 report "Religion in America," 89 percent of Americans single out a religious

preference, with 82 percent reporting that they are Christian, and 2 percent, Jewish. Two-tenths of 1 percent are Muslim, while one-tenth of 1 percent hold Hindu beliefs.

In legal cases brought before U.S. courts by employees who were made to attend training programs of various kinds, the employees noticed that there were "religious" differences between their own beliefs, which are constitutionally protected, and the cosmology or philosophy put forth by these training programs. These citizens were the first to alert the public to this encroachment on our freedom in the workplace.

Clarification of *New Age*

Since I refer on occasion to *New Age* programs or groups, I feel that a clarification of my use of the term is necessary to avoid misunderstandings. This is not a book critiquing New Age philosophy. But I do call attention to what I think of as the dark side of New Age thinking, to show how some so-called New Age techniques and ideas are in some instances used to exploit people and induce them to join cults. Countless theories, activities, practices, and events are included in the broadest definitions of New Age. For example, discussions of New Age thinking can range from interests in acupuncture, crystals, tarot cards, channeling, meditation, alternative health care, special diets, wavy music, health-food restaurants, and a variety of self-actualization books and programs to specific theological critiques of the reasoning underlying certain New Age beliefs—such as the central theme that "all is one"—and to thoughtful philosophical critiques of what such thinking is bringing into the educational, medical, and religious arenas.

Many persons today dabble in such New Age ventures as going to holistic health practitioners, engaging in supposed native practices, attending inspirational lectures, going on wilderness treks, and collecting crystals. Many aspects of the New Age can be entertaining, beneficial, and informative, as long as people don't get caught up with someone using these ventures to entrap them into a thought-reform group or a cult or to psychologically coerce them into turning over their lives to a leader who is exploiting them personally or financially.

How does this relate to the business world?

Many people of goodwill, with a desire to improve the lot of humankind, have explored and continue to explore how our thinking influences how we conceptualize the world. There has been an effort, under the New Age umbrella, to introduce the notion that the thought models we use—now widely called paradigms—should be examined to see if advances can come from our taking new vantage points from which to look at both our daily life and our world of work. Unfortunately, much of the writing and discussion about New Age ideas is put into esoteric, hard-to-follow language, which has made it possible for con artists and cult leaders to latch onto the phrases and concepts for their own purposes.

I often think of Ludwig Wittgenstein's statement from his well-known *Tractatus Logico-Philosophicus*: "Everything that can be thought at all can be thought clearly. Everything that can be said can be said clearly." Many manipulators and cult leaders have used New Age ideas and phrases to imply that they have secret knowledge, something new and wonderful to offer. They use such terminology as

"Achieving ultimate reality."

"Death is the final stage of growth."

"Your beliefs are what stand in your way."

"Transformation through psychotechnologies."

"Myths must be eliminated before new consciousness
is achieved."

Exploiters prosper by exploiting ignorance, fear, and guilt to manipulate us. In that vein, they have appropriated some of the notions of New Age thinking and used them as leverage in their self-serving ventures. The very notion of "new paradigms," for example, sounds both scientific and esoteric, even mysterious. New Age language can be baffling while also implying that the speaker has specific knowledge: the answers, the lore of the ancients, or the one path to transformation, specifically, in the case of this chapter, transformed and improved cooperation and productivity in the workplace.

A Clash in the Workplace

How many reading this book recall attending a large group awareness training, either on your own or at the behest of employers or friends, where you repeatedly heard the trainer or so-called facilitator shout at attendees that what was getting in their way was their "beliefs"? Without being told what was happening, you were being taught a new belief system about the universe.

People do have the right to try to persuade others to think as they do. But participants should know ahead of time when a program teaches a new belief system, and they should be able to choose whether or not to participate. The majority of complaints about this kind of training have centered around the fact that employees weren't informed either about the intensity of the psychological attacks that would be made upon them as individuals or about any underlying belief system or philosophy being taught. And the biggest concern always remained that the training "had no real application to my job!"

The criticisms come from many parts of the country and from employees in a variety of work situations. The most frequent criticisms are that certain programs make concerted attacks on employees' moral and ethical values and spiritual beliefs. Claims have been made that these training programs seek not only to convert employees to accept specific spiritual philosophies but also to recruit employees to cults. Among the recruitment programs are those that lack any markedly visible spiritual content but that are used to get into business, educational, and industrial settings, at the company's or the government's expense, where large numbers of people can be contacted. Once their foot is in the door, cultic groups will attempt to get as many employees as possible who take the first course to join the cult. Cult leaders and trainers assess individual participants in their seminars as potential recruits, already partially converted.

Cultic programs that tend to be purely commercial ventures generally aim at selling more and more courses. Again, persons met through the program are regarded as potential buyers and as links to a whole company. Shortly after taking one course, individuals are contacted by agents of the training program to purchase additional courses and to get their companies to send more employees to the introductory seminar.

All these programs raise several general areas of concern:

- They are religious and philosophical in nature and thus don't belong in the workplace.
- They use thought-reform techniques and methods of psychological coercion and can cause psychological breakdowns.
- They produce social friction in the place of business.

I have mentioned that those for whom religion or a personal belief system is an issue are deeply offended by having what is essentially another religious belief foisted upon them under the guise of job betterment. Also a plethora of allegations has been raised, some in civil suits, pointing out that individuals have suffered mental breakdowns and psychological harm as a result of participating in certain training programs.

In addition, negative social consequences in the workplace have arisen from these programs. In certain workplaces, you find an in-group and a group of outsiders. The insiders are those who have attended the program and, through compliance and adherence, have taken on the jargon taught in the seminars. They act in unison with others who have bought into the content of the program and go with the flow.

Moreover, there are inherent inequalities in any job situation. The power and influence that owners, supervisors, and superiors hold by their very roles is greater than that of workers of lower rank. Roles bestow power, and power determines the direction of the flow of influence. Few will quibble with the view that those at the top of the hierarchy have the power to see that their directives are carried out. In other words, if your boss sends you to a seminar, you go.

Thus, the workplace has become an arena where several social and psychological phenomena are converging. The New Age movement, business's desire to compete in the world marketplace, and our nation's propensity to believe in self-improvement are intermingling in our corporations. This situation is further complicated by the intrusion of certain cults and thought-reform groups that take advantage of this milieu.

Violation of Civil Rights

As a result of the prevalence of programs that are not what they appear on the surface, a number of complaints have been filed with the Equal Employment Opportunity Commission (EEOC) by employees who describe how the course content violated their rights under the Civil Rights Act of 1964.

Such programs were addressed by the EEOC in its 1988 policy statement, issued to employers as a warning. The statement reads in part:

Employers are increasingly making use of training programs designed to improve employee motivation, cooperation, or productivity through the use of various so-called "new age" techniques. For example, a large utility company requires its employees to attend seminars based on the teachings of a mystic, George Gurdjieff. . . . Another corporation provides its employees with workshops in stress management using so-called "faith healers" who read the "auras" of employees and contact the body's "fields of energy" to improve the health of its employees. . . . The programs utilize a wide variety of techniques: meditation, guided visualization, self-hypnosis, therapeutic touch, biofeedback, yoga, walking on fire, and inducing altered states of consciousness. . . .

Although the courts and the Commission have not addressed the particular conflicts raised by the "new age" training programs, this issue can be resolved under the traditional Title VII [Civil Rights Act of 1964] theory of religious accommodation.

Thus, the EEOC clearly regarded these matters as religious accommodation issues between employers and employees, to be handled on a case-by-case basis.

Several training programs around the country use programs called ropes courses, in which participants (often employees sent by their companies) climb high onto a platform, up a tree, or onto a promontory. There, they are strapped into a safety harness and given a hand strap to hold as they zip down and across a chasm or open space. Persons with fears of high places reportedly suffer great anxiety but feel compelled to participate in front of the other employees and managers at the program.

One of the most spectacular rope lines is said to be at the Wilson Learning Corporation in New Mexico. Employees attending the course launch themselves off a cliff, hanging onto a pulley that races down a zip line stretching to the other side of the Pecos River. While the person is zipping to the bottom, other attendees jump up and down, yelling, "Hug, hug, hug," and welcome the person. Most of these programs encourage much hugging and "sharing" of personal histories during certain sessions.

Some of the other procedures used in certain of the large group awareness training (LGAT) programs and their offshoots contain processes to humiliate people (they resemble fraternity hazing events). The only rationale that I can conjure up for these is to imagine that someone thought that humiliating people would get them over their shyness, which is not true. Nor can I see a correlation to work or anything that might be remotely helpful to employees in exercises that have an obese woman don a bikini and go out on the street singing and trying to get a band of men to follow her, as one woman reported, or that have people cross-dress and act out caricatured opposite-sex roles, as others have reported.

In the nineties, we're even seeing a renewed interest in firewalking. One of my colleagues recently observed that "firewalking is sweeping the oil fields in Canada." Employees are sent to these programs (imported from the United States) and are told they will be able to traverse pits of hot coals without being burnt as long as they *think* properly. They are told that after firewalking, no job will look difficult.

Such programs seem designed more to get participants emotionally pumped up, suspending their judgment and following the orders of the "trainers," than to impart anything connected with job performance, communication skills, and profit margins. Many programs are described as simply providing "unforgettable experiences." And no one asks what you really learned and thought about the event or whether it had any useful application back at the office or factory. Yet the promoters claim these exercises produce "openness and confidence."

Having observed a number of LGATs and having interviewed many persons who attended variants of these programs as part of their work assignments, I am astonished at the gross childishness and unkindness of humiliating anyone under the guise of education, experiential learning, or the claim that participation in such travesties enhances work performance. Nor do all participants find sessions of "sharing" personal details helpful. Because of the popularity of training programs and seminars, countless employees are sent to courses thinking that they are going to learn management techniques or specific job-related skills. Instead, they find themselves in high-confrontation, psychologically intense programs that are supposedly going to transform them—not just train them but literally make them over into a new breed.

Many employees realize that certain managers and bosses either are desperate to improve production or are captivated by the promises made by the sellers of these programs. These managers and employers don't want to hear that the programs are less than welcome. Often, frank evaluations are produced only with the aid of an outside agency and a promise of anonymity to informants, as was done by the California Public Utility Commission when it investigated the Pacific Bell Krone program, which is described later in this chapter.

In some cases, there is no training program per se but simply outright pressure to join the background organization. For example, a $30,000 settlement with ILWHA American Corporation was reached in December 1989 after charges by a former employee of True Nature Health Food Store, a subsidiary of ILWHA, that he was pressured to join the Reverend Moon's Unification Church. The Illinois Department of Human Rights had found substantial evidence of a civil rights violation by True Nature, ILWHA, and the Unification Church. Several former employees of True Nature reported they were told that unless they agreed to join the Unification Church of America within two years of beginning employment at True Nature they would lose their jobs. They said that during their employment they were sent on religious retreats and to church-connected stores in other states.

Besides making complaints to the EEOC, many employees have filed civil suits objecting to training program content or related pressures at the workplace. Some lost their jobs by objecting. Other employees have suffered psychological decompensation as a consequence of what occurred in the training programs; still others have complied and gone along with the programs, even saying they enjoyed them.

What Goes On in an LGAT?

On federal court orders, I have attended six large group awareness training sessions (sponsored by est, the Forum, Lifespring, and PSI World) and have interviewed dozens of persons who have attended these and such other programs as Silva Mind Control, Actualizations, and Direct Centering, as well as the myriad of other programs now available, some started by former employees and even, on occasion, attendees of the larger well-known LGATs. I have studied the training manuals and videos used to train trainers and have interviewed a number of trainers.

I have also served as an expert witness for various persons who sued corporations selling this training. These persons, or their survivors, alleged in civil suits that they had been harmed by particular programs. Therefore, the lawyers in these cases asked the court to order the corporations to permit me and another expert to attend the relevant programs as observers, sitting in the back of the large hotel ballrooms or other facilities where the training takes place. Because most of these programs are made up of highly scripted, standardized procedures, seeing one unfold gives a good picture of the processes and the attitudes of the trainers, as well as some experience of the group process that occurs when 250 to 300 people are being psychologically and emotionally aroused into becoming, on occasion, sobbing masses on the floor.

The other expert and I needed to view and study the training the plaintiff had attended and form an opinion whether any connection existed between the conduct and content of the training and the alleged damages. These damages ranged from death by drowning and suicide to both brief and prolonged stays in mental hospitals. I have kept track of the individuals involved in the nearly sixty legal cases in which I was a consultant. Some of them have gotten their lives going again, although with the fearful recall of what it was like to completely lose mental and emotional control. A few are still hospitalized as long as ten years after their breakdowns during or immediately after the training.

LGAT programs tend to last at least four days and usually five. They are described as seminars and sound very much like special college courses. The highly confrontational and psychological aspects generally are not mentioned beforehand. Nor it is mentioned that a whole new theory of how the world works will be inculcated in attendees.

The program trainers and leaders typically get agreement from participants that they will not tell anyone about the processes that occur. To do so "will spoil it for your friends, family, co-workers when they take the course. Tell them what you got out of it," trainers advise. This means be vague about the actual content and provide glowing endorsements telling others that the training turned your life around, but do not tell them how emotional, dramatic, confrontational, and unnerving the sessions can be for some people. Because of this promise, consumers who buy and attend these seminars do so without information about how psychologically, socially, and sometimes physically stressing the event can be.

The following outline description is a composite of what goes on in the course of many LGAT sessions. Based on my attendance at several LGATs, consultations with former attendees and trainers, and my research, it also reflects my professional interpretations.

Day One

Day one is usually devoted to demonstrating the leader's absolute authority. The leader, often called a facilitator or trainer, immediately takes control of the setting with a demeanor that suggests he is a powerful, in-charge person and no one is to challenge what he says. "This program works," the trainer proclaims. "It's all up to you to obey and get the maximum benefits." He remains totally in charge, acts knowledgeable, and is practiced in verbal skills, so that he never loses an encounter. Anyone who challenges the trainer will be humiliated and verbally mashed.

New customers are unaware that most LGATs allow or even encourage those who have taken the training before to reattend. These people serve as a claque or modeling section. They clap, speak the same jargon as the leader, make endorsing statements, and are models for the new customers to pattern themselves after. Because the returners talk the talk and walk the walk, they get good responses from the trainer when they make comments. New customers begin to pattern their language and demeanor after the behavior of these others who, they notice, receive praise for using certain language or revealing personal material. The leader trains the group to clap after every sharing, no matter how inane, off target, or incoherent it is. For many, it is heady stuff to have a couple of hundred people clap when they speak a bit to the group. At the same time, new customers also see how the trainer berates and decimates opponents.

Day Two

Day two focuses on instilling the new philosophy the LGAT is teaching. The well-known LGATs claim that you have caused everything that ever happened to you, from choosing your parents to breaking your leg, from getting yourself jilted to having been molested by your stepfather as a child. Trainers use the terms *accountable* and *responsible*, but not with their ordinary meaning. Trainers mean that you will, if you "get it," start to make your choices patterned after the way the organization advocates. They create guilt and fear in you that you have caused all the bad things that have happened in your life. "Your life is not working!" the trainer or leader yells, while he implies his is. If you just "get it," you'll be able to "make your life work." What they teach about how to get your life to work is that there is a magical thinking that allows you to create whatever you want. You are told that you can create parking spaces, money to buy the next courses, and so on. Since creativity is in, you create just by thinking.

Day Three

Day three is usually devoted to exercises, often trance-inducing guided imagery, in which attendees are urged to recall all the disappointments of life since early childhood. Exercises about your mother and father, the promises you've broken, and the promises to you that others have broken—all the sad memories of your life up to now are brought forth. By the end of the third day, participants have been opened up psychologically.

Day Four

Day four is one in which much group sharing occurs, and the leader begins to change from the stern, domineering taskmaster into a seductive, charming, loving daddy or mommy who wants you to buy the next courses. Legal cases have revealed that trainers' promotions and even their very jobs hinge on how many of those in the first course they lure into purchasing the next courses.

Day Five

Day five is one of lightness; there is dancing after rest room and lunch breaks. Much effort is put into getting you to sign up for the next and more expensive course. All participants are told to come back for a posttraining meeting with the company staff, where again a great effort will be made to sell subsequent courses. At the end of the day, a surprise is staged, with friends and family unexpectedly appearing to congratulate "the graduate."

The Impact

What can be upsetting to certain people in such LGAT sessions is that, in these four or five intense, exhausting days, they become flooded with more emotion and conflict than they can handle all at once. Up until this time, they've handled their lives in their own way, but at these training sessions they've had to look at their entire past, in a brief but enforced way. This is quite different from psychotherapy, for instance, where the therapist and the patient progress more slowly in order to allow the patient to deal with whatever she or he wants or needs to at a manageable pace.

If they had known ahead of time the intensity and psychological depth of some of these exercises, many have told me, they never would have bought or gone to the training. They had no true idea of the intensity of the situation, the effects of group pressure, or the personal fatigue that comes from LGAT sessions, and they simply expected an ordinary educational experience. Even though printed statements are now given out to participants by several of the LGATs and training programs, it is my opinion that these statements don't meet the criterion of truly giving the consumer full information about the intensity that will be experienced and about the potential surfacing of extremely personal past material. In California, for example, where residents have seventy-two hours to decide not to make purchases elicited by high pressure, people have more protection from door-to-door magazine salespersons than they do from being taken in and pressured by cults and recruiters for LGATs.

I have included LGATs in this book because they represent forms of coordinated programs of intense persuasion and group pressure. I am not discussing here the many excellent skill-training, educational, and motivational programs that are used in business and industry for practical results. But apart from those programs, there are many training schemes that employ thought-reform processes that can harm employees and engender lawsuits for employers. They are a modern-day, corporate version of social and psychological influence techniques that make people deployable without their knowledge or consent—precisely my objection to cults.

Development of a New Age Training Program: A Case Example

One personal development program quite popular with educated professionals was Insight Seminars. Some defectors from the organization have charged that Insight was used to recruit members to the background organization, the Movement of Spiritual Inner Awareness (MSIA). The founder of Insight and head of MSIA is John-Roger Hinkins (although he rarely uses his last name), and his story is an interesting one.

Hinkins graduated with a degree in psychology from the University of Utah in 1958. Subsequent to a postoperative coma in 1963, he claims he awoke to say he felt there were two people within him: a "new" John and the "old" Roger. For a while, J-R, as he called himself, sold his spiritual insights for three-dollar love offerings. Then he studied Eckankar, a New Age spiritual system, and declared himself the "holder" of the Mystical Traveler Consciousness fighting the Red Monk (the devil). He is said to have considered himself in line with Jesus, Moses, Noah, and the like. Blending the old and the new, J-R created MSIA and gained quite a following. By the early 1970s, he was teaching seminars four nights a week.

Later in the same decade, some of his devotees convinced him to adapt Lifespring training to MSIA's needs. (Lifespring has been one of the more popular LGATs since the early to mid 1970s, along with est and Actualizations.) Working with a person who had been key in the development of Lifespring, J-R inaugurated his Insight training seminar with 120 MSIA ministers, who spread it first to MSIA's own church cells then to public seminars. J-R is reported to have called Insight both his "ministry" and his "money machine."

The seminars were a cross between a motivational course and an intense group encounter session. They eventually became an orgy of self-exploration, full-body hugs, and love letters to oneself. Guilt was purged, fantasy was indulged, and love was in the air. One exercise, the "Cocktail Party," has been described as a mass primal scream session in which people shout blunt, honest expressions at one another for about two hours nonstop, while assistants hand out vomit bags and exhort participants to keep going. The session evolves into a "rebirthing" process, with peaceful guided imagery and calming music. Then participants act out their most anxiety-producing fantasies in front of each other. This is followed by "cradling," meant to let participants know that their new "family" loves them unconditionally, despite their revelations of deep personal vulnerabilities. Lights dim and certain individuals are hoisted in the air and gently rocked to heavenly music, with everyone else beaming angelically into their eyes.

Afterward, participants have attested to feeling "awesome" and experiencing an emotional high that lasted for days. Some say they had to use special "grounding" procedures just to carry on with normal life after this "transcending" experience. At some point, a "Gift of Giving" session was added to the five-day Insight seminar. During this session, it has been reported, some people were so euphoric they made out checks for $10,000 to the group. Numerous Insight graduates were said to have been recruited to MSIA, although the link between Insight and MSIA was not generally known to seminar attendees.

In 1983, allegations of sexual abuse surfaced from two top aides. Some staffers said J-R used his spiritual authority to seduce them. According to reports, J-R discouraged marriage and ordered his personal staff to abstain from sex; but former devotees said that they were forced to engage in sex with J-R to maintain a "smooth relationship with the Traveler." Hinkins denied these allegations and no legal or law enforcement actions resulted. Because of these charges and other negative publicity, however, many devotees and Insight trainees became disillusioned and quit. Some described the period afterward as a "spiritual shattering," and in some cases, it took years for these former followers to patch up their psyches. Meanwhile, some staffers have remained loyal, continuing the Insight seminars.

A recent annual brochure from the Insight Consulting Group (ICG) claims that over fifty thousand people have participated with Insight, and boasts worldwide expansion, noting seminar locations in twelve U.S. cities and London, Sydney, Toronto, and Vancouver. The partial list of clients includes Abbott Labs, Beth Israel Hospital, Campbell Soup, Lockheed, McDonnell Douglas, NBC, Pillsbury, Rockwell, the Social Security Administration, UCLA Graduate School of Management, and the United States Navy, and "a host of small and medium-sized companies." As recently as 1990, J-R's book, *Life 101*, was on the *New York Times* best-seller list.

Problems with Being "Transformed" at Work

The following cases illustrate some of what has happened when employers sent employees to certain training programs. In part of these cases, the employees sought redress because they felt they had been coerced by their employers to attend and/or had been harmed by the programs.

Aside from complaining that they were being put through programs tantamount to a forced religious conversion, employees also objected to specific techniques being used: meditation, neuro-linguistic programming, biofeedback, self-hypnosis, bizarre relaxation techniques, mind control, body touching, yoga, trance inductions, visualization, and in some cases, intense confrontational sessions akin to the "attack" therapy methods that emerged in the 1960s and 1970s. Using intense psychological techniques, some of these programs "induce ordinary people to suspend their judgment, surrender themselves to their instructors, and even adopt new fundamental beliefs." Trainers using confrontational techniques create a sense of powerlessness in the seminar attendees. Once this sense is achieved, it becomes a lot easier to erase old patterns of thinking and behavior.

From a tire factory in Albany, Georgia, to a car dealership in Tacoma, Washington, workers began to put up resistance to the imposition of religious values and the intense influence techniques used in the workplace training programs.

Management Courses and Worker Responses

Sterling Management Systems, a consulting firm in Glendale, California, offers programs to dentists, chiropractors, optometrists, osteopaths, veterinarians, and other medical professionals to teach them how to expand their practices and increase their income. Sterling claims to be a secular organization, but one lawsuit filed by three dentists alleged that a $17,000 seminar turned out to be a weeklong "Scientology workshop" aimed at recruiting them into the church. One of the dentists alone said he spent $65,000 in less than six months on the Sterling course and further Scientology counseling.

A promotional brochure asserts that in a single quarter 109 Sterling Management clients "went Clear at Orange County Org" (group jargon that indicates they went through Scientology courses). And a review of a dozen brochures, mailings, and flyers put out by Sterling shows a clear link to Scientology founder L. Ron Hubbard, but none makes mention of the Church of Scientology. Sterling representatives assert that the training is nonreligious. A lawyer for Sterling has stated that they have secularized the teachings of the church.

In October 1993, the Nassau County (New York) Commission on Human Rights made a determination that promises to protect large numbers of employees against potential religious discrimination in the workplace arising out of such seminars. The commission found "probable cause" in the case of two employees of a physical therapy firm who were discharged by their employer for refusing to take training courses given by Sterling Management Systems. The attorney for the complainants regarded the commission's ruling as a "ground-breaking precedent . . . greatly advancing the protection of employees' rights throughout the country to resist religious indoctrination and solicitation of membership in another church."

Here are three additional examples of companies affected by this issue.

Applied Materials. In September 1992, Applied Materials, a California computer chip manufacturer, settled out of court for an estimated $600,000 with three former employees who alleged that they were driven out of the company after they complained about courses given on the job by Applied Scholastics, a management consulting group basing its work on Hubbard's writings. In 1989,

Applied Scholastics listed General Motors, Hewlett-Packard, and the United States Army as some of its clients.

Applied Materials admitted it had "lacked sensitivity with regard to the controversial nature of L. Ron Hubbard." A legal affairs writer commented that the case "is a typical one in a growing number of EEOC complaints and lawsuits throughout the nation over a host of management training programs linked to a host of religious sects."

Cocolat. In 1991, an investment firm owned by Joel Feshbach, an acknowledged Scientologist, purchased Cocolat, a West Coast candy company that was having some financial troubles. Then, in early 1993, thirteen management and administrative employees told local newspapers that they had quit their jobs at Cocolat because their employer was using management techniques based on the teachings of L. Ron Hubbard. The company reportedly fired an additional six managers after they had resisted the company's management philosophy. Feshbach denies ever having pushed Scientology onto Cocolat employees, but once again claims of religious harassment were filed with the EEOC by employees.

Former Cocolat employees said that references to Hubbard and his terminology had begun to pervade the company training and in-house communications. They said outside consultants brought in Hubbard's philosophy, complete with workbooks, saying they were going to make the employees' lives better. One former store manager said, "It was like Scientology came in disguised as a management course. All the red lights went off for me. I felt like I was being brainwashed or something." In April 1993, the popular chocolate maker announced a reorganization and the closing of its entire San Francisco Bay Area retail chain.

Stryker Systems. According to a 1990 lawsuit filed against this California software company, employees claim they were ordered to read and complete written exercises in the books *Introduction to Scientology Ethics* and *Personal Integrity*. The plaintiffs, who were allegedly fired for refusing to adopt the Scientology practice of "writing up their overts and withholds" (meaning confessing bad thoughts and actions), won an undisclosed settlement. The company acknowledged no wrongdoing.

The Forum and Transformational Technologies

Around 1971, Werner Erhard established est (Erhard Seminars Training), which in 1985 reemerged as the Forum. Although Erhard sold his interest in the Forum a number of years ago, the program is still being offered. A recent promotional brochure describes the Forum as "a lasting breakthrough," its method a "challenging, rigorous inquiry." It says that "the actual breakthrough of the Forum is generated by the participants themselves, as they individually come to grips with their own profound possibility of *being*."

Like other training programs, the Forum is sold worldwide. For example, the public sector in Great Britain was targeted by Landmark Education International offering the Forum course. After the director of education in Britain's largest municipality attended an introductory session, he warned his staff that Landmark was working through the city councilors, getting those who had taken the initial course to recruit more participants. In another region, at least one former employee filed a lawsuit against her employer, claiming that she suffered a nervous breakdown as a result of a four-day course.

Transformational Technologies, or TransTech, a 1984 offshoot of est and now of the Forum, describes itself in a brochure as "a network of independent professional management consulting firms . . . bringing about a breakthrough in the field of organization and management" and "creating a formal method of inquiry. . . . As our name suggests, we use and transfer a technology which produces a qualitative shift for clients."

This TransTech brochure is a high-end example of the personal transformation trend gone corporate. The talk here is of performance, productivity, and proactive behavior; and organizational culture, accountability, and teamwork are the subjects of this training program. The brochure tells us that breakdowns are necessary for breakthroughs: "Through a carefully designed process of questioning," participants can begin to look into what "is really possible at work. . . . In the process of this examination, people recognize all breakdowns as interpretations. As a result, people are empowered with respect to breakdowns and are able to consider new pathways of resolution."

"Rigorous action-inquiry," as the brochure calls it, is "a well-designed inquiry [that] reveals the deeper structure of thinking and perception that shape the way people act." But does it belong in the workplace?

With a network of affiliates in thirty-eight U.S. cities, as well as in Sweden, the West Indies, and Canada, Transformational Technologies says it wants to work with companies who want to "produce changes at a very basic level." According to the brochure, they have already worked with AT&T, Eli Lilly, Ford Motor, Gannett Publications, GE, General Foods, Home Box Office, Lutheran Church of America, McDonald's, Monsanto, Procter & Gamble, RCA, Scott Paper, Syntex, Touche Ross, TRW Systems, Westinghouse, and six departments of the U.S. government.

Erhard franchised Transformational Technologies shortly after its founding in 1984. Two years later, he licensed fifty-eight small consulting firms for a fee of $20,000 each and 8 percent of the gross; within another year the total was up to seventy affiliates. By 1987, these companies had sold these techniques to Allstate, Sears, General Dynamics, the Federal Aviation Administration, IBM, Boeing Aerospace, Lockheed, and dozens of Fortune 500 companies. Even NASA was reported to have paid $45,000 for a group of managers to go through three sessions led by Erhard himself.

Here is what has happened at two companies using these programs.

Ohio Children Services Agency. The Forum gained notoriety in Franklin County, Ohio, when staff members at the Ohio Children Services Agency complained about being encouraged to attend three-day sessions that some considered "cultlike." In this incident, the agency's executive director had previously participated in a Forum seminar, and since that time had sent twenty of her managers to similar sessions at a cost to Ohio taxpayers of $4,800. Although some who took the seminars called it a "profound experience," others complained of pressure to take the course and on-the-job discrimination against them if they didn't. Because of the feedback and the controversy, the agency stopped sending staff to the sessions.

DeKalb Farmers Market. Possibly one of the most celebrated cases related to workers' rights concluded with an out-of-court settlement reached between the DeKalb Farmers Market and eight former employees who were allegedly fired or forced to resign for refusing to participate in Forum sessions, in this instance allegedly led by a Miami-based consulting firm said to be affiliated with Transformational Technologies. The consulting firm denied involvement in the courses named in the suit; the DeKalb Market denied the allegations; and the Forum, not named in the suit, said it would never sanction coercing people to participate in its programs.

The plaintiffs said that the training program's espousal of the supremacy of man violated their belief in the primacy of God or other higher beings. The lawsuit contended that supervisors who declined to participate and to recruit their employees were harassed, humiliated, and interrogated. The lawyer handling the case for the employees said the case had "made employers come to grips with the legitimate boundaries of employee training."

Dong Shik Kim, one of the plaintiffs, worked at the DeKalb Farmers Market, a large produce market near Atlanta, Georgia. When his boss asked him to attend a special training seminar, Kim thought it would help him learn to increase sales and improve morale among fellow employees. Kim reported that the training sessions lasted as long as fifteen hours and became a nightmare. The outside consultants who ran the program "bullied employees into tearful confessions about intimate and heart-wrenching episodes in their lives." Kim said, "The sessions put people into a hibernating state. They ask for total loyalty. It's like brainwashing."

Faced with staying in the program or losing his job, Kim quit. He and seven others sued the DeKalb Farmers Market and the consulting firm, claiming they were forced out of their jobs for objecting to a "new age quasi-religious cult."

Jumping on the Bandwagon

Werner Erhard's thinking, as put forth in est, the Forum, and Transformational Technologies, was, in fact, the inspiration for many of the training programs that became popular in the eighties. In a sense, these programs were successful at injecting into the corporate world a fascination with New Age thinking that remains present to this day. Lifespring, Actualizations, MSIA/Insight, PSI World, and the many affiliates of Transformational Technologies, among others, all incorporate techniques modeled after those introduced by Erhard.

Krone Training at Pacific Bell

One of the most notorious New Age employee programs espousing "leadership development" was instituted at Pacific Bell after its divestiture from AT&T. Pacific Bell brought in a program directed by consultant Charles Krone that was based on the philosophy of G. I. Gurdjieff, causing Jacob Needleman, a San Francisco State University philosophy professor, to comment, "I'm a bit amazed to see [Gurdjieff] being used [in business] because it is one of the most uncompromising spiritual teachings I know of."

The program attempted to change employees' thought patterns by changing the words they use—for example, a "goal" was to be called an "end-state vision." Employee complaints, exposure in the local newspapers, and a study instituted by the California Public

Utilities Commission (PUC) put an end to the program. Outside evaluators who went in at the PUC's request reported that they found some positive features, but "unfortunately these benefits are heavily outweighed by strongly negative influences." The influences listed included fear, intimidation and mistrust, decreased productivity, wasted time, a split in the culture, introduction of obscure language and phrases, and a loss of morale.

Pacific Bell had spent $50.6 million on the program in two years, and would have spent an additional $135.6 million to send all 67,000 Pacific Bell employees through the program. The PUC disallowed recovery from ratepayers of half the expenditures actually made.

PSI World

Another out-of-court settlement was reached in a case that involved PSI World, a consulting group based in San Rafael, California. The plaintiff claimed that he was impaired after having his emotions manipulated in a five-day PSI World training program and that this caused him later to lose control of his car, crash, and get hurt. He said he was physically and mentally exhausted after what he described as emotional ten-hour sessions in which participants were asked to act out mostly negative situations. He also went without sleep on two nights in order to complete homework assignments. "There was no clock and no one was allowed to wear watches," he said. "We were going long periods of time without eating and without breaks."

While PSI World admitted no guilt, and its lawyer said there was no merit to the claims, PSI World was reported to have paid a six-figure settlement to have the case dismissed.

Lifespring

"Jane" took two Lifespring training programs in the late 1980s. Lifespring's philosophy maintains that people are to "take a stand" to be responsible for *whatever* happens to them. By the end of the

Level-I training, Jane had begun to accept this idea. During the Level-II program, Jane was required to reveal a brutal knife-point rape that happened three years earlier, when she was sixteen. Jane had never before discussed the rape except in a few counseling sessions immediately afterward. Neither her culture nor her family had treated the rape as a dishonor, since she had done nothing wrong. She felt her family had supported her right to continue to regard herself as a virgin. For three years, she functioned well, both psychologically and at school.

During the training, Jane was urged to release emotions associated with the rape. She forced herself to express anger and to describe the experience publicly. In a subsequent exercise, she was urged to express the emotion she felt toward her father who had died shortly after her birth. In response to this exercise, Jane began assaulting herself and chewing on a styrofoam bat used in the training. Nevertheless, she was allowed to continue the program.

Later, the trainer instructed Jane to role-play a $10,000-a-night prostitute. She believed the assignment had special meaning because of what she'd been led to reveal about the rape. She was further upset, perceiving herself as having been singled out for special humiliation. Although she had no history of psychiatric illness prior to the Lifespring training, afterward Jane underwent a period of growing depression that culminated in multiple suicide attempts. She was hospitalized for three years and remains on medication.

Jane sued Lifespring, and the case was settled for a large amount.

Psychological Casualties

As we have seen, coercive psychological influence may be operating in the workplace at the time an employee is assigned to attend certain training programs, and/or it may occur in the actual training program. Consequently, the psychological ramifications of some training programs have led to employees' filing legal suits. Some of these suits were described in the previous section, and three additional cases are described here.

Psychological Breakdown

"Gerald" a forty-year-old man, applied for a job as a store manager. The owner told Gerald he would hire him only if Gerald purchased and attended a specific large group awareness training. The owner, who had become a devotee of the group, abides by the group's policy of not revealing what the training is about. Thus he failed to describe to Gerald its philosophy, the extremely emotional and confrontational quality of the program, or how psychologically upsetting the procedures can be for some attendees.

Because taking the course was a prerequisite to employment, Gerald assumed it would be a skills-training, job-related program, and purchased it at a price he could ill afford. Once the five-day program began, he realized he was in an emotionally intense, high-confrontation, encounter-group situation. It appeared to him puzzlingly unrelated to managing a small store. The content was an amalgam of New Age philosophy, guided imagery, personal confessions, and confrontational attacks by the trainers. Gerald had never seen people break down emotionally to the extent that he saw in these sessions. His anxiety mounted by the hour, much of it growing out of the conflicts he was feeling between his religious beliefs and the New Age philosophy he was hearing in the training. Adding to this stress was his fear that he would not be hired unless he completed the program. He felt himself coming apart psychologically and asked to be excused, but the leaders of the program insisted he remain. By the fourth day, he was in a mental hospital experiencing a brief reactive psychosis. Gerald had no prior history of mental illness and nothing related to such illness in his family history.

Psychological Deterioration

"Joyce" was a top marketing executive in her firm. Her supervisor told her she would get ahead only if she attended the New Age training program that he urged her to take. She thought it was a skills-training, job-related program but instead came upon the same stresses experienced by Gerald. Joyce found the psychological and social coercion so intense that she has no remembrance of just when she deteriorated, but she was admitted to a psychiatric ward with almost continuous panic attacks. As time passed, she developed numerous and incapacitating phobias and became house-bound and unemployed or underemployed for more than three years. She had no prior history of mental disorder nor was there any in her family.

Intense Psychological Stress

A dozen female technical employees of the same minority ethnic background were sent to a seminar after being told that success there would determine who would be promoted in the corporation. The course was run by a Caucasian male who had been a security guard before becoming a seminar trainer. None of the women could link the seminar with on-the-job demands either during or after the training. However, each suffered greatly during the program because of the humiliation and degradation heaped upon each of them by the trainer.

The trainer ran the program in the manner of an attack therapy group. He had no appreciation of the women's ethnic values and, in fact, seemed particularly insensitive to their ethnicity. Additionally, he apparently had no awareness or concern about the impact of the intense psychological techniques he was using. He was described as a rude, confrontational, and menacing figure. He called the women to the front of the room and had them stand on a table while he criticized their bodies and their clothing and taunted them for their conformity and cultural ways.

The psychological coercion was intense, the humiliation great, and the fallout was that each of the attendees suffered marked psychological stress, most resigning from their jobs within a relatively short time after the seminar. One woman suffered an enduring major depression, requiring medication and psychotherapy, and took her case to legal hearings and subsequent settlement.

Buyer Beware: Thought-Reform Processes at Work

Because of my involvement in psychological and medical research over the past fifty years, I have worked in a variety of hospitals, clinics, and universities. For more than fifteen years, I have served on the Kaiser Permanente Medical Institutional Review Board, evaluating and reviewing informed-consent procedures for all research involving humans that is performed under the auspices of the Kaiser Permanente system. I sat on the National Academy of Sciences, Institute of Medicine Committee to survey the effects of mustard gas and lewisite after a government testing program was revealed in which sixty thousand World War II military personnel were exposed to those gases without their consent. Data from this testing had not been made public until 1991. So I have been sensitized to fighting for and sustaining the laws that protect human rights in biomedical and behavioral research.

The combination of these review responsibilities and my professional work with cult survivors has given me an avid appreciation for the need to protect and uphold the practice of informed consent. I am dedicated to individuals' having informed consent over their lives, their choices, and their beliefs, and I believe that employees have the right to know what they are being made to attend. This perhaps has made me particularly aware of how deceptive many training programs are.

Thus I call attention here, as I did earlier in describing cult recruitment, to the uninformed state in which many employees and individuals are sent or go on their own to various training programs and work-related or self-improvement seminars. They learn what the program is about only after it becomes difficult to leave it. The primary barrier to leaving, of course, is that they might lose their jobs by offending the boss who sent them to the program and perhaps seems enamored of it. Yet in the examples just given, we can sense the devastation that can be wrought when employees are made to attend training programs that are not the excellent ones that exist for skills training and job-related behavior but instead are meant to "transform" (and in some cases recruit) employees for less than noble purposes.

Religious issues aside, the pronounced psychological nature of many of the exercises within many of these programs is of concern. We cannot deny the fact that they grew out of the highly confrontational group therapy techniques introduced by the encounter, sensitivity, and large group awareness training movements. And in many ways, these psychological techniques are little different from the influence processes used in today's cults to achieve attitudinal change. This is apparent in the psychological and behavioral effects produced, and in the appearance of a certain number of psychological casualties during and after participation in some of these training programs.

A further result is that the majority of participants experience varying degrees of alienation and instability because they are urged to give up old norms, goals, and ideals. They also suffer a type of culture shock as they try to reconcile pretraining values with what they learn in the training and with the realities of their posttraining existence. Importantly, a certain number of participants will be seriously harmed as these stresses precipitate a handful of psychological conditions, such as brief psychotic episodes, posttraumatic stress disorder syndrome, a variety of dissociative disorders, relaxation-induced anxiety, and other miscellaneous reactions including phobias, cognitive difficulties, and stress-related illnesses.

In light of such consequences, the fact that most of these programs do not provide the skills training they advertise is the least of their problems. Unfortunately, the decision to buy a training scheme is often made on an emotional rather than a rational basis by an executive who is still high on his own introductory experience of the training.

While some people decry the number of legal suits filed yearly in the United States, it appears that it has been the recent legal cases filed by employees and EEOC rulings that have given employees the hope that they have some leverage over the types of training programs they can be sent to. The hue and cry has *not* been over employees' finding themselves at authentic skills-training programs, but over their finding themselves at programs that impinged on their religious or personal beliefs and that did *not* train them for their jobs but that attacked and decimated their personalities and very selves.

In short, lack of informed consent, use of hidden agendas, and use of various forms of coercion characterize the criticisms of both cults and certain modern-day training programs among those who have experienced them. Buyer, beware.

9

The Threat of Intimidation

Many cults are small, remain small, and have as their goal the fulfillment of the idiosyncratic whims and desires of their leaders. Such groups usually do not aspire to rule the world. Many other cults, however, are large and growing, have international branches, and use deceptive ways to increase their size, wealth, and power through financial, social, and political avenues. In their quest for power, they employ a variety of tactics, which I will explore in this chapter.

One tactic is to recruit and exploit the professional sector, co-opting those who by their training can serve the cult's goals. Another is to scare off critics—be they researchers, journalists, or private citizens—with threats, intimidation, lawsuits, and other acts of harassment. And yet another is to spread themselves world-wide and attempt to hold themselves above the law. By gaining footholds in government, the media, and the educational system, cults seek credibility and power and feign acceptance into the mainstream.

Co-opted Professionals

When we confide our ills and secrets to a doctor, dentist, psychologist, psychiatrist, attorney, or nurse, we presume confidentiality. We assume that their prime obligation is to us, not some third party. Tradition and the law lead us to expect that these helping professionals will keep our welfare and not someone else's foremost in their transactions with us.

Cults and thought-reform groups tend to seek out the allegiance of many professionals within various fields. To varying degrees these co-opted professionals become information pipelines to the leaders, and they are used to manipulate and exploit members at the leaders' behest. Their prime allegiance is to the cult leader, not their patients. It's shocking to think that your doctor or psychiatrist is blabbing your secrets to a cult leader or sharing them with a facilitator, trainer, or guru of some group that uses thought-reform processes.

The use of professionals as pipelines to convey information is generally kept hidden from cult members. Instead, some leaders claim to have superhuman knowledge or special talents and powers for knowing this information; others state that they read minds, know everything, or have infinite wisdom. Eventually, a member may catch on to how personal secrets become known. Even then, the member's discovery is handled by condemning him or her for having such thoughts and complaints. The member is put down and punished for "doubting." As we've seen in earlier chapters, the system is never wrong, only the member.

Health Professionals

Numerous ex-members have reported that psychologists, psychiatrists, nurses, and physicians who were cult members often acted in key dual roles: as information gatherers and as the ones who tried to talk people out of complaining or leaving. Not only have I heard such reports from former rank-and-file members but I have also interviewed nearly two dozen professionals who have told me of their purposeful activities on behalf of their cult leaders. Here are some prime examples.

"Jed" was a licensed mental health professional with a doctoral degree; he was also in a Bible-based cultic group. Other members were encouraged to meet with him for therapy regarding child-rearing problems, marital concerns, and work issues. The cult leader instructed Jed that he had three missions: to report the contents of all his sessions to the leader, to "smooth people out" and convince them to obey the dictates of the leader, and to prevent members from leaving the group.

After he left the group, Jed was guilt stricken that he had been so malleable as to have deserted his personal and professional ethics and on occasion actually to have violated the law. He said it was as though he had dimmed out his conscience from his earlier religious, parental, and educational training and blindly obeyed the leader by providing information and using his authority and training in psychological techniques of persuasion to keep people in the group.

"Eric" entered a cult with his parents when he was fourteen and left at nineteen. The group had started as a country-living vegetarian life-style commune peopled with college-educated, upper-middle-class members, many living on income from trust funds. Over time, it evolved into a cult, with the leader in total control and members thinking he had the secrets of the universe. The leader was "sharing his knowledge" about all kinds of esoteric philosophies, diets, and mind-expansion methods, and claimed to have "the 3 O's"—omnipresence, omniscience, and omnipotence. Eric was in awe, believing the leader could read his mind, as he always seemed to know how Eric was feeling and what his plans and doubts were.

Eric left the group soon after realizing that the in-house psychologist was telling the leader everything members reported to her in their "counseling sessions," which followers were urged to attend. People confided in her, naturally assuming that their conversations were private. Instead, the woman provided written reports to the leader about each conversation. By accident, Eric saw some of the reports while cleaning the leader's office. He said it was as if a light went on around him; suddenly he "saw" how the leader created the aura of reading minds and knowing everything.

Another licensed mental health professional was a member of a group that has about 250 live-in and 1,100 live-out members. The professional worked in town at a clinic during the week and went to the cult's farm on weekends and vacations. Investigation revealed that, at the behest of the cult leader, he recruited from among his patients. He referred patients with trust funds and independent means, telling them they should enter the group for rehabilitation.

The group is best described as a life-style cult that regards the leader as the Great Teacher, obeying him unswervingly. The leader changes the members' names to more "classic and cultured" names: Frances becomes Francine, Ben becomes Broderick, Tom becomes Theodore. Members who enjoy the better life-style in the group either have family money or savings from past employment. Those without such funds are the cooks and cleaners. The leader claims he will teach members how to control their thoughts and social behavior, promising them near-perfect self-improvement. One of the leader's most powerful control mechanisms is to allow followers to speak only at certain times and in a stilted pedantic jargon. Rebellious ones are put on word diets, not allowed to speak for days on end.

"Doug," a young man who had been referred by the mental health professional to the group, was visiting his mother when I happened to be there interviewing her as a witness in a legal case. She herself had been in an abusive confrontational life-style cult for some time. After we finished the interview, she told me her son had been sent home by the cult and that cult leaders had phoned before bringing him home to inform her that he was on a word diet as well as a food diet. She was concerned about Doug's visible weight loss and his muteness; since coming home he had barely been able to get out of bed.

Doug appeared cadaverous when I saw him. Speaking as a layperson, I told the mother that her son looked in dire need of quick medical evaluation. During the interview, I had realized how subdued and submissive she was because of her years in a cult; now she felt helpless to do anything about Doug. Luckily, she was relieved to be told what she really wanted to do—act on behalf of her obviously sick son. She phoned me a few hours later to let me know that Doug had been hospitalized immediately when seen by a physician. Without revealing the mother's or son's names, I checked with the mental health facility where Doug had seen the therapist who had recruited him to the cult. The director of the clinic said they were aware of this particular staff person's practice but felt there was nothing they could do, since the patients he was referring to the cult were all over twenty-one.

Some ex-members of a health-fad psychological life-style group reported that, while they were in the group, a medical professional who had considerable power as a helper of the leaders and who followed the leaders' orders would not allow members to seek outside medical help. Instead, the medical professional instructed members to take the cult leaders' directives as medical advice, including advice to do such things as lie in ice packs outdoors in winter in Washington state.

Members said they were instructed to drink their urine, take repeated coffee enemas, and give each other anal exams. The members believed that a hepatitis outbreak was related to the latter practice. A man who had been a long-term hospital worker was reportedly derided and not allowed to be of help because the male leader appeared to regard the man's training as a challenge to the leader's power. Capitalizing on members' trust of medical personnel, the nonmedical leader of the group allegedly had ordered four pregnant women to have cesarian sections. Former members reported that he commanded the four women to appear nude before him, and then examined them, including pushing his fist strongly into one woman's left pelvic region until she screamed out in pain. The leader was then said to have diagnosed her need for a cesarian delivery due to her unwillingness to bear pain.

Two physicians performed vasectomies on a number of men sixteen and over. They were members of Synanon, a group that began as a drug rehabilitation group, incorporated as a religion, and became a cult. When I interviewed the two physicians later, they had considerable remorse and misgivings about putting the desires of their leader above their Hippocratic oath and ethical obligations to serve their patients.

Although some men in the group volunteered for the operation, many were set against the vasectomies. Several men who protested reported that other men had grappled them into submission, saying it was for the good of the group. At one point, it was reported that "within a week nearly two hundred men had undergone vasectomies performed in Synanon by Synanon's own cadre of doctors working ten hours a day, seven days a week." At the same time, women who became pregnant in Synanon were pressured to have abortions or leave. The abortions were performed by in-house doctors. All this was done because the leader had decided that it was too expensive to allow members to procreate. He accomplished his goal by exploiting the physicians in the group, and members acquiesced or left.

"Sarah," an experienced paramedic, got involved with a small cult in California, in which the cult leader conducted many "marathon experiences," usually beginning on a Friday evening and continuing into Sunday. During these experiences, the leader and his followers of all ages indulged in a smorgasbord of alcohol, marijuana, cocaine, and amphetamines, with little sleep. The leader had a circle of so-called wives, and when he retired with the wives to his private quarters in the course of these sessions, he often became physically violent during sexual games.

Sarah was not in the circle of wives but was called upon after these events to fix the bruised and otherwise hurt women. Even though some needed more serious medical treatment, they were retained in the cult compound. After leaving the group, Sarah became depressed and deeply self-blaming over not having had the courage or ethical fortitude to leave sooner or to help the other women to leave the abusive situation. She would say over and over, "I kept fixing them so they could stay."

Jim Jones had medical professionals in Jonestown: a young physician, Larry Schacht, and several nurses. Massive amounts of medicines were procured from San Francisco to use in the cult's "extended care unit," where rule breakers or those who wanted to leave were confined and sedated. Schacht and Peoples Temple nurses used drugs to punish, intimidate, and control Jones's followers. It was Dr. Schacht and the Jonestown nurses who stood at the tables preparing the potassium cyanide–laced Fla-Vor-Aid drinks and filling the syringes used to kill the followers. The doctor and nurses also lost their lives in this massacre. After the deaths there, an investigator found over eleven thousand doses of Thorazine, a powerful major tranquilizer, and massive amounts of Quaalude, Demerol, Valium, and morphine. Jones's medical personnel seem to rank second only to the Nazi doctors in the World War II death camps in abandoning their ethical obligations to preserve life and aid their patients.

Numerous similar unsettling tales of professionals functioning as pipelines to cult leaders and as henchmen carrying out bizarre and sometimes life-threatening orders have and continue to come to light as members leave cultic groups. Many cults and thought-reform groups have set out specifically to recruit doctors, nurses, psychiatrists, psychologists, and lawyers, for both their skills and their prestige value. Cults believe that visitors and outsiders will be impressed that people with such credentials belong to the group. Additionally, these professionals can be induced to recruit for the group from among their contacts.

Most of the large group awareness training programs (LGATs) have psychiatrists and psychologists involved with them. These professionals are available when the programs are given, so that they can cool down anyone who decompensates, or comes apart emotionally, during the training. They can also try to convince participants and their families not to sue the group for any damages incurred during the intense and psychologically upsetting seminars. These same programs also specifically recruit professionals to take their courses, in order to add prestige to their seminars' image and to use these professionals to obtain new members from among their patients and colleagues.

Sometimes, medical professionals may find themselves unwitting accomplices to an LGAT recruitment when they are asked to sign a release form for a patient to take a particular seminar. Even if a medical professional has personally been to an LGAT and fared well, this doesn't mean he or she should sign a release for someone else. If you are a medical professional asked to sign such a release, my suggestion is that you consult your hospital or clinic legal department, as you may risk having yourself or your medical facility named as a codefendant in a legal case should the patient be harmed by attending the LGAT. Remember, what transpires in a person's head can be very powerful, and you may not know your medical patient well enough or know enough about the way the seminar leader will treat your patient to predict the outcome.

All these examples illustrate that professionals can be led to violate not simply their personal values but especially their professional ethics as they carry out the bidding of their leaders, act as informants, prevent defections, break doctor-patient confidentiality, and compromise the health and welfare of those who have sought professional help. The bottom line is that the role of such professionals is to support the leader in all ways. Not unlike the Nazi doctors of whom Robert Jay Lifton has written, these professionals have sold their very souls.

Academics

Some people committed to cultic groups become downright illogical in their support. For example, there is a small claque of social scientists who have become procult apologists. Some have been given trips to exotic places by large, wealthy cults; some fear revealing critical findings because certain cults have paid for research and underwritten trips to professional meetings.

For example, Eileen Barker, a London sociologist, wrote a book called *The Making of a Moonie*, in which she presented an idiosyncratic version of thought reform or brainwashing, apparently attempting to get readers to discredit the idea that thought reform could occur and to absolve the Moon organization of criticisms alleging deceptions in recruitment. This apologist stance left Barker hard pressed to handle the issues she was left with.

Initially, Barker alleges that Moonie (as she calls them) recruits join *freely*, but this leaves unaddressed the fact, which she also reports, that recruits are deceived by members not revealing that they are Moonies. Barker claims that this deception has no bearing on recruits' decisions to join. Most people, however, believe that true free choice has to be based on full information. Later, Barker remarks on "another form of deception . . . a failure to disclose the true nature of the movement to potential members," saying that "some information is for members only. . . . Moonies are unlikely to present their guests with statements such as, 'Moon . . . lives in the lap of luxury, and has control over an enormous amount of money,' or 'The movement has been the subject of close scrutiny by several government agencies.'. . . [The recruit] is unlikely to understand the amount of time that he will be expected to spend on fund-raising," and so on. Barker rationalizes this deception by saying that most religions work in this way, and she concludes that "it is probably true to say that the factual information Moonies give their guests is usually a fairly accurate account of what the overwhelming majority of members do *themselves* believe to be the truth."

In 1989, the Religious News Service carried a story that Dr. Barker's book was funded by the Unification Church, saying that Barker "freely admits that the Unification Church paid all her expenses to attend 18 conferences in Europe, New York, the Caribbean, Korea, and South America. 'My university and the SSRC (a U.K. government grants council) regarded this attendance necessary for my research,' she said. 'They thought if the Moonies paid the bills it would be a big savings for the taxpayer.'" Not everyone felt that way. One member of Parliament said, "Any academic who allows themselves to be manipulated to lend credence to a cult does harm to families all over the world."

According to a press release from a member of the House of Commons, Barker's organization, INFORM, lost its U.K. government funding in 1993 after much criticism from churches, parents, and former cult members, and Barker resigned as the organization's director and chairperson.

On the one hand, a number of academics are unwilling to inspect the deceptive recruiting practices and membership policies of many cultic groups. On the other hand, they try to discredit researchers who do. They also shelter the cults by trying to discredit the reports of ex-members who try to tell the world what it was like to be in a cult. The apologists disparage these former members, calling them bitter apostates, disgruntled, defectors, disloyal, and turncoats.

For example, sociologists David Bromley and Anson Shupe published the book *Strange Gods: The Great American Cult Scare*, in which they blamed former cult members and their families for generating "hysteria" about cults, implying that these citizens were more dangerous than the cults themselves. Treating former cult members with utmost disdain, Bromley and Shupe throw demeaning labels at ex-members' first-person accounts, calling them "tales of atrocity that include lurid themes of exploitation, manipulation, and deception." They write that former members are merely publicity seekers wishing to stand in the limelight and profiteers looking to make money by writing books about their cult experiences. "In sum," write Bromley and Shupe, "apostates and the horrific stories they tell are necessary, to provide fuel to attack unpopular movements, but, more important, to absolve families (and themselves) of any responsibility for their actions."

Cult apologists blame the victims and protect the villains. Like the mad kings of old, they shoot the messenger bearing bad news.

One of the most illogical positions taken by the apologists is their claim that only current cult members tell the truth. However, the findings of many researchers, as well as my own numerous interviews with former members, show that cult members are so dependent on the group while they are in it that they dare not tell the truth, dare not complain.

Co-opted academics not only defend the cults but may also serve as recruiters. Like their medical counterparts, some cult members and sympathizers who teach in high schools and universities have been known to funnel potential recruits to cults. Students are sent by professors on field studies to cult groups or referred as interns in cult businesses. Being referred in this way tends to make students all the more vulnerable to cult recruitment as they believe that the group has the teacher's approval. In some cases, professors start their own cults, as the teachers in the following example did.

Two male teachers in an art department of a small college started a cultic group of twenty students. The professors, who touted themselves as the most advanced teachers of the generation, who trained only "the best of the best," said they would sponsor only the careers of students who were dedicated to them, but they promised these dedicated students fabulous training and superb jobs in the future. Student dedication was shown by taking classes from the teachers, paying room and board to live in a suburban home owned by one of them, avoiding contact with friends and family, and living a cloistered life with the group. For some students, it also meant having sex with the teachers.

This group lasted five years, until the death of the older teacher and the discharge of the second man from the college. The group broke up when the students exchanged information about their private relationships with the teachers and came to see that the men were not the world-class teachers they claimed. The students then realized that, instead of completing their college requirements, they had spent their college years providing a sense of glory and a following for their teachers' grandiose notions.

Intimidation and Harassment of Critics

From university professors and students to journalists, reporters, and writers, those who study cults have consistently come upon one particularly disturbing aspect of the cult world. It has become apparent over time that, when researchers are critical of certain cult activities or features, some of the groups attempt to suppress such findings and opinions and silence their critics through both subtle and overt intimidation in a variety of forms.

Intimidating Scholars

Recently a professor who has published several books and articles and who lectures widely was working on a book about cults. He wishes to remain anonymous here because he's "had enough trouble already." But he related to me having been mystified to learn that one of the cults had obtained a copy of his manuscript while it was still in its early stages. He was alerted to this when a letter arrived at his home, not at the university, saying the sender had a copy of the manuscript, as well as the professor's other publications, and a list of his upcoming lectures.

In essence, the letter said to the professor: My group and I know that you have a forthcoming book. You are not to use the following references, ideas, and persons that are in your current manuscript, which my group and I oppose. The writer of the letter offered himself as the expert to guide the book. He concluded by advising the professor to call him at the soonest possible time, within the week. And he ended with, "Yes! We do go into court and sue." The writer cited some cases and continued: "This is a war against evil and you may have allied yourself with Evil." As a result of this harassment, the professor went very lightly on the group in question, then steered away from any further studies of that group, concentrating instead on others.

In another instance, at a national meeting of the American Psychiatric Association (APA), six APA members who had been studying the cult phenomenon and treating patients who had left cults each received a registered package of material from two of the larger cults. An identical letter accompanying each package warned each speaker that if he or she did not base his or her presentation on the material in the package, the groups would take "appropriate action" against him or her. Each speaker read portions of the letter to the audience of hundreds at the meeting. The recipients condemned the efforts to abridge freedom of inquiry that such ploys represented. In this case, the cults' effort backfired.

One group sent two aggressive individuals into the research office of the chairman of the department of psychiatry at a large university medical school. They said they wanted access to all research and reference files of the department in order to inspect everything and make sure that there were no negative statements about their group in any of the institution's files. The university lawyers and campus police had to be called to end this foray.

A recent egregious occurrence was the blocking of publication of a well-conducted scientific study because a cult threatened legal action against the publisher if the study were printed. Respected Canadian sociologist Dr. Stephen A. Kent has studied cults and published his findings for some years. He submitted an article that was a psychohistorical study of a particular cult leader who has been around since the sixties. Prior to carrying out the research, Dr. Kent's proposal had been reviewed carefully and thoroughly to see that it met the strict ethical and scientific standards of the Edmonton's Ethics Review Committee at the University of Alberta, which it did. The article went through detailed editorial and peer review and was accepted for publication in a respected academic journal. Dr. Kent received final page proofs for the article, and advance advertising indicated that his article would be included in the forthcoming volume.

The article never appeared, however. Individuals who claimed to represent the cult and others wrote letters to the journal editors asserting that Dr. Kent's research methodology for the article was not ethical. The writers made other unsubstantiated allegations about Dr. Kent's conduct, and viciously attacked his character. They requested that the article be withdrawn and threatened legal redress if the article were to be published. As a result, Dr. Kent was advised that his article was to be removed, and the journal was published without it.

Afterward, a university official pointed out in a letter to the publisher that the issue of academic freedom, highlighted by this incident, was central not only to the university but to the entire international academic community. Agreeing wholeheartedly, I would add that not only should the academic community be concerned but so should all citizens.

In a number of instances, it has been only because some publishers and authors were financially able to withstand efforts by certain cults to prevent the publication of studies of the cults that the books in question ever saw the light of day. Many of the large international cults have nearly unlimited financial resources and the power to intimidate publishers, newspapers, television producers, academic researchers, professionals, and any of the public who may speak up about cults.

If cults and their sympathizers block publication of scientific studies about their groups, the histories of their leaders, and fair comment from scholars, the cults become the arbiters of what the world hears about them. Without a free press, scientific publications, fair comment, and the ability to express opinions, all of us are at the mercy of cult leaders who would determine what we read, what we say, and what we think. Orwell's 1984 could become a reality.

Harassing Journalists, Reporters, and Writers

There are many examples, too long to tally, of magazines and newspapers receiving letters threatening legal action for even mentioning the names of some cultic groups.

• Journalists Marshall Kilduff and Ron Javers wrote about the ordeal of a *San Francisco Chronicle* reporter who was due to visit the Peoples Temple to interview Jim Jones while he was still in California. Knowing the reporter was a plant fancier, Jones ordered houseplants brought in. A small coterie of members was instructed "to compliment [the reporter] on her earlier stories and to stay close to her at all times. After the interview, Jones took to calling [her] at home late at night for long, wandering discussions. He would let suggestions drop about how she could give him better and fairer coverage." His staff sent her thirty letters asking for fair treatment. "When the final story ran, another innocuous and complimentary account, the reporter was showered with three hundred letters." She reportedly rewrote the story six times, progressively deleting hints of criticism.

• A metropolitan newspaper's desk editor was harassed after he ran a piece critical of a local cult. He and his family had to move out of their home after receiving seventy-two hours of continuous phone calls from cult members.

• The *National Enquirer* was threatened with a $20 million lawsuit by the Peoples Temple when it published aerial photographs of the inadequate housing for the twelve hundred followers living in a supposed paradise.

• Andrew Skolnick received the 1992 Responsibility in Journalism Award from the Committee for the Scientific Investigation of the Paranormal for his investigative reporting in the *Journal of the American Medical Association* (JAMA) about the Maharishi Ayur-Veda products. The *Columbia Journalism Review* awarded JAMA one of its coveted Laurels, for having the integrity and fortitude to publish Skolnick's article. The National Council on Health Fraud said the article was "a classic in the literature of consumer health education, and is *must* reading." Yet, Skolnick and the editor of JAMA were sued for $194 million, plus legal expenses, by two groups affiliated with the Transcendental Meditation movement. The case was dismissed without prejudice in March 1993, and thus can be refiled in the future by the plaintiffs.

• More recently, a large New York publisher, St. Martin's Press, was greeted with "blasts of hostility and threats of a libel suit" when it announced plans to publish a new critical account of the rise and fall of est founder and New Age guru Werner Erhard. Similarly, in 1992, Erhard's attorney filed a libel suit against CBS News after "60 Minutes" aired a program critical of him. The lawsuit was withdrawn three months later.

• Not long ago a large international cult attempted to force Switzerland to ban distribution of a *Reader's Digest* issue that contained a reprint of a popular news magazine's article about the group. A Swiss judge lifted the ban and newsstand copies were distributed. In May 1992, a judge denied the group's appeal and ordered it to pay court costs and the *Digest's* legal fees. The group also filed suits that are still pending against *Reader's Digest* in four other countries.

• Freelance writer Paulette Cooper went through what she describes as "a nightmare," after nineteen lawsuits were filed against her for the book *The Scandal of Scientology*, which she wrote and published in 1971. Cooper and her publisher were sued separately but simultaneously in several U.S. cities, England, Canada, and Australia. As two authors wrote:

> According to documents later recovered from Scientology files at the New York headquarters, "Operation Freak-Out" was designed to "get P.C. [Paulette Cooper] incarcerated in a mental institution or jail or at least hit her so hard that she drops her attacks." Among other plans for this campaign were bomb-threat calls to an Arab consulate in New York City by a member of Scientology who had a voice like Cooper's and written bomb threats written on personal stationery stolen from her with her fingerprints on it.

As a result, Cooper was indicted by a federal grand jury. Those charges were finally dropped in 1975 when Cooper volunteered to take sodium pentothal tests to establish her innocence. By that time, Cooper weighed only eighty-three pounds. All the lawsuits were finally settled in 1984.

• Most recently, an associate of one of the political cults sent a letter containing a veiled threat to all twenty-one contributors to *Recovery from Cults*, a book brought out by W.W. Norton, one of America's most respected publishers of professional books. The letter was also sent to the senior editor at the publishing house and to the professionals quoted on the book's jacket endorsing the book. The list of names attached to this letter revealed a joint effort by cults and their sympathizers from both ends of the political spectrum to silence and harass their critics.

Manipulating the Public Image of the Cult

Cults have found many ways to restrict and control public information about them. Some groups have brochures, handouts for the press, and written overviews and endorsements of the group, often prepared by sophisticated public relations firms. In essence, these materials imply that "you need go no further. Here is who we are. Here is all you need to know to understand us perfectly. Take this material and use it. Everything is fine." The implication is that the material is objectively represented and relatively comprehensive.

An illuminating example of cults' efforts to control how they are viewed by outsiders is revealed in the blatant discrepancies between a film made under the auspices of the Rajneesh group and the observations of that same group by a prominent behavioral scientist. A young San Francisco filmmaker related that, one year, "a strange sum of money appeared in his bank account." A few days later, he received a letter requesting him to use the money to go to India and make a film about the group, which he did. The film, which I have seen in the company of ex-members of the group, depicts a series of pastoral scenes and people singing and dancing, the guru walking among them, people sitting in the courtyard of a palace, and so on, and the film won some acclaim at an art film festival.

According to former members, who later testified in legal proceedings concerning some allegations against the group, this film does not reflect the realities of the group as they experienced them. The former members' views were supported by Richard Price, then head of the Esalen Institute, who went to India to see what the group was about. On the occasion of his visit, *Time* magazine carried an article on the group prepared by the magazine's New Delhi bureau chief. The article cited Price's presence in India, labeled him the group's "best-connected disciple yet," and implied that Price endorsed the group.

Shortly after the article appeared, Price wrote to both the editors of *Time* and Rajneesh, saying that he considered the encounter groups taking place at the ashram to be authoritarian, intimidating, and violent. He observed and had learned from former members that violence was being used to enforce conformity to an emerging new order rather than to facilitate growth. Price described witnessing broken bones, bruises, and abrasions. He remarked that Rajneesh's professed compassion was not reflected in his groups.

If slick handouts and packaged films don't keep inquiring folks away, the group may have to provide conducted tours. The master among tour guides was Jim Jones. Kilduff and Javers reported that "Al Mills, formerly the official church photographer, said Jones would try to set a trap for obliging politicos when it came time for the perfunctory handshake snapshot. 'If it was someone Jones wanted to compromise, he would have a group of members standing behind the podium and on cue they would raise clenched fists and I would take a picture,' Mills said. 'They would look like revolutionaries. He just wanted these pictures on file if some politician ever turned against him.'"

The tours were entirely staged, with church members rehearsed in their roles, outfitted in borrowed clothes to look the part, and coached ahead of time on what to say. Then the visiting big shots were introduced to supposedly recovered heroin addicts, recovered cripples, and tough little street kids happy to be fed a decent meal at Jones's bountiful table. If a visit went off successfully and the outsider went away impressed, Jones would switch to a new role. He would stand before the congregation and mock the visitor, imitating his or her voice, repeating questions asked and laughing at how the women visitors had brushed against him suggestively.

Restricting and Controlling Research

Another way to control views of a cult is to control the research about it. Researchers in the behavioral sciences rely on informants or interviewees for much of their basic data. However, what cult members talk about to outsiders may be controlled and restricted. Generally, only certain members are designated as spokespersons for the group. Others are commanded not to talk, not even to nonmembers among their own families and friends. Members are taught that nonmembers are either too "uninformed" or "uninstructed" to understand what the group is about, and members are trained to pass inquiries upward within the system.

When asked by a parent or friend about a certain aspect of life in the group, more than one cult member has replied, "I can't answer that—that's 'need to know.'" Members are not only trained how to respond but are often expected to report fully—either verbally or in writing—on interactions with outsiders and are often chastised if they do not perform as instructed. This explains why many cult members' answers are strikingly similar, devoid of normal emotion, usually monosyllabic, and quite often not truly responsive to the questions asked. It is no wonder that cult members are often considered programmed. Hundreds of former cult members have described role-playing sessions in the cults during which members rehearse how to answer questions from outsiders.

An extreme example of this was experienced with a small lifestyle cult in California that claims its members have melted and intermingled. When one distressed family visited the headquarters and asked to see their daughter—a small, dark female in her twenties—they were greeted at the door by a large blond middle-aged male saying, "I'm your daughter now. We are interchangeable, intermingled, and melted together." The family tried for several months to see their daughter alone but never succeeded. The group banded together like a large flock of birds, chirping occasionally to one another, but only the leaders conversed with outsiders.

Because of such restrictions, a cult researcher who hopes to obtain a broad-based, representative sample of responses will be stymied. In fact, the researcher may not discover for some time that she or he has been exposed to a carefully selected sample of hardcore trained members who know how to respond according to the leader's wishes. Thus, the researcher will hear only those things that group members are taught to say they think or believe, and she or he will hear those things only from a designated few.

Cult leaders also typically intimidate researchers by threatening to withdraw the availability of research subjects. Normally, a researcher approaches the group's leader to secure access to members. Access may be given, but as time goes on and the researcher becomes dependent on securing the rest of the needed sample, the leadership suddenly intimates or sometimes openly states that if the researcher offends the group by coming upon any "wrong" findings or engages in any disapproved conduct such as criticizing anything about the group, then the completion of her or his study will be threatened because future access to this and allied groups will be withdrawn. This type of threat has succeeded in keeping a number of researchers and academics from making truly objective statements about cults and thought-reform processes.

In one case, a well-known university professor was asked by a publisher to review former cult member Barbara Underwood's book, *Hostage to Heaven*. The professor wrote the publisher extolling the book, saying that it was "one of the finest and best written of the entire genre"; yet he would not submit a positive review for general publication as it would, he said, "jeopardize my delicate relationships to any of them" (meaning the cult and its allies). Out of fear, the professor chose to withhold his positive endorsement of the book, which makes one question the objectivity of his writings about cults and groups that use thought-reform processes, about which he is often consulted.

Persecuting Therapists and Lawyers

Psychiatrists, psychologists, social workers, and lawyers have had a variety of things happen to them as a result of helping and treating current and former cult members. These range from attempts to defame these individuals' character to efforts to have their licenses revoked.

• A psychiatric social worker in Massachusetts who has helped many ex-members was a steady target of harassment. One of the more picturesque incidents occurred when a bundle of red roses was delivered to her workplace with a card thanking her for her efforts to destroy religion and signed "the American Nazi Party."

• Two psychiatrists in California who had treated former cult members learned that several cults had written to the board of state medical examiners making outrageous and false claims against the physicians simply because they had been the therapists of cult defectors.

• "A severely sick, extremely troubled member of an unusual cult, which routinely rejects its adherents who cannot continue to contribute money, was finally admitted to a hospital. Subsequently, she was discharged [at the request of] the cult, whose members removed her at gun point," according to reports received by the parents from hospital staff who were present. The hospital offered no help to the family and never brought the incident to the attention of the police. The hospital administrators "officially denied" what the staff had told the parents, illustrating "the degree to which panic can compromise professionalism."

• In a much-publicized event, a California lawyer was attacked by a rattlesnake placed in his mailbox by members of Synanon, the alcohol and drug rehabilitation program that evolved into a multimillion-dollar cult as it moved from nominal charitable corporation into a religion. Paul Morantz, an attorney in Pacific Palisades, had fought Synanon in three civil cases as well as a child custody case in which the judge ruled that a grandmother could get her three grandchildren back from Synanon.

Previously, Morantz had won a $300,000 judgment for a twenty-five-year-old woman whose husband was planning to take her to the UCLA Neuropsychiatric Institute when he got off work, but during the day she became so anxious she went to a clinic in Santa Monica asking for tranquilizers. From there she was referred to the Santa Monica Synanon facility for counseling. "Once inside Synanon, she was not allowed to leave. The organization informed her husband by phone that his wife was now living in Synanon and that he would not be able to see her for ninety days." The husband went to Paul Morantz for help. After nine days of private legal negotiations, Morantz got the woman back. "Her hair had been shaved off, she had been convinced by Synanon members that her husband wanted to divorce her," she had been told she couldn't leave, and she reported being pulled around by the wrists and yelled at. At the husband's request, Morantz drew up a lawsuit. The "Synanon attorneys so angered the judge in the case by disobeying court orders that he placed Synanon in default," and after a doctor testified that the woman had been subjected to "rape of the mind," the judge made a $300,000 award.

On the afternoon of October 10, 1978, Morantz went home, reached into his mailbox, and was bitten by a four-and-one-half-foot diamondback snake that had been placed there. Its rattles had been removed so he would hear no warning. He reportedly cried out, "Synanon got me!" as he was taken off by ambulance. Morantz barely survived the attack, requiring eleven vials of antivenom serum to pull him through. He continues to have some deficit in the bitten hand. Witnesses who had seen two suspicious men at the Morantz house had taken down the number of their car license, in spite of someone's attempt to alter the plate with tape. The car was registered to Synanon. Two of the Imperial Marines from Synanon's strong-arm force, Lance Kenton and Joe Musico, were arrested and later pleaded no contest to conspiracy to commit murder.

A month after the rattlesnake attack, law enforcement agents with search warrants confiscated documents and tape recordings including the one with Charles Dederich speaking of "greedy lawyers" trying to "bleed Synanon dry." "We're going to play by our own set of rules," he said. "I'm quite willing to break some lawyer's legs and break his wife's legs and threaten to cut their child's arm off. That is a very effective way of transmitting information. . . . I really do want an ear in a glass of alcohol. Yes, indeed."

Threatening Legal Suits

Legal suits are costly affairs. But some cults have developed large in-house legal staffs, including huge numbers of paralegals to help the resident lawyers. Thus legal actions are not very costly for the cults to pursue, whereas the people who must defend themselves can easily go broke battling against such tactics.

Among the more litigious stances taken by cults against critics was that shown by Synanon. Both local and national media had been frightened away from reporting on Synanon after the Hearst Corporation, in a two-year period in the 1970s, settled two libel and conspiracy suits filed against them by Synanon for $2.6 million. This is part of what Dederich called his "Holy War" against the media. Synanon also sued *Time* magazine for more than $76 million for an article that ran in late 1977, and sued ABC television for $40 million. They sued the Health Department for $35 million, and when a Marin County grand jury called for an investigation of Synanon, the jurors were served with a $55 million lawsuit. Other suits and hundreds of threats of suits followed. After that, the media were effectively muzzled and left Synanon in a silent void—until a series of articles ran in a small weekly, the *Point Reyes Light*.

In April 1979, David and Cathy Mitchell, coeditors of the *Point Reyes Light*, and their colleague, University of California sociologist Richard Ofshe, won the Pulitzer Prize for Meritorious Public Service for their research and exposure of Synanon. In nominating them for the prize, Ralph Craib wrote, "Major news organizations were unwilling to risk the inevitable litigation certain to be pursued by an organization with a 48-member legal staff. Meanwhile David Mitchell and his co-publisher wife Cathy were printing week after week stories of beatings, of weapons, and of other strange practices in which this cult was involved."

Only after the Mitchells and Ofshe won the Pulitzer did the National News Council, acting on a complaint from United Press International, investigate Synanon's efforts to silence media coverage of problems at the group. The council found that Synanon lawyers in 1978 and 1979 alone had on 960 occasions threatened libel suits against various media.

Soon after the three researchers won the Pulitzer Prize, Synanon filed three legal suits against them, which grew out of their discussing their findings about Synanon in the media. When CBS television was going to make a movie about the work of the Mitchells and Ofshe, Synanon threatened to sue and prevent the movie from being made. Synanon lost each of the suits and the three researchers countersued and collected damages, which was only possible because of the pro bono services offered to the Mitchells by San Francisco law firm Heller, Ehrman and because of the University of California's defense of Ofshe.

These events and the snake in the mailbox were turning points for Synanon. The media no longer held back writing about the group for fear of legal retaliation. Synanon lost its earlier suit against Time Inc., and Time countersued for its costs. ABC countersued Synanon; three young men beaten by Synanon members sued, as did Paul Morantz; a family that lived near the organization sued for harassment and other issues; and a number of other cases were filed.

Individuals' and organizations' fear and reluctance to speak are not unfounded, given the record of cult harassment of critics. Not only professionals but also citizen groups stand to be bothered and tormented. The volunteer-based Cult Awareness Network (CAN), a nonprofit organization devoted to educating the public about the harmful effects of mind control, has been the target of countless attacks. Between 1991 and 1993, the Church of Scientology alone filed more than forty-seven lawsuits and dozens of human rights complaints against CAN and/or its affiliates and individual members. Some of these were efforts to have the courts force CAN to let Scientologists work in the CAN national office or attend CAN conferences. This stated purpose is as absurd as having Nazis sue for the right to work in the Anti-Defamation League!

As of October 1994, all but four of these cases have been terminated, and the Scientologists have not prevailed in any of them. As former CAN president Patricia Ryan, the daughter of Congressman Leo J. Ryan who was assassinated at Jonestown, said, "The American courts were never meant to be used as a weapon available to those with money to destroy with frivolous legal actions anyone perceived as their enemy. Scientology has a long history of using the courts this way, and it has to stop if justice means anything in our courts today."

Forcing Relatives and Friends into Silence

A variety of tactics are used to try to keep inquiring relatives and friends from exposing cults or even asking too many questions. For example, if relatives contact public officials or the media, their family member in the cult is often forbidden to have any further contact with the family. Younger cult members have been known to write letters to their parents or grandparents with such statements as, "I am sorry to hear you called the radio station, but since you did, I will not be writing you anymore."

Many groups have reputations for sending members out of the area, out of the state, even out of the country, if relatives inquire about them, seem negative in any way toward the group, or talk with the media, authorities, or researchers. If the person in the cult is presented with information about the cult by the family, again the cult member is usually removed from sight and the negative family members are kept away from cult offices. This, however, has not stopped some families from successfully exposing cults in the media and picketing their facilities in order to gain access to their relatives in the cult.

One woman who wrote to her daughter in an international guru-based cult was startled to receive the following letter from a stranger in return.

It so happened that I got your letter in my hands that you actually was [sic] sending to "Barbara." At this moment I don't know her exact whereabouts, but very soon I will find out and will see that she will get your letter. . . . The last I heard she was in Nepal. Nepal is a neighbor country to India. By now she must have left for another country. You can keep communicating with me, and I will see that you will hear sometimes how Barbara is doing. So if you feel to do something good and loving, you can send us your good Christmas cookies and a check. And I am sure if I could tell this to Barbara she would be glad as if she would have the cookies herself.

Sometimes when the heat gets to the boiling point, certain groups move the entire operation to another part of the country or out of the country altogether in order to avoid an investigation or further inquiry and negative publicity. Group after group has been known to do this, moving to Europe, Hawaii, Australia, or countries in South America.

Extraordinary Harassment

Those who criticize or oppose cults become accustomed to a plethora of harassing actions. They get phone calls from people posing as reporters, seeking information on local anticult activities. Neighbors, relatives, and employers are likely to get calls and visits, sometimes from fictitious persons on various pretexts who accuse the anticult activist of all sorts of crimes. Meetings sponsored by CAN and similar grass-roots educational and research organizations have been infiltrated and disrupted. Participants' hotel and airplane reservations have been canceled and files have been ransacked, mailing lists stolen, garbage cans and waste baskets inspected, and scheduled speakers accosted. False fire alarms and bomb threats at locations of such meetings are not uncommon.

In my own work, I have been pestered, threatened, sued, and harassed often by cults because I have testified against a number of them in legal cases and because I have spoken out against certain of their practices.

Once, when I had been invited to speak in241 the British House of Lords, I was detained at the London airport because some anonymous person had informed customs officials that I was an IRA terrorist! The matter was quickly settled but perhaps gives a picture of what life is like for those who try to educate the public about cults. While still in London, I was invited to give a talk in a church. When I began to speak, a man much like a messenger delivering a singing telegram ran down the aisle with a big bouquet, singing a dirty song to embarrass me. He later identified to the authorities which cult had paid him to do it.

A young woman appeared several years ago at my university office, posing as a student. She volunteered to help in my office, as a number of students did, filing news clippings and articles for me and other instructors. She disappeared one day, but soon I began to get letters and phone calls. She had made photocopies of students' term papers and, imitating my handwriting, on the front pages of the papers had written such notes as, "This student would make a good CIA operative." This was done to make it appear as though the term paper had been sent by me to some secret agency, as though I were recommending the student to government agencies behind his or her back and as though I were a government agent myself! She then mailed these papers to the students by getting their addresses out of the student directory.

Some time later, through the Freedom of Information Act, I obtained documents that the government had retrieved when that young woman's cult had been raided. Among the documents were *security reports*, as this cult called them, including lengthy, fabricated reports signed by this woman in which she named everyone who had visited my office during the brief time she was around. She obviously had been sent to harass me and spy on me, and she made up some weird stories of the kind her cult wanted, but which were total fabrications.

I have learned to travel and book hotel reservations under assumed names because one cult used to have a man monitor my work and the lectures and meetings that I would be attending. He would then cancel my plane.and hotel reservations. When he left the cult, he wrote an apology and asked forgiveness for all the inconveniences he had caused me when he was doing the cult's bidding.

At one point, I received repeated phone calls every night at 1:30 A.M. until I had a police officer come over. He waited and answered the phone, giving the caller his badge number and saying if the caller wanted to talk, to call the Berkeley Police Department and talk with them at night. That ended those calls.

Once, while I was doing a series of interviews with two former cult members who were suing a large cult, someone would put a large dead brown rat, its heart skewered with a lollypop stick, on my steps each morning before the ex-members were to appear—no doubt to convey to them and me that we were all "rats." During that same period, two dozen of the same large brown rats—only live ones this time—were put into my house one day. I surmise that the cult wanted the rats to run loose throughout my home, but the rats had been put into a duct to the attic. So I had a herd of rats scampering about the attic until they could be caught and taken away.

I once testified in a lawsuit in which the jury gave a former cult member a multimillion dollar award against the cult. My testimony had described how the conduct of the cult and the ways the man had been treated had been so stressful to him over such a period of time and with such devastating outcomes that he had become psychotic. The day after the jury made the award, the cult started an ex parte suit on some trumped-up charges, against the man, his attorneys, and the experts who appeared for him, merely to harass us and cost us all a lot of money. Their case was eventually tossed out by a judge in Southern California, but only after years had gone by.

In that same case, I was escorted by an armed guard during the entire trial, even to the rest room during court breaks, in order not to be assaulted by cult members who were picketing the courthouse holding long pointed sticks with placards and crowding the court corridors. I was on the witness stand two and a half days for direct examination, but the cult lawyers kept me on for twelve and a half days of cross-examination—so the corridors and court area were quite a spectacle.

My office has been broken into and hundreds of video and audio interviews of ex–cult members and others have been stolen. My garbage and trash were continually being stolen, so I am now on my third paper shredder.

On numerous occasions when I was giving lectures, various cults have sent members to picket the university or organization sponsoring the program. One time when I was giving a talk at a local hospital to dentists, a cult known for sending people in Nazi uniforms to picket me sent their usual troop of about fifteen "Nazis," carrying placards stating that I was a Nazi neurosurgeon! When the hospital security guards came in and asked me, "Who are those jokers out in front with those pointed sticks, screaming your name?" I told them the name of the cult and explained that I was not a Nazi neurosurgeon and that I was there simply to talk about hypnosis for pain and anxiety reduction in dental care. I also explained that I had testified against the cult in several legal cases and that they wanted to destroy my reputation and ruin me. The security people went outside. I don't know what they said, but the group took their pointy sticks and placards and loaded themselves into two vans and sped off, looking confused.

The attempts to humiliate me and destroy my reputation are also part of an effort on the part of several of the large, international, and very wealthy cults to make me into a symbol. I have heard from colleagues that they and other professionals have been told, "Look what we do to Singer and others who speak out. It could happen to you. So you, professor, or doctor, better not say anything we don't like unless you want to be treated like Singer."

I have not given up, and the harassment goes on, for what I have listed here is only a small part of what has transpired.

There are many frightening examples of cults' stark and widespread efforts at silencing and intimidating critics. Not only have researchers, journalists, authors, and ordinary citizens been intimidated, attacked, and sued, but cults have also attempted to frighten professionals away from the courts, waging concentrated attacks on professionals who have testified on behalf of ex-members. In the hope of stifling attorneys, physicians, psychiatrists and psychologists, social workers, child welfare evaluators, and any others who might aid cult victims in legal suits or child custody cases, certain cults have stooped to vicious ends and terror tactics. In addition, they have filed unfounded and downright ridiculous charges against lawyers with their respective bar associations, against physicians with state medical boards, and against psychologists with their professional organizations.

So far, honesty, dedication, and integrity have usually prevailed, and victims of cult abuse can still find more and more professionals coming to help, in spite of the unending attacks on them.

PART THREE

How Can We Help Survivors to Escape and Recover?

10

Rescuing the Children

Each year since 1978, on the anniversary of Jonestown, I have participated in a memorial service, either in the Bay Area or in another city. My favorite of the various locations is the Evergreen Cemetery in Oakland, California. I go early to have some time alone to think about why I keep studying cults and why I want to help people who leave them.

One major reason is that I want to be a voice for those children lying beneath the grass who were never allowed to grow up. Who never went to real schools. Who never had the opportunity to choose what kind of work they would do. Jim Jones's mad ego ended their lives before they had a chance.

Standing next to the huge area of unmarked graves, where 406 bodies are buried, I think of all the pictures of smiling children's faces that are in my office. These were given to me by Jeannie and Al Mills, who spent six years with Jones, and who were mysteriously murdered in Berkeley about three years after the Jonestown tragedy. I have other mementos given to me by Charles Garry, a lawyer for the Peoples Temple who went to Guyana and was hiding in the jungle when the end came. Being on that hillside in Evergreen Cemetery alone, thinking of all those little smiling kids, thinking of all the letters I have read that they wrote to "Dad" (which is what Jones made them call him), is a solemn reminder to me of the effects of cults on children.

I have interviewed or counseled a number of ex–Peoples Temple members, who survived because they were either in Georgetown, Guyana, or back in the United States when the final White Night, as Jones called the cult's preparation for suicide, came down. For them and for relatives who lost families there, the memories are painful. Each year, these families call out for the public to face what cults are. And each year, they go away puzzled that cults keep growing and that thousands of children and parents are still in bondage.

The most recent Jonestown memorial had an interesting pair of participants: Stephan Jones, son of Jim Jones, and Patricia Ryan, daughter of the U.S. Congressman killed at Jones's command at the Port Kaituma airstrip. These two young adults met in hope that no more Jonestowns occur. They both know in their hearts that it could happen again and again.

At one memorial, a girl who survived spoke of her friend who died. Her friend didn't know what the outside world was like, said the girl, but she'd sometimes talk about it, saying, "Just for a day I'd like to know how it is in the outside world." She wanted that chance but never got it. She had no way to get out. Nobody to turn to.

It has been estimated that there are thousands of small children in cults, with five thousand young children in one cult that moved from the United States to base itself in Europe and elsewhere. The Tony and Susan Alamo Foundation was known to advertise nationally, asking pregnant women to give their children to the foundation to raise instead of seeking abortions. Some cults insist that their female members act as "breeders" to bring more children—that is, cult followers—into the world. Yet the work of a number of researchers attests to the deplorable status of children in certain cults—the use of extreme discipline; the rearing of children by others in the group rather than the parents; the sheer neglect, poor schooling, emotional and psychological abuse; and the lack of adequate medical, dental, and nutritional care.

No matter how youngsters get into a cult, they are even more powerless than most neglected and abused children on the outside because they are hidden from the protection of general society.

Abused, neglected, and mistreated children in ordinary U.S. society are often around schoolteachers, neighbors, and relatives. Once the abuse is noted, child protective services, the police, and others can use legal channels to rescue these children. Children in some cults are more like prisoners in another country, although they lack even workers from Amnesty International or the International Red Cross to come to their aid.

Some groups send families to recruit and fund raise overseas, where the children are beyond the jurisdiction of U.S. child protection laws. For a number of years, parents who leave a cult while their spouses remain in the group with their children have found that the cult spirits the children away, often out of the United States to a location abroad where locating the children is difficult if not impossible.

Cult children are powerless. They are total victims—even the parents on whom they should be able to depend are controlled by the cult leader, and thus the children's fate is in his hands. In cults, parents do not function as they do in the regular world. They are more like middle-management personnel in a business: the cult leader dictates how children are to be reared, and the parents simply implement these orders. This can be illustrated first by the children of Jonestown and Waco.

Children of Jonestown

Of the 912 members of the Peoples Temple cult who died, 276 were children. At the cult's jungle settlement in Guyana, the children lived in crowded physical conditions that resembled quarters on slave ships. Food was barely edible; medical care and clothing inadequate. Children were separated from parents and siblings and cared for by day care and nursery school teachers and house parents, who supervised the children in groups of about twelve.

Children were allowed to see their parents only briefly at night, so that they would place their allegiance instead with Jones and his wife and look upon them as father and mother. Children were rewarded for spying on their parents.

Those above the age of six had to do "public service"—hard labor including working in the jungle fields and on construction crews from 7 A.M. to 6 P.M. in temperatures as high as 100 degrees Fahrenheit. Teenagers did over half of the heavy construction work at Jonestown.

As punishment, children were thrown into a dark well after being told that snakes awaited them there. They were kept in a plywood box measuring six feet by three feet by four feet for weeks at a time. They had teeth knocked out in public beatings, were forced to dig holes and then refill them, and were imprisoned in a small cellar. Jones often watched security guards beat children with switches, belts, and a long wooden board. Young girls were stripped and forced into cold showers or a swimming pool. Children had electrodes wired on their arms and were administered electric shocks. In one case, two six-year-olds who had tried to run away had chains and balls welded to their ankles.

Peoples Temple children were frequently sexually abused. While the group was still in California, teenage girls as young as fifteen had to provide sex for influential people courted by Jones. A supervisor of children at Jonestown had a history of child sexual abuse, and Jones himself assaulted some of the children. If husbands and wives were caught talking privately during a meeting, their daughters were forced to masturbate publicly or to have sex with someone the family didn't like before the entire Jonestown population, children as well as adults.

Jones gave children powerful mind-altering drugs. They were also subject to the terror of forty-two mass suicide rituals. Until the last one, the final White Night, they never knew if the ritual was a practice or the real thing.

Jones had begun to plan the ending of the cult as a murder-suicide at least five years before it happened. In 1973, he told cult member Grace Stoen, "Everyone will die, except me, of course, I've got to stay back and explain why we did it, for our belief in integration." Jones told teenage member Linda Myrtle, "We're all to commit suicide, killing the children first, then ourselves." By late

1975, Jones began the White Night suicide drills in which members were given drinks and then were told they had been poisoned and would die in a few minutes. Guards were around and no one could leave. These drills began in San Francisco and continued in Guyana.

About 5 P.M. of the last day, Jones assembled everyone at the compound. The camp doctor and two nurses had filled hundreds of syringes with a cyanide-laced sweet drink—yellow for infants, pink for children under ten, and purple for the older children and adults. Jones had audiotaped the last hours to memorialize them, and on the tape cult member Christine Miller can be heard protesting, "I look at all the babies, and I think they deserve to live . . . I have the right to choose and I choose not to commit suicide."

I noted as did others who studied the tape that Jones turned it off, then on again, repeatedly. Soon Jones was yelling: "I want my babies first. Take my babies and children first. Get moving, get moving, get moving. Don't be afraid to die." The nurses reportedly took the syringes and squirted the cyanide down the throats of the babies. Stanley Clayton and Odell Rhodes, who hid and survived, provided accounts of the last minutes. Clayton reported that "the nurses plucked babies right out of their mothers' arms." The infants gave out piercing, tormented screams, and a nurse called out: "They're not crying from the pain. It's a little bitter-tasting. They are not crying out of any pain." Mothers poured cyanide-laced Fla-Vor-Aid down the throats of their infants and young children. On the final tape from Guyana, Jones's voice tells mothers, "Hurry, bring the little ones up here. Hurry, mothers, hurry."

The Jonestown settlement is gone, but the nightmare of cult life lingers on for many small children and teenagers caught in other cults.

Children of Waco

Twenty-five of the more than eighty who died in the fiery burnout of the Branch Davidian cult in Waco, Texas, were children. Earlier, during the stand-off with agents of the federal government, cult leader David Koresh had released twenty-one children, ranging in age from five months to twelve years. These freed children have been carefully studied by Bruce D. Perry, M.D., Ph.D., a research professor of child psychiatry at Baylor College of Medicine in Houston, Texas. His background in studying traumatized children and adults prepared him well to observe and conceptualize what he and his colleagues found among the Branch Davidian children.

Physically, psychologically, emotionally, cognitively, and behaviorally, these children demonstrated that their development was far from normal. For the first few weeks, they showed physical signs of the mental stress they were feeling. Even at rest, their hearts raced at about 120 beats a minute, 30 to 50 percent faster than normal. "These kids were terrorized," Dr. Perry said. Their terror grew out of having been taught by Koresh that everyone outside the cult was evil and likely to hurt or kill them. The assault on the compound reinforced that teaching. Research shows that traumatic experiences actually change the physiology of the brain, resulting in mental or emotional problems.

Free of the cult's structure, the children organized themselves in a manner similar to the life they knew in the compound. Boys and girls formed separate groups, each with a leader who spoke for and made decisions for the other children in the group. Many children drew pictures of Koresh as God; others made doodlings that said "David is God."

The children had been taught what Dr. Perry called "malignant stories" about life, and they had no concept of families and family relationships as do children raised in the broader world. They referred to Koresh as their father because couples in the cult were routinely broken up, families were split, and Koresh made himself the father figure for the entire cult. Most of the children thought of their parents merely as adult members of the cult and treated siblings as friends or acquaintances. When Dr. Perry asked children to draw pictures of their family, they drew pictures of random groups of cult members or of Koresh, even though they were not related to him. Some children lacked even a vague idea of family.

Not only were their views of family distorted or undeveloped, so were their own self-images. When asked to draw a "picture of yourself," most children could manage to draw only a small, primitive figure, often in a corner of a full sheet of paper. Most importantly, Dr. Perry and his team of child trauma specialists noted that the children found it nearly impossible to think or act independently. They did everything as a group, even simple tasks such as deciding whether to eat a plain peanut butter sandwich or one with jelly. The boys' group leader and the girls' group leader made such decisions for their respective groups.

These children were not mentally retarded, but they were limited by the cult environment in which they were reared. They could not recognize a quarter but were able to recite long quotations from biblical scripture. Some were fascinated with indoor toilets that flushed, devices they had never seen until leaving the cult compound. Likewise, indoor running water was new to them.

The children raised in the Branch Davidian cult knew only the distorted, violent world created by David Koresh and the illusion of the enemy world in which he cast all outsiders. Dr. Perry's report on his work emphasizes the human rights issue for children in cults who suffer in many ways—from distorted self-images and distorted, unreal ideas about the outside world to the traumas of the cult life that actually change their brain functions.

Children of Other Cults

Each cult regards itself as above the laws of the land, as a sovereign state with its own superior rules, and in many cults, children are treated as though they were expendable. The cult leader may not want to "waste" money on children. Or the leader may rationalize the group's practices so that parents no longer heed the practices they once knew were good for children. Often cult parents are led to regard children as creatures similar to wild ponies, who must be "broken."

Physical Abuse

Extremely strict and punitive behavioral controls are exercised over children in many cults. Severe beatings to "break the will, beat out the sin, overcome the demons" are accepted means of handling children. In some cults, exorcisms are performed on children to drive out evil spirits, devils, and such. These can be brutal, terrifying events.

Discipline can be meted out without regard; at times, lives are taken by the punishment.

• Five-year-old Luke Stice died of a broken neck in a survivalist cult in rural Nebraska. Reportedly, his neck was broken either during a regular "discipline session" or deliberately, to force Luke's father to return because he had fled the cult leaving behind Luke and two other children. Before Luke died, the leader had made him spend most of his time in undershorts and forced him to wallow naked in mud and snow.

• Twelve-year-old John Yarbough allegedly was beaten to death in a Michigan cult, the House of Judah. Before his death, when John had been beaten several days in a row and could not eat or walk, the leader tried to pick him up by the ears with pliers. Another boy reported that he was burned on the face for punishment; one testified that another boy had hot coals put in his mouth and on his hands.

Moreover, child sexual abuse is promoted in certain cults, either as a reflection of the leader's deviant desires and a way of satisfying his fantasies or with the leader rationalizing the abuse as a way to recruit new members. Child-to-child sex, adult-to-child sex, and incest are encouraged in some cults.

Inadequate Schooling

Many cults limit contact with nonmembers, creating an invisible wall around the group. As part of this practice, a number of cults decry school and formal education, although others do allow the children to go to outside schools. These children, however, are often ridiculed by their classmates because of their strange clothes or odd habits.

Some cultic groups have members earn money by ferrying cars across the country for people who don't want to make the drive themselves, and children are taken along on these drives. Such children do not have regular schooling or the chance to make normal acquaintances with other children in their apartment buildings or neighborhoods. Always on the road, they don't have playmates. Eventually, when a parent leaves the cult and takes the child out also, the child is usually behind in school and doesn't know how to fit into a normal environment.

Poor Health Care

Births and deaths among cult members may not be legally registered. Prenatal and delivery care are scorned or prohibited, with infant mortality and maternal mortality rates reaching staggering proportions in some groups.

Health care is generally lacking in cults. Depending on the philosophy of the cult, personal health care, including that of the children, may be nonexistent, denigrated, or overtly prohibited. Children often do not receive proper immunization shots or regular checkups. Cult members lack such normal medical care as dental work and braces, glasses, and orthopedic care.

Children have also participated in drug use in cults that promote such behavior. There are instances of children using marijuana, cocaine, heroin, and amphetamines.

Inadequate diets are the standard in many cults. In some groups, odd, imbalanced diets are used as punishment or to keep costs down. In general, food may be poor or improper for children. Small children in nomadic cults like the Garbage Eaters are carted about the countryside. They eat the same food their parents scrounge from the trash found behind restaurants and supermarkets.

As a result, children in cults are nearly always hungry—both for food and for nurturing, tenderness, and normal caring from the adults around them.

Emotional and Psychological Abuse

Children in most cults lead restricted, isolated lives. Some become part of the cult when their parents join, some are born into the cult while their parents are members. Children born before their parents joined the cult often are treated even less kindly than their siblings born within the cult: the latter are "blessed" while the ones born earlier are typically regarded as "satanic," lesser beings, or unenlightened. Still other children, as was the case for a number of children in the Peoples Temple, come into a cult because they are unwittingly assigned by welfare departments to a cult group for "care." They are often considered nobody's children.

Even the offspring of those cult members who remain in the regular world and work at normal jobs suffer. The children have little time with their parents and often must attend countless adult meetings that interfere with the children's sleep and playtime and prevent them from ordinary mingling with other children. In many cults, either by intention or because the adults are functioning on a frenzied cult-controlled schedule, children are sometimes kept awake as long as seventy-two hours on end.

Other kinds of emotional and psychological abuses prevail as well.

• In the Democratic Workers Party, a political cult, the three-year-old daughter of two of the members was denounced in front of adult members and expelled, prohibited from ever coming again to one of the cult's buildings.

• In 1992, an Indiana judge ordered four children removed from their mother who was a member of the Church Universal and Triumphant. Among other reasons, the judge stated that the children's health and educational needs weren't being met, and that "a clear threat to the children's emotional health has been demonstrated regarding the children's presence in underground shelter drills or visits, and in the imposition upon them of a fatalistic approach to life and a fear of the end of the world." The three oldest children had been kept out of public school for one and a half years and spent much of their time each day "decreeing," which the judge described as "intense, repetitive chanting of prescribed prayers of a self-hypnotic nature, for extended periods."

• In a custody battle related to a nameless religious sect in Gwinnette County, Georgia, members testified that they sing to their children and offer encouragement during beatings with wooden rods or refrigerator hoses and insisted that they didn't strike in anger. According to child welfare investigators, one girl said "the only way she knew her daddy loved her was because he whipped her. He would tell her he loved her while he was doing it."

Children coming out of such environments are very puzzled about who they are and whether they are good or not good.

Children in cults also witness the abuse of others. They see bizarre and violent exorcisms and punishments meted out to their parents and other children and adults. In some groups, it becomes common knowledge that the leader can decree the murder of members who leave the group, including children. Some children who witness such brutality and harshness identify with those doing it and imitate it, while others become terrorized and docile to avoid such a fate befalling them.

A former member of Moon's Unification Church wrote, "It was very difficult to draw most of the children out of the consuming melancholy which engulfed them." It is surely an understatement to say that cult life is almost never pleasant for the children.

Role of the Cult Leader

The abuse of the Branch Davidian children is shocking but in fact similar to the many accounts I have heard both from children raised in other cults and from parents who have left cults. The anecdotal evidence has been accumulating for years and coalesces into the following: submit, surrender, and obey is the theme and yardstick of successful adaptation in the cult.

Since the structure of a cult is authoritarian, children are socialized to that world, not the mainstream democratic society. Children see their parents submit and surrender to the dictates of the leader. Their parents and others simply carry out orders, doing what the guru or leader says.

Parents in cults are like offspring of the leader and are expected to be his obedient children. This was evident in one case in which I testified concerning a ten-year-old boy who was held by four grown men over the arm of a sofa and hit with a large wooden paddle 140 times, with the group calling out the count. The boy's mother stood by and watched. The cult leader was in a nearby building directing the beating over the phone. The leader of a cult in the northeastern United States had all adults carry large wooden cooking ladles and strike any child who deviated from group rules until the child "surrendered."

A cult is a mirror of what is inside the cult leader. He has no restraints on him. He can make his fantasies and desires come alive in the world he creates around him. He can lead people to do his bidding. He can make the surrounding world really *his* world. What most cult leaders achieve is akin to the fantasies of a child at play, creating a world with toys and utensils. In that play world, the child feels omnipotent and creates a realm of his own for a few minutes or for a few hours. He moves the toy dolls about. They do his bidding. They speak his words back to him. He punishes them any way he wants. He is all-powerful and makes his fantasy come alive. When I see the sand tables and the collections of toys some child therapists have in their offices, I think that a cult leader must look about and place people in his created world much as the child creates on the sand table a world that reflects his or her desires and fantasies. The difference is that the cult leader has actual humans doing his bidding as he makes a world around him that springs from inside his own head.

The cult leader's idiosyncratic notions permeate the system he puts into operation. There is no feedback. No criticism is allowed. When he finally gets his followers to be sufficiently obedient, he can wield unlimited power and get his followers to carry out whatever acts he directs. He becomes the most powerful director one can imagine. Not merely a director of toys and actors, but a director of real lives in real acts based on his desires and fantasies. As the child moves toys about an imagined landscape, the cult leader moves, directs, chastises—even kills—those who disobey.

Role of Cult Parents

Usually, cults do not respect the parental role. As I have described, parents are just intermediaries who see that the children obey the will of the leader. Even in many Bible-based cults, respect for parents is not extolled as might be expected. Rather, the leader positions himself as the gatekeeper between parents and their God.

Parents must get their children to submit to them and to the dictates of the leader in order to prove that they themselves are submitting to the leader, who becomes the sole person to be given high respect, obedience, veneration. There may be high-level functionaries in the cult who must also be obeyed, but they are really just tools of the leader also. Moreover, in many cultic groups, especially the Bible-based and psychotherapy cults, parents' dedication is measured by their willingness to abuse their children at the leader's request. Parents are taught that the leader is their only avenue to enlightenment, God, mental health, or political rightness, and that unless their children submit to them, and they to the leader, they will be cut off from the promised result.

"We were taught that we must not be attached to our own children," wrote a mother describing her three years in the Unification Church. "We were also taught that these children came from satanic relationships and that although it was horrible to have 'attachments' to any other person, it was most terrible to be 'attached' to our own children." She describes "tremendous guilt for even considering the welfare of the children."

In some cults, parents who give even the slightest attention or thought to their children may well be verbally attacked and chastised in other ways for "spoiling their children." But as this same mother writes, "How could you spoil a child who was in a situation of almost total emotional deprivation, a child who never knew from one day to the next whether she would even see her mother, a child who was, with no apparent consistency and depending upon who was caring for her at the moment, disciplined either not at all or with great severity?"

Poignant tales about children in cults also come from grandparents. One grandmother visited her relatives in a life-style cult that now has offshoots around the world and that has been the subject of publicized reports of abuses and other cultlike behavior, such as separating children from their parents. While the grandmother was visiting, she asked her grandchild if there was a room where the children could read books and play. The child appeared not to know the answer and replied, "I must get a stupid one. Ask the stupid ones"—meaning the parents.

Another set of grandparents told me that David Koresh had taught the small children to refer to their parents as "dogs." The grandparents in both instances felt that the children did not grasp the extent of derision and bizarreness inherent in calling their parents stupid ones or dogs.

While parents may be in the same locale as their children, cult duties and meetings occupy so much of their time that they get little personal time with their own children. Moreover, anger and frustration is engendered in the parents by the cult leader's actions, but because they dare not express this anger toward him, when they do see their children they often act out their anger on their children instead.

When one parent leaves the cult and the other remains, the absent parent is called satanic or other derogatory names, and the child is discouraged from having any relationship with that parent.

When children do see their noncult parent, they may feel extremely uncomfortable and fear punishment or shunning upon returning to the cult environment. This also causes undue stress for children.

Because cult parents in essence turn over the custody of their children to a third party, so that the leader or the group becomes the actual custodian of the children, children in cults may also be assigned to live with adults other than their parents or may be sent to other states or other countries to cult-run facilities. Some cults openly proclaim that the family must be destroyed, that children must be reared by the group, with no particular ties to their parents. Often, children are taught to hate grandparents and other relatives not in the cult.

One example of this thinking was seen in the Sullivanians, a psychotherapy-political cult begun by Saul Newton, a longtime leftist who said he fought with the Abraham Lincoln Brigade in the Spanish Civil War. He led members to believe that mothers unconsciously hated their children and that the nuclear family is the root of all evil. In the guise of eliminating these destructive forces, Newton allegedly took complete control of procreation within the group and selected pairs of followers to mate. Children were not to have special relationships with their parents, and adult Sullivanians were not to talk with their own parents.

The thought-reform milieus and totalist thinking found in cultic groups play a major role in influencing parents to stand by while their children and others are severely abused, sometimes even killed before their eyes. It appears that several factors enter into these situations.

There is an interplay between the ideology of the group and the authoritarian role of the leader that has a particular impact on parents' thinking and behavior. The authoritarian ideologue, through his control of the social system and social environment, is able to gain compliance and obedience from the parents. The shared ideology of the group is a set of emotionally charged convictions about mankind and its relationship to the world. Once parents have made overt commitments to follow the ideology of a particular leader, then social psychology tells us that their open declaration solidifies and increases the likelihood that they will follow through on whatever behavior is expected of them. Certain behavior may be in total opposition to what they previously subscribed to—not to mention morally reprehensible. But like other cult members, cult parents assume pseudopersonalities, brought on by the cult's training and thought-reform processes. This alteration in the way they think allows them to perform as desired by their cult leader.

What Children Learn in Cults

Children see no modeling of compassion, forgiveness, kindness, or warmth in cults. Since all members are expected to idolize the leader, so are the children. Children either identify with the leader's power and dominance or capitulate and become passive, dependent, obedient, and often emotionally subdued and flattened.

Children adopt the cult's right-wrong, good-bad, sinner-saint starkly polarized value system. They are taught that a divided world exists—"we" are inside; "they" are outside. We are right, they are wrong. We are good, they are bad. In this us-against-them world, children (like the rest of the members) are taught to feel paranoid about nonmembers and the outside society.

Cult children have no opportunity to observe the compromising, negotiating, and meeting on middle ground demonstrated in ordinary families. They do not see people resolving disputes or adjusting to the wants and desires of others, the trade-offs that are so central to learning how to play, work, and live in a family or in groups that have been socialized in democratic ways.

Cult children do not see adults having input in decision making or making ideas and plans together. Instead, they witness and are taught that critical, evaluative thinking; new ideas; and independent ideas get people in trouble. From this, they learn simply to obey.

In many cults, normal aggressiveness, liveliness, and assertiveness in children are labeled as sinful or as signs of demons, and often warrant severe punishment and suppression. Thus like their parents, children learn to be dependent on the leader and his system. As a result, anxious-dependent personality traits can be built into cult children's developing character.

After the Cult

As cults vary in their demands, the help given to children coming out of cults must be tailored to fit the varying needs of each child. For example, acting out roles they learned from adults in their cult, some children emerge flat, melancholic, and phobic, whereas those raised in militant, confrontational groups may be more defiant and assertive. The later appear to be small aggressive caricatures of the demeanor built into the group's culture by the leader.

Adults and older teenagers who join cults take with them a personality that is already developed. The cult pseudopersonality is imposed on an existing personality and some knowledge of how the world works. When these persons leave the cult, they can draw on both their former personality and their memories of precult days. They can begin to integrate their precult, cult, and postcult experiences. Unfortunately, children raised in cults don't have that earlier personality or knowledge of the world to build upon when they come out of the cult.

Compared to other children, many children raised in isolated cults emerge with restricted learning, fewer skills, and below-average socialization. Because cult children are told that the cult's people are chosen, elite, and superior, afterward it can be difficult for them to form opinions, express themselves, and sort out conflicts between cult beliefs and new postcult experiences. Certain cults teach racial, religious, or political intolerance, which the children bring with them into the outside world.

Thus children raised in some cults will have learned ideas and practices that the broader society may regard as bizarre, bigoted, and antisocial, and casually expressing these ideas after leaving the cult can lead the child to be ostracized. This is particularly likely to be the case for children leaving cults that promote free sex or sexual contact between adults and children. For example, children who openly masturbate at school or when visiting other children because masturbation was an accepted practice in the cult become instant pariahs and are regarded as "monsters" by teachers and other parents.

Many cults teach children that lying to or deceiving nonmembers is the correct thing to do. The tenet that outsiders are lesser beings is the cults' justification for such actions. Children in cults also learn a kind of groupthink and a language, or jargon, that have to be unlearned upon leaving the group if the children are to speak with the rest of the world.

As we have seen, cult leaders establish spy networks so that the leader can claim he omnipotently knows all about everyone, reads minds, and perceives things that others cannot, when in fact the information is provided by members' tattling, reporting, and spying on one another. Children so taught in cults become school "rat finks" and talebearers when they carry out such reporting in the outside world.

Teenagers emerging from certain cults, especially those with extremely controlled environments, tend to act out: they sample sex, drugs, alcohol, fast cars, fast living, total rebellion, and rule breaking. They are often at high risk for sexual diseases, AIDS, and pregnancy, and are often preyed upon by delinquent and criminal youths.

Some teenagers have seen their parents put down so often that they absorb that attitude and continue to express it toward their parents when the family is no longer in the cult. These teenagers have identified with the cult leader's harsh attitudes toward others.

Many cults are anticareer and induce members to accept low-level jobs in order to keep members available to work for the leader. Higher education, or sometimes any education, is devalued. Afterward, it's difficult for teenagers to fathom what to do—Go to school? Get a job? Get into an apprenticeship program? Personal talents, skills, and interests have probably never been recognized or developed.

Children Are Survivors

In the past decade, we have seen more and more children coming out of cults. They either escaped on their own in their teen years or left with the rest of their families. These children are in great need of support and comfort, for they face extraordinary adjustment problems.

Initially it is helpful if the parents of these youngsters go to the schools, the pastors, and other available counseling facilities and help the professionals in those environments and agencies understand cults and the particular difficulties of children who were raised in a cult.

Because cult children are taught to dislike people who aren't in the group, it can be beneficial to help them reconnect with grandparents, aunts and uncles, cousins, and other family members. This will lessen the impact of cult thinking and broaden their potential support network.

Because many cults have skeptical or negligent attitudes about health care and education, it is vital for children coming out of cults to get a thorough medical examination and an objective evaluation of their educational level.

Often these children will need instant instruction that some attitudes learned while in the cult just do not go over well in the outside world. Many children coming out of cults are ill-trained in the general social skills that other children learn in school and through their family and friends. These children's prejudices, biases, and tendencies toward severe judgmentalism ingrained by the cult's philosophy must be countered. Learning to cope and function within a diverse, egalitarian, democratic society will be a challenge for these youngsters. This is especially true for those born or raised in a cult, who have no life experience outside the cult and no precult personality, values, or belief system. These children must be helped to shed their elitist views, their dogmatic and rigid thinking, and their self-blaming and hypercritical attitudes.

Although they face enormous tasks, and sometimes face them alone, children coming out of cults do survive, become healthy and happy, and lead productive lives, proving once again the resilience of the young. The story of "Ethel" is a case in point—and an inspiration to us all.

Ethel was raised in a West Coast life-style cult which her parents joined in the late 1960s after having lived in two hippie communes. They had met a woman who owned a huge spread of land with many small cottages on it and who had started a highly controlled communal living group that evolved into a cult. The woman recruited each person or couple herself from among those who had already adopted alternative life-styles. She sold them the idea that they could "return to the land" by coming to live communally on her property and, with her, creating a new order that supplanted the family and society as we know it.

The woman determined who would have children and when and directed child rearing, even though she had no children of her own and had never married. She convinced them, much as the Sullivanian group had convinced its members, that families, especially parents, were the root of all human suffering and that communal rearing would alleviate this evil. The followers broke contact with their families, and children raised in the group were permitted only the most infrequent and supervised contact with grandparents. Some grandparents never passed the leader's inspection and were not allowed to see the children anywhere but on the property.

Luckily, over the years, Ethel had been permitted some time with her paternal grandmother, who understood how impossible it was to try to wean her son and his wife and child away from the cult leader and so was content to keep the tie with the granddaughter alive.

Anyone who went off the property, even briefly, was interrogated by the leader in front of the whole group, for there were to be no secrets among them. Even people who went on food-buying trips to town had to "share their experiences." Ethel said later that, somehow, she caught on early that whenever she had been off the property with her grandmother she should report what the leader wanted to hear, not what she and her grandmother really did and talked about. So she reported that the grandmother admired the leader and remarked what good care the group took of her son and his little family. Ethel never varied these positive reports and would also relate details of her grandmother's colds, the state of her headaches, and such trivia.

The few cult children that there were went to public schools in the area but were not to talk in detail to teachers or classmates about their lives. They were not permitted to visit other children or participate in after-school events. Someone from the cult would pick up the children and bring them home.

All through high school, Ethel hid from the cult that she had been befriended by a school advisor, with whom she spoke freely. The entire surrounding community knew about the cult and felt sorry for the children and members, but could do nothing to help, for they soon learned that the children got in trouble if asked to play or do other normal activities after school. Ethel said that without that one advisor and her grandmother, she would still be back on the land, subservient to the leader and docile like her parents.

Even now Ethel describes how hopeless she felt all her young life as she watched her parents always give in to the leader. In spite of preaching avant-garde ideas, the leader was very old-fashioned in her practices: for example, girls were taught to be subservient to boys and men, and women had to be ultrafeminine and obedient, especially to the leader.

Ethel, a high-energy, athletic young woman with a high IQ, wanted to go to college, and she was the first child permitted to get an education beyond high school; however, the cult wouldn't pay anything toward Ethel's college education as it was against the "plan." The leader allowed Ethel to go only because she promised to return and because she asked her grandmother for help. With some money from her grandmother, Ethel began college and worked hard at jobs and school.

As soon as she got to college, though, she went to the counseling service and signed up for help. She knew she had to have someone help her make decisions because she had never made any herself other than deciding to hide her special relationships and knowing that she *had* to get out and go to college. She said she didn't know how to "think" about everyday life. She could think about books, do schoolwork, anything someone else directed, but never having had any role models for decision making, she felt desperate about her lack of knowledge about how to live on the outside.

I have had contact with Ethel episodically during the past two years. She is now twenty-two years old, just graduated from a state college, and is working far from the cult. She has found another counselor who helps her think through decisions and make specific plans about buying clothing and a car and about the concrete details of living an ordinary family would have taught her. She sees her parents only during specially arranged events, as the leader wants her back. Ethel wants to get her parents away from the group some day but cannot even hint at this idea with them now. Ethel's greatest concern is that her parents are hopelessly bound to the cult leader and will only be freed when the woman dies. She says, "They are even more ill equipped for life than I am now," and she plans never to return to them as long as they are "on the land."

Many children reared in cults are truly victims who are especially alone and without advocates. They may be living in the United States where daily comforts, education, and medical care are among the best in the world, but within the cult these benefits are rarely available to them. Those who are abused or neglected are even more hidden from the help of general society than the ordinary abused or neglected child because of the secrecy and tight boundaries many cults place on their members.

Compounding this isolation, cult children are usually not protected by their own parents, for the cult leader dominates and parents are powerless. The fates of both parents and children are determined by the whims and philosophy of the leader. I have not yet heard of any cult leader who has exuded care, warmth, and concern for the children in his group.

Despite such odds, children like Ethel leave cults and survive. They may have seen and lived through the worst, yet they carry on to be the best. Our responsibility is to give them support, love, and understanding.

11

Leaving the Cult

Sometimes people ask former cult members, "Why didn't you just get up and walk out?" There is no simple answer to that question, for a variety of factors contribute to keeping a cult member bound to the group. In most cases, there is no physical restraint, although some groups do punish and imprison those who try to leave. But in all cases, there is a psychological bond that becomes most difficult to sever.

Why It's Hard to Leave

When a person is taken in by the coercive psychological and social influence of a cult, she or he experiences what I call the five D's.

1. *Deception* in the recruitment process and throughout membership

2. *Debilitation,* because of the hours, the degree of commitment, the psychological pressures, and the inner constriction and strife

3. *Dependency,* as a result of being cut off from the outside world in many ways

4. *Dread,* because of beliefs instilled by the cult that a person who leaves will find no real life on the outside

5. *Desensitization*, so that things that would once have troubled them no longer do (for example, learning that money collected from fund-raising is supporting the leader's lavish lifestyle rather than the cause for which it was given, or seeing children badly abused or even killed)

All of these factors, which I expand on in the rest of the chapter, enmesh and work together to keep the cult member from seeing a way out.

Belief

Among the many influences that reinforce the difficulty a cult member has in just getting up and walking out, belief is probably the starting point. Your belief or sense of commitment is a very powerful force—whether that belief relates to a specific god or religion, a certain brand of politics, animal rights, living in the country and being free, your family, or the existence of magic. Being able to carry out their beliefs and act on their ideas is very appealing to people. It seems to be the normal human condition that we want to believe in something; we need beliefs that help us understand our universe.

In the world of cults, belief becomes the glue that binds the person to the group. You begin to go along with things, no matter what group you are in, because you believe in the group. You believe in the goals and in the people who are doing these things with you. You believe in the leader. You believe you are going to accomplish something.

In most cults, you are told that, in order to live out the group's belief, you must make certain changes in yourself. So you say, "Okay, I accept that. I believe this, I agree with it, and I'll make those changes," and slowly those changes begin to have a radical effect on your thoughts and actions, though you are not highly conscious of this effect.

Decency and Loyalty

A second major influence that keeps people in cults is that most people are decent, honest beings. They want to do good, be altruistic, and achieve something in their lives. And they are loyal. Once most people make a commitment to something, they don't easily renege on that commitment.

So when you make a commitment to a group and it's a group you believe in fervently, it's very hard to go back. Later, when you begin to see things going on around you that you don't understand, you may say to yourself, "Well, I said I was going to do this, and I was told that it was going to be hard. Now, some of this doesn't seem right to me, but I said I would go along with it, and I made a commitment. I'll stay in a little bit longer." All this time, of course, the leadership and everyone else around you are telling you that you better go along with it—in either subtle or not-so-subtle terms.

The fact that people don't like to just stand up and say "I quit" is also significant. Rather than be quitters, they will stick with it and stick with it. The longer they do, the harder it is to get out, so not wanting to be a quitter becomes yet another element that keeps them in the cult.

Authority Figures

Another major point of influence is that we're brought up to respect authority figures, leaders, people who are going to give us answers. We are told when we are young, and all through school, that there are answers and authorities. We are supposed to listen to the answers and look up to people who "know better."

So, when you are told not to question your cult, your rationale for doing as you are told is that doing otherwise would be disrespectful to the leader, who knows all. The leader knows better. The leader has the all-powerful answer. Your questions and doubts are discouraged.

To reinforce this rationale for obedience, each group usually has some kind of punishment pattern for violators. In particular, when you question, you may be made to look ridiculous and called a renegade, a spy, an agent, a nonbeliever, or Satan, or whatever disparaging terms are used in your particular group. There's always an internal language with terms to ridicule and denigrate. In some way, you are made to feel bad for doubting or questioning. You're convinced by the closed logic of the cult and by peer pressure that to question means you don't believe enough. So you stop questioning.

Ultimately, human beings do whatever they need to do to survive in a particular environment. When you're a cult member, a great deal of your environment and many of your life choices are controlled: your financial resources, access to information, the work you might do, your free time, your social circle, sometimes even your sex life is controlled. You adapt and learn to function and survive in order to remain part of the group. It's easier to conform, to go along with the flow and try to be a good believer and a good follower than to resist.

Peer Pressure and Lack of Information

Peer pressure is a critical factor in keeping people in cults. Former members have told me, "In my group we had doctors, lawyers, social workers, people with all kinds of advanced degrees, intelligent people. I would look around, and I'd think, Well, Joe's still doing it. Mary's still doing it. It must be me; it must be me. I just don't get it. There is just something wrong with me; I just have to try harder."

Cult members feel that way because nobody else is speaking out—because nobody *can* speak out. The one who does feels alone, isolated, contaminated, wrong. Directly or indirectly, all the cult members actively encourage each other to behave in certain ways. Since we are social animals, it is difficult to resist such pressures.

In addition, the cult's dishonesty about many things keeps members from knowing what is really going on. Members are not only kept from sources of outside information but are also told lies and misrepresentations about the cult, the leader, and the group's activities. The importance or influence of the cult's actions is made larger than it really is; the leader's reputation is embellished, if not fabricated; the number of members or followers is often exaggerated to make the group look larger and more popular; and world events are distorted, as are the outside world's attitudes toward the cult. All these myths about the cult and the society at large are generally perpetuated not only by the leader but by his inner circle of leadership as well. The resulting lack of knowledge among most members helps prevent them from making a real assessment of the situation they are in.

Exhaustion and Confusion

Exhaustion and confusion increase cult members' inability to act. In most groups, members are made to work morning, noon, and night. It's no wonder they become exhausted and unable to think straight. After several years of sixteen to twenty-hour workdays, seven days a week, no vacations, no time off, no fun, no hobbies, and no real, intimate relationship with your spouse, even if you have one, you're living in a fog world. Some former members describe feeling as though there were a veil over their eyes, as if they were not in touch with the physical world. They functioned by rote. Some people tend to laugh and say, "Oh, such-and-such cult members have glazed eyes." Well, in fact, they do. And that effect is partly caused by the sheer exhaustion the person is experiencing.

When you can't think, when you feel as though you can barely survive each day, all you want to do is get through that day without getting battered in whatever form that takes in your group—repetitive, meaningless work; criticism or exorbitant fund-raising quotas; or sexual abuse or other violence. You plod along and plod along and plod along. You are incredibly confused but don't know any way of dealing with your confusion.

You may have asked questions early on, but once the pace is set, you don't even have time to think what those questions were or what they might be now. All you want to do is get through the day and maybe get some sleep. And, you hope, survive.

Separation from the Past

Another notable factor that keeps people in cults is that they have been separated from their pasts. In almost every group, over the course of time, you break with your past. You no longer see family or friends who did not join the group. Maybe you tried to recruit them, and they weren't interested. In many cases, you no longer have much contact at all with the outside world.

Some people work internally in the group for the entire duration of their membership. They don't go to an outside job every day. They have little or no human contact other than with members of the cult. If they go on a recruitment drive or an organizing assignment or to a public event, they are out in the world for a purpose. What contact with others they do have is completely superficial and controlled by the group, with briefings beforehand, debriefings afterward, and meticulous reporting mechanisms to monitor members' behavior when they are away from the cult.

In this way, your entire universe becomes the people you are with, what you are doing each day, the meetings you go to, and the house you live in, probably with other members. You are completely surrounded by that, and eventually forget about your past.

You even forget who you were before you joined. In some groups, people take on new names and often don't know the real names of the other members. Even those who share living arrangements aren't allowed to tell housemates their real names. Everything is to be kept secret: members are instructed to get postal boxes for their mail, use pseudonyms when possible, and maintain a low profile. Another name, a completely new identity, and very little connection to your past—these are strong influences that keep people bound to the group.

After living in an environment where everyone thinks and acts alike, even if you aren't as sequestered as those in the more restrictive cults, your outlook shrinks and your ability to communicate atrophies. If you do happen to see your family, it's so alienating that all you want to do is rush back to the group. Even though cult life is miserable and deprived, in some bizarre way the group is where you are comfortable because it's what you've come to know. It's familiar; it's your daily environment, your home and family.

In this context, to think about leaving becomes completely overwhelming. If escape even crosses your mind, you think, Where would I go? What would I do? Who would accept me? You have lost so much self-esteem that the thought of leaving is unbearable. You can't imagine abandoning your protected little universe to go out into the horrible world that all this time you've been trained to believe is the other, the evil, the bourgeois society, or of Satan. The nonbelievers are not going to accept you. The minute they find out you were "that," you are going to die on the spot or be chased away. Nobody would hire you; nobody would want you; you will never have a relationship. You are a loser.

All this is going on in your mind because, one way or another, you were told those things in the cult, and you've internalized them through the training sessions and the power of the cult milieu. Because of your profound separation from the world, you think you can never leave, and you enter a kind of emotional and psychological paralysis. (Not to mention that many cult members have little access to money, and just on the practical side, don't think they could get very far even if they did leave.)

Fear

Another reason people don't leave cults is simply that they are afraid. Many groups chase after defectors. They threaten them, punish them, put them under house arrest. If members try to get away, they are stopped by the cult; if they make the mistake of telling someone they are thinking of leaving, they are suspended from group activities, ostracized, and punished. They are criticized, put in the hot seat, and in most cases rather quickly "convinced" to stay. As a member of the group, you come to know of these occurrences and dread such a fate befalling you. Once again, leaving does not seem like a feasible option.

In some cases, members are expelled. They are literally thrown out of the group or deposited in front of a psychiatric ward or their parents' home. Then, back at the cult, they are denounced and defiled. They are entered on a roster of enemies and nonpeople. Horrendous lies are told about them to reinforce the cult's line on why they are no longer members. Such denunciation is not a pleasant prospect for someone thinking of leaving. The pariah image takes on enormous proportions and coming to fit that image seems a fate worse than death.

Guilt over Participation

The final factor that closes the trap's door is the cult member's active participation. Whether or not you care to admit it, you have invested in cult life. It's hard to leave that—partly because there is still part of you that wants to believe this really is going to work, and partly because of the shame and the guilt you feel. You've been party to activities that in normal life you'd probably never have considered—acts that are morally reprehensible, actions that you never would have believed you could have carried out or witnessed. That kind of guilt and shame keeps people in cults. It keeps them from simply saying, "I'm going to get up and go now."

Through the cult experience and all these influences, an *enforced dependency* is developed. You may have started out as a completely autonomous independent individual, but after a certain amount of time, even though you may not want to admit it, you become completely dependent on the group for all your social needs, your family needs, your self-image, and your survival. To varying degrees, you are told every day what to do, and so you regress. You become like a child for whom any thought of independent action is totally confusing and unbearably overwhelming. How can a child get up and leave after being led to believe that she or he could not function without the grace of the leadership and the group?

Because of the powerful combination of belief, loyalty, dependency, guilt, fear, peer pressure, lack of information, and fatigue, all of which probably have equal psychological weight, members do not readily leave cults. Decent, honorable people do not easily give up on commitments, and the cult environment is such that it makes leaving practically impossible.

Many cult members, especially those who remain at a low status within the group, endure a state of mental conflict and torment for years. Others rise in the cult hierarchy and are taught to perpetuate the manipulative system. They learn to fake miracles, fake cures, give false presentations on cult victories, and cover for the corrupt leader. Their role is to enforce obedience and dependency, and they learn to rationalize their own behavior as well as that of the leader. Despite knowing the falsehoods, they stay because of the status and power they enjoy. They also stay because they are trapped by the same influences as the others, plus they feel enormous guilt and fear blackmail and retribution from the cult.

In a number of cults, armed guards see that defectors and those being punished do not leave. One woman I counseled who had tried to leave her cult was held by armed guards in the cult compound for a year before she finally escaped. For two years afterward, she slept with her clothes on so she would have a chance of getting away if the leader sent his guards after her.

Great trauma is associated with the experience of imprisonment. The degrading of members that is central to most cults is especially intense during punishment and even more intense during various forms of cult imprisonment. Former members who have had such experiences often break down while telling about the hopeless, lonely, fearful time they had while imprisoned. Even when eventually freed, they usually remained in the cult for long periods afterward because of fear coupled with emotional devastation. Some ex–cult members I have counseled described being held under prisonlike conditions in their cults for periods from a few months up to seven years, sometimes on several occasions before they finally were able to leave. These detentions have been documented in legal cases and verified by other ex-members.

One of the most illustrative stories about the difficulty of leaving a cult concerns two people who had been high in the power structure of a cult and deeply inculcated with the group's routines and rules. When they finally ran away, they were so dutiful that they called the home base of the cult from the airport, not only to say they were leaving but also where they were going. The cult official they spoke to rented a private plane to be flown to their destination, met them there, and took them back to the cult. Friends have not been able to locate them since this happened.

Ways of Leaving the Cult

The good news is that eventually most cult members leave their cults. They tend to do this in one of three ways.

First, many leave of their own accord because they become disillusioned, fed up, or burnt out, or they realize the cult is not what it said it was. The contradictions simply become too glaring and can no longer be ignored. They muster up their courage and make the break. Often a particular incident sparks their move. For example, one cult member whose mother came to visit from two continents away was not allowed to see her mother for more than one hour because of her cult duties. Although she went along with the delay at the time, it continued to grate on her until she eventually succeeded in a plan to escape. Cult members who leave in this way are known as *walkaways*.

Second, some members are thrown out by the cult for various reasons ranging from a policy of discarding members who break down mentally or physically from the stresses of the cult life to deliberate programs in which the cult leader decides for economic or other reasons to cut back the size of the group or to get rid of someone. Sometimes the leader is willing to sacrifice a few disaffected or "independent" members in order to teach a lesson to the others that he can discard them, too, if they don't behave. Often these purges instill immense fear in the remaining members, who may be totally dependent, guilt ridden, and convinced that they cannot function in the larger world. Cult members who leave in this way are sometimes called *castaways*.

Third, nonmembers—usually family or friends and a team made up of exit counselors and former members—may meet with a cult member and give him or her information and support that makes it possible to make a fully informed choice about membership in the group. That is, the cult member is given the opportunity, through what is now called an exit counseling session or intervention, to reevaluate her or his membership and commitment and decide whether to remain or to leave the group.

Leaving a cult is for many one of the most difficult things they will ever do. And it's especially difficult to do alone. That is a prime reason for the success of family interventions, exit counseling, and other methods of providing the cult member with support and information.

Deprogramming and Exit Counseling

I first heard the term *deprogramming* in 1972. Before that, I had listened to many parents and families describe how one or more members of their family had joined one of the new cults. After just a few days or weeks of cult membership, the family member seemed unable or unwilling to respond freely in conversations. Instead, the new cult member answered questions mechanically and responded in stereotyped, rehearsed jargon that had just come into his or her vocabulary. The cult member made pronouncements, spouted slogans and dogma, and didn't participate in give-and-take conversations as before.

Families chose the term *programmed* to describe the rapid changes they were noticing in their family member's personality, changes that were not typical of the person they knew. It was not that their relative had taken up a new religion or joined a communal group that caused these families concern; it was the *types* of changes they were seeing: abrupt changes that did not suggest growth but rigid, inflexible thinking and a constriction of feeling. Previously warm, outgoing young adults with many interests and friends and a plan for the future suddenly dropped school, hobbies, and goals, and shunned their families.

Families also noticed that the cultic group itself was preventing them from talking with their relatives. Some families tried for years to learn where to mail letters, send a present, or phone. Other families hadn't seen their offspring at all for six to twenty years, and some still don't know if these people are alive. Many parents and grandparents have died without ever knowing what happened to their loved one who joined a cult.

In those instances in which a family could meet with the cult member or speak with him or her on the phone, the family had the distinct impression that the person was cutting them off and no longer seemed connected to the family or the past. Conversations with the cult member were like listening to tapes, with the person lecturing dogmatically, trying to recruit the rest of the family into the group.

Sometimes parents could tell that phone calls were being monitored, with the cult member rather obviously being instructed what to say. Parents with children who had been in graduate school showed me letters from them that seemed like the products of grade school children. These families witnessed a marked regression in almost all areas of behavior from speech to writing to appearance. Sometimes they also noted a great reduction of knowledge about current events. For example, young adults who previously had been politically active in liberal causes began spouting right-wing dogma. Others seemed unaware of occurrences in the world since joining the cult.

Families were baffled and concerned. They felt that their children's life plans, attitudes, ways of talking, and value systems had changed too greatly and too rapidly. These families were without words to label what they saw, but they desperately wanted to convey their experiences and concerns. They often made such comments as "spacey," "programmed," "not herself anymore," "a different person now," "they changed him somehow," and "she has a ten-mile stare in her eyes."

Parents took every avenue they could think of—talking to university student affairs offices, school counselors, pastors, mental health professionals, the police, private investigators, and their elected officials—in efforts to bring attention to this problem. In 1976, U.S. Senator Robert Dole, of Kansas, responded to a petition signed by fourteen thousand citizens from various states, asking for an investigation into such matters. Approximately four hundred persons—parents, former cult members, and concerned citizens—from thirty-two states met with a panel of federal officials to speak out against cults. Senator Dole presided and was assisted by U.S. Senator James Buckley, of New York, and U.S. Congressman George O'Brien, of Illinois. A transcript of this meeting was produced and distributed; however, no legislative action followed.

Between 1974 and 1976, three state legislature hearings—in New York, California, and Vermont—also produced testimony and reports about cult members and brought out descriptions of the way cult members' "dependence on the group and the thought structures it offers results in gradual changes in the language base in which discourse and thought are carried out. Old, emotion-laden words are given new, rigid, simplified meanings. The new vocabulary is at once literal, magical and task-oriented. Converts' speech patterns demonstrate a lack of humor and an inability to appreciate and use metaphor. Critical thinking and the asking of questions are discouraged; converts are taught to feel rather than think."

In this same period, psychiatrists, psychologists, and psychiatric social workers dealing with cult members suggested behavioral changes they labeled the *cult indoctrinee syndrome*. These changes included:

- *Sudden, drastic alteration of the individual's value hierarchy, including abandonment of previous academic and career goals.* These changes are sudden and catastrophic, rather than the gradual ones that result from maturation or education.
- *Reduction of cognitive flexibility and adaptability.* The cult member substitutes stereotyped cult responses for her or his own.
- *Narrowing and blunting of affect.* Love feelings are repressed. The cult member appears emotionally flatter and less vital than before.
- *Regression of behavior to childlike levels.* The follower becomes dependent on the cult leader and accepts the leader's decisions uncritically.
- *Physical changes.* These changes often include weight loss and deterioration in physical appearance and expression.
- *Possible pathological symptoms.* Such symptoms can include altered states of consciousness.

A number of families noticing such dramatic changes became desperate about what to do. In an effort to counter what they considered to be the cult's programming, they arranged meetings with the cult member to try to reawaken the person's critical thinking abilities so that he or she could rethink the decision to stay with the cult, and it was this process that came to be called deprogramming.

In the late 1970s, families were also occasionally able to find legal recourse through gaining conservatorships. In this legal procedure, parents or family go before a judge to attempt to establish that a person, in this case the relative in the cult, lacks the capacity to care for herself or himself or fails to show a degree of judgment adequate to conduct her or his daily life. Therefore the family requests that a family member be allowed to take over the care of that person to protect the person's interests. Courts in various states granted such conservatorships for short periods of time.

This legal recourse was especially effective when the cults deceived families about the whereabouts of relatives, because the cults had to produce these relatives and allow them to be with their families for the period decreed by the court. Often, during that time, the person would meet with deprogrammers and would not return to the cult. The cults soon worked to get legislation changed to make conservatorships more difficult to obtain, so today this method of locating a cult member, particularly a relative who has been hidden or moved about, is extremely limited.

Beginnings of Deprogramming

Around 1972, as parents and others with relatives or friends in cults began talking about the deprogrammings occurring here and there around the United States, two names—Joe Alexander, Sr., and Ted Patrick—began to be associated with deprogramming efforts. In order to give a practical description of deprogramming, I will explain first how these men became involved in the world of cults and then present the details of the revised form of deprogramming known as exit counseling that is used today.

Joe Alexander's brother had an only son who in 1968 had just completed college. Between graduation and the beginning of medical school, he was recruited into the Tony and Susan Alamo Foundation, a Los Angeles–based group that eventually spread to other areas. The young man was in the group from 1968 until 1970 when Mr. Alexander, who had been in contact with two other families who had information about the group, planned a debriefing and got his nephew to meet with him, the young man's father, and the two sets of parents.

By the time they all met, the older adults had educated themselves about the Alamo Foundation, its leaders, and how influence and manipulation worked in that particular cult. They successfully presented information and reasoning, and the young man decided to leave the group. Before long, word of this success spread, and parents were seeking out Joe Alexander to help them. Mr. Alexander told me that during a five-year period he deprogrammed six hundred individuals.

Next on the scene, in 1971, was Ted Patrick, who was California Governor Ronald Reagan's Special Representative for Community Relations in San Diego and Imperial Counties. On the Fourth of July of that year, Mr. Patrick rented a hotel suite on Mission Beach in San Diego. His family, his nephews, and their friends came along, and the young people went to Belmont Park to watch the fireworks. Mr. Patrick's son, age fourteen, and one of his nephews did not return with the others. About half past midnight, just as Mr. Patrick was calling the police, in walked the boys.

Mr. Patrick said that he thought his son had been smoking marijuana or drinking: he looked vacant, glazed, and drifting. The nephew was less spacey and described being stopped by people with Bibles and guitars. The boys said that "there was something about them. We couldn't leave." The group (later learned to be the Children of God) wanted the boys to go with them and reportedly promised that they wouldn't have to work anymore, they'd never be sick again, they wouldn't have any problems, and they wouldn't have to go to church or school even—because those things "are of the Devil and [your] parents are of Satan."

After getting the two boys settled and safe, Ted Patrick went out and allowed himself to be recruited by the Children of God (COG). He spent some days with the cult in order to see how it operated. He concluded from firsthand observation that COG was "programming" people to its ways and ideas. This reinforced the growing idea that cult members were being programmed and that the antidote was deprogramming—that is, providing members with information about the cult and showing them how their own decision-making power had been taken away from them. Mr. Patrick says that over several years in the mid 1970s he deprogrammed about one thousand cult members.

This is not the place to go into details about the multitude of events that have transpired since. During the early years of deprogramming, desperate parents and dedicated deprogrammers were occasionally arrested for abducting cult members off the streets and conducting what came to be called involuntary deprogrammings, and a number of court cases ensued. But on the whole, most of the deprogrammings of that era worked, and the cult members elected to leave the groups, while the legal complications involved with abductions or the forcible restraining of cult members from leaving their homes or the deprogramming sites caused many people to seek other methods of getting their friends or relatives out of a cult.

The term *exit counseling* first came into use to distinguish voluntary interventions from deprogrammings. Today, exit counseling identifies the educational process that takes place in efforts to get cult members to reevaluate their membership. In fact, "deprogramming" is in many ways a more accurate description of the process of getting the cult member to recognize what has happened to him or her, but since that word is now tinged with memories of the early snatchings and restraint, most people are reluctant to use it.

As the early deprogrammers presented their materials to cult members, these people left their cults to become informed, happy-to-be-out *former* cult members. Hundreds of these young adults, scattered across the United States and elsewhere, most of them with some college or even professional training, saw what had happened to them and wanted to share this knowledge.

Today, to make a long history short, these and other cult veterans are for the most part the people who meet and work with cult members' families and who participate in the multitude of voluntary exit counseling sessions that now go on regularly around the world. And when I say families, I am not talking simply about parents concerned about their children. People in many family roles are working with exit counselors and cult information specialists in the hope of gaining access to a parent, a cousin, an aunt or uncle, a grandparent, a good friend, or a spouse who is in a cult.

Exit counselors assist these people to learn about cults in general as well as the specific group they are involved with and about manipulative influence techniques and thought-reform processes. They work with families to see if a voluntary meeting with the cult member can be set up. These meetings are sometimes called *family interventions*, and they are similar to family interventions with alcoholics and drug abusers. An intervention or exit counseling session includes the person in the cult, an exit counseling team, and select family or friends. If the cult member does not agree to meet, the meeting does not happen.

What Goes On in Exit Counseling

Exit counseling is a process of providing and exchanging information. Exit counselors have to be expert on thought-reform techniques and on the particular cult the person is in. Usually a member of the team is a former member of that cult and can provide specific details and an insider's knowledge. The team must know the cult's language and idiom and its history and content and have extensive documented data about the leader. The team comes prepared with documents, videotapes, audiotapes, and as much information as possible related to the group and its activities.

Beyond knowledge, however, there must be a fit, or match, between the team and the cult member. The effectiveness of exit counseling hinges as much on rapport as skill and knowledge, and all present must participate in the information process.

The team has a plan of what material to present, but generally what comes first, second, and third will depend on the reactions and openness of the cult member as she or he is presented with the information.

The members of the exit counseling team do two things: they present details about the cult and cult leader that have not been available to the cult member, and they explain thought reform and the systematic social and psychological influences that have been used to get the person to reject the past and take up the ways dictated by the cult. The idea is to offer access to such information in a safe atmosphere, where a free discussion can occur and where the cult member is protected from the pressures and influences that have led her or him, a step at a time, to give up her or his freedom and become dependent on the group and distrusting or rejecting of the world.

In this environment, the cult member can ask questions, respond, and deal with feelings and attitudes toward the information. The advantage of having former cult members present is that they will be able to talk about their experiences, describe how they made the decision to leave, and share what they now know about the group and why they want the current member to have access to information that will allow for an uncoerced choice about continued membership.

Simply the presence of a healthy, thriving former member will make a big impression on the cult member, since most groups instill fear and guilt so that members think they can no longer make it on the outside or that they or their families will be threatened or harmed if they leave the group. When the cult member sees that another member has left the group, is surviving, and perhaps even performing the altruistic activities the current member thought she or he was going to be performing by becoming involved with the cult, the member is greatly reassured by this proof of life after the cult. Former cult members are a solid and lively antidote to the cult's induction of phobia.

Many exit counselors will also have reading material and videos on thought reform and coercive persuasion available, and the content of this material can be discussed in an atmosphere of acceptance. In the cult milieu, the member can never discuss how bad she or he feels about deceptive fund-raising or luring others into the group, how disenchanted she or he often feels, or nagging questions about certain activities, since cults condemn such concerns. But here the cult member has the opportunity to evaluate what happened in the cult and how it happened, and can ask all the questions she or he wants.

As information is shared and discussed, the counseling session might extend from several hours to a series of meetings and discussions over several days. Generally, as the cult member grasps the content of what is being presented, she or he will want to hear more and will decide to stay in the session. At first, the person may be defensive and resistant, then slowly she or he will become a more active participant in the process—asking and answering questions, expressing suppressed doubts, and providing more examples of what is being discussed.

This is not an easy process. It can be highly emotional, very stressful, fatiguing, and full of conflict. The support and understanding of the family members and the team are key to the progress and outcome of the session. Also, as the reader can see, this work requires specialists with the right kind of knowledge and skill. This is not therapy. The team is not there to change behavior but to provide and discuss information and be able to follow up on the reassessment that may occur. The cult member sees and hears in a respectful, nonargumentative setting some things that range from interesting to appalling. Exit counselors must know how to deal with a cult member's growing recognition that she or he wants to get out of the group.

One man who had been in a cult for three years told me he had a phenomenal experience partway through his exit counseling. He said he suddenly felt that his mind was like a muscle that he was beginning to exercise. He said he knew it sounded odd to describe thinking actively, as if it were exercise, but that's what it was. Many individuals begin to mentally emerge during the exit counseling. Others, such as this man, have a real "aha" experience.

Another man, whose mother and sister came from Australia to be with him during his exit counseling, said that when he met them in their hotel room where the session was to take place, he realized something odd about himself that he had not put into words until then. He felt at first that he was inside a glass booth in which he could hear them, but the invisible barrier was preventing him from feeling connected or attached. But at some point during the exit counseling, he suddenly began to weep and feel. For the first time in ages, he felt real feelings, knew he was back in the real world, and was not about to leave it again.

Although no one can make guarantees as to the outcome of a session, most exit counselors agree that if they are given sufficient time to present their information—usually three days—the cult member will decide not to return to the group in about 90 percent of the cases. Of those who choose to go back to the cult—generally because they do not stay to hear enough information and discuss it—60 percent eventually leave the cult at a later date.

After a cult member decides not to return to the group, he or she may benefit from spending a week or two at a rehabilitation center that specializes in cult-related cases. Over the past decades, a number of rehab centers have existed for those coming out of cults although only one is currently available: Wellspring Retreat and Resource Center in Albany, Ohio. This facility is run by Dr. Paul Martin, a clinical psychologist and cult expert. Some years back, Dr. Martin was in a cult himself. Therefore he also has the advantage of personal experience.

Ex-members may spend one to three weeks at the rehab center, receiving further education about cults and being debriefed about their time in a cult, a process that is extremely useful for recovery from the experience. They have contact with professionals and cult experts who are able to discuss the information the former members have received either in exit counseling or in the course of their own departure from the group, they view educational videos on cults and thought reform, and explore options for the future in an unpressured environment. All the guests at the center are in the same place in their lives—coming back into mainstream society. Families can also join in and learn more about how the cult experience affected the cult member and gain some appreciation of what transpired in the cult.

Who Becomes an Exit Counselor

In 1981, I interviewed ninety persons to ask how they got into exit counseling, what it was that they did, and the results of their efforts.

Fifteen exit counselors were mental health professionals, and four of these professionals had been in cults themselves. Two had walked away from their group, the other two had been picked up by their families and taken to a deprogramming. Eight others had no personal connections to cults but had been therapists to ex–cult members and thus had learned how the cults used social and psychological manipulations to change behavior and attitudes. These professionals worked primarily with former cult members as co-partners in the exit counseling sessions. The remaining three professionals had gotten a son or daughter out of a cult through a conservatorship and subsequent deprogramming and later used their knowledge to help others.

Forty-five of the ninety exit counselors were ex–cult members who had been deprogrammed themselves by one of the pioneer deprogrammers and then worked as assistants in those early efforts. The remaining thirty were either relatives of former cult members or clergy who had become knowledgeable about the cult problem. They knew the details of certain cults intimately and had read and gathered information about thought reform.

The early exit counselors said they learned the importance of preparing families for exit counseling and also helped them understand the necessity of their participation in the actual process when it occurred. Parents, friends, and family were present or nearby at all those early exit counseling sessions, as they are today. Through planning and discussion prior to the actual meetings, families learned what each family member might have to contribute both during a session and afterward. This is an important step, since families often do not do enough planning for what needs to be done when the cult member leaves the group: Where will the person go? Where will the person live? How will the person be supported financially until he or she is able to be fully employed and on his or her own again?

Choosing an Exit Counselor

Many families begin their search for assistance with an investigation by telephone, finding out who knows about cults and who can help them. (In the back of this book are a list of further readings and a list of resource organizations that can provide general information.)

Through their research, families learn the names and phone numbers of one or more exit counselors by talking with friends, professionals, and ex-members of cults. Each family selects the exit counselor who seems to best fit its needs, basing the selection on an assessment of the counselor's manner, experience, and knowledge, as well as on personal recommendations. Then the planning begins.

Most exit counselors have family members take the time to fill out history forms in addition to the information they give the counselor over the phone. Often family members feel a lot of pressure to rescue their loved one and want to act right away. Without good planning with an experienced exit counselor, however, much can be lost and little gained.

The exit counselor's initial consultation with the family, typically on the phone, will likely cover the following questions:

- How long has the person been with the cult?
- What is the name of the group? What is the leader's name?
- What information does the family have about the group and its leader? (Some groups are large and well known, and much literature exists about them. Other groups are small, new, and unknown.) Is it a nomadic group or a stationary group? Where is its home base?
- What occurred just prior to the person's entering the group— what setbacks, losses, disappointments?
- How was the person recruited? What were the circumstances?
- How much has the person changed and in what ways?
- How much family consensus is there about the member's condition?
- How unified is the family's view of the cult?
- What in general would the family like to see occur?
- Where is the cult member now?

- What agencies and individuals have been contacted and what was learned?
- Has the family spoken to college authorities, friends of the cult member, parent support groups, ex–cult members, other exit counselors, pastors, the police, the immigration service, and so on? What was learned?
- How informed are family members about thought reform and coercive persuasion?
- What related books and articles have been read?
- What actions have been considered to contact and aid the cult member?

After this information-gathering stage, if the exit counselor has agreed to work with the family and fees have been settled, additional possible team members will be discussed, as well as who else (immediate family, friends, or other relatives) will be involved. Usually the lead exit counselor will suggest one or two persons to be present when the actual meeting with the cult member takes place. The exit counselor then teaches the family members who will be present how to communicate with the cult member and how to set the meeting in motion. Each case is very complicated and involves close cooperation and responsibility on the part of the family and the team.

Exit counselors typically charge between $500 and $1,000 a day, plus expenses—a fee schedule similar to that of many other consultants. Exit counselors have to study and keep abreast of the ever-changing cult scene and collect data, films, and documents from and about the various groups. Many exit counselors do not charge for the extensive phone time that is involved. Most offer free clinics for ex-members and donate hundreds of free hours lecturing to schools, churches, and other organizations. Their typical workday is twelve to sixteen hours. Often they are "on call" for some time while the family sets up the meeting time and place. In addition, many exit counselors are targets of harassment, verbal abuse, and threats of spurious lawsuits by cults. As described earlier, many of the large international cults have nearly unlimited financial resources as well as in-house lawyers to intimidate exit counselors and their other critics.

Before contracting with any exit counselor, a family should inquire as to exactly what the counselor's process is like and what the potential pitfalls and successes are. Books and other material written by exit counselors are available that describe the process in detail. They explain not only the necessity of family preparation but also outline what the family can expect from the exit counselor.

Mental Health Professionals and Clergy as Counselors

For the most part, mental health professionals and clergy who are not expert in cults are also not the best professionals for exit counseling. They are often the least informed about what is involved, at a time when families need real information about cults and groups using thought-reform processes, as well as an objective evaluation of family options.

Families who call upon these clergy or mental health professionals are almost always told some variant of "It's just a passing stage; he will outgrow it," or "There is nothing to be done; she is forty years old (or seventy)." Because in most cases these professionals don't recognize how intense influence, social pressure, and cult interactions affect cult members, they simply turn away or misdirect the family.

Clergy who are not knowledgeable about cults may resort to arguing doctrine with a cult member. Experience shows that such an approach is not the way to begin. Indeed, it merely reinforces the cult leader's propaganda. A person in a religious cult, for example, will have been taught that mainline clergy, the outside world, parents, relatives, and friends are evil, simply wrong about everything, and should be disbelieved. If the cult in question is not a religious group, a member of the clergy may not make the best impression on the cult member because his or her interests are not religious.

Similarly, mental health professionals who are unaware on the whole of the procedures and effects of cults do not grasp what is needed to help cult members and their families. Rarely is a family seeking family therapy when contacting a mental health professional about a family member in a cult. Rather the family is seeking information and consultation in order to determine the best way to respond to the situation. Whether the parental or marital family is involved, the family's psychoeducational and referral needs should be met before traditional psychotherapy is considered. The family wants to learn about the reality of their concerns and then gain information about their options.

Exit Counseling Versus Therapy

Most persons leaving cults are not severely mentally ill, but those occasional ones who are should, of course, be referred to a psychiatrist or psychologist knowledgeable about cults.

From my interviews with many former cult members—some who have received exit counseling and some who have not—it has become apparent that participation in an exit counseling session is far better than ordinary psychiatric or psychological treatment, both for assisting people who are in cults to evaluate whether they want to stay in, and for helping those who have already left but are having trouble understanding and handling what went on during their cult days and the types of problems they are experiencing in the aftermath of their cult involvement.

There are two reasons why exit counseling is preferable. First, former cult members need information and explanations about what produced changes in them while they were in the cult. Since exit counselors understand how coercive persuasion works and how group influence and social pressure affect people's thinking, behavior, spirit, and emotions, they can educate the former member. They also understand and are able to explain some of the typical aftereffects of meditation or trance induction, intense coercion, past-lives regression, extensive blaming sessions, the destabilization of a person's sense of reality, and other persuasion techniques used by cults.

Second, ordinary psychiatric and psychological counseling focuses almost exclusively on early life experiences and childhood history and the impact of these early years. Not only do most of us have a blind spot that prevents us from realizing how we are being influenced all the time throughout our lives, but professional training programs for psychotherapists have also overlooked this significant phenomenon. They have become locked into inspecting only early childhood influences and experiences and give almost no training that focuses therapists on adult experiences of intense social influence and group situations.

Thus both mental health professionals and clergy need to educate themselves about cultic influences. In particular, clergy need to be aware that many people suffer spiritual abuse in cults and need special education when they seek to reconnect with nonmanipulative spiritual and religious groups. It is my hope that this book and others addressing recovery from cultic experiences will be of use to professionals as well as former members and their families.

Exit Counseling Today

Recently, I again surveyed who is active in exit counseling, and over the decade since my original study there have been many developments of interest. Just as it is difficult to estimate how many people are in cults, it's equally difficult to ascertain how many exit counselors there are today. Nevertheless, there are a few developments we can review.

A group of exit counselors has formed an association with bylaws and ethical standards. The counselors' purpose was to spell out the appropriate arrangements and understandings between counselor and client, and to elucidate just what will and will not occur as part of an exit counseling. Because of the controversy surrounding deprogramming, much effort is being made to educate the public about ethical exit counseling.

Also according to my most recent survey, a great majority of those providing exit counseling services now are former cult members, and in many cases have been exit counseled themselves. There are exit counselors in the United States, Canada, England, France, Spain, Sweden, and Denmark, and probably many more in other countries.

Most exit counseling is done by small groups of two or three persons—usually the lead exit counselor and one or more former members, especially former members of the group in question. However, there is no way of estimating the number of these former members who participate on exit counseling teams in collaboration with experienced exit counselors. Whenever work begins with a family, the lead exit counselor generally contacts former cult members to benefit from their participation in the entire process.

From the very early days of my work with ex–cult members, I have noticed that those who have been deprogrammed or counseled out make the easiest, best, and quickest returns to normal life. Other professionals have found the same thing, which suggests that the education and information provided by exit counseling may be extremely valuable, helping those leaving cults to understand their own situation and feelings and to adapt to life in the regular world.

Obviously, it's not possible to speak for the thousands upon thousands of walkaways from cults. But among those I've counseled and heard about from others in the field, it appears that individuals who leave groups on their own must debrief themselves of the cult experience through reading, contact with other ex-members, and in some cases therapy dealing with cult-related issues before they come to understand the impact that the cult experience has had on their emotional and daily life. This pattern also suggests why exit counseling is of value.

Relatives and friends who set up an exit counseling are not doing it to control or thwart the cult member. They become desperate as they learn more about the group in question, and they merely want to give their loved one in the cult some choice. And exit counseling is voluntary; it is not a badgering and attack program. It is an educational exchange of information about thought reform and about the cult. Exit counseling is a time of thinking and of illuminating ideas. If successful, it sparks in cult members the desire to evaluate their commitment to the group, to assess their goals and what they want to do with their life. This assessment can only occur away from the pressures and fears of the cult.

I keep seeing in my mind pictures in a California home not too many miles from my house. They are the photos of two beautiful young women in the Koresh cult in Waco, Texas, whom the family was hoping to meet with in an exit counseling session. But Koresh sacrificed the group before the family could complete the plans.

12

Recovery: Coming Out of the Pseudopersonality

Just as cults vary greatly, so do their members, their after-effects, and the duration of those effects. Yet those who help former cult members have seen certain patterns in the types of trauma, damage, and emotional and cognitive difficulties. This has been true for former members of a variety of cults and groups that use thought-reform processes.

Not everyone who is exposed to thought-reform processes is successfully manipulated, however; nor does everyone respond with major reactive symptons. An evaluation of what a person may experience after belonging to a cult requires study of the group's particular practices, social and psychological pressures, and conditions. Nevertheless, groups using thought-reform processes can be usefully classed into two main categories: those that primarily use dissociative techniques and those that primarily use emotional arousal techniques. Each category produces characteristic negative psychological effects.

Former members of groups relying mainly on the use of *dissociative techniques*—meditation, trance states, guided imagery, past-lives regression, and hyperventilation—have tended to exhibit these aftereffects:

- Relaxation-induced anxiety and tics
- Panic attacks

- Cognitive inefficiencies
- Dissociative states
- Recurring bizarre content (such as orange fog)
- Worry over the reality of "past lives"

Eastern-based cults and New Age groups doing past-lives work and channeling fall into this first category.

Former members of groups using primarily intense *aversive emotional arousal techniques*—guilt and fear induction, strict discipline and punishments, excessive criticism and blame—have tended to experience these aftereffects:

- Guilt
- Shame
- Self-blaming attitudes
- Fears and paranoia
- Excessive doubts
- Panic attacks

Bible-based, political, racial, occult, and psychotherapy cults typically fit into this category.

However, although cults tend to focus on one category or the other, they often use a multitude of techniques and do not restrict themselves to one or the other of these major groupings. For example, the large group awareness training programs and some psychotherapy cults use both kinds of techniques. Moreover, a group relying heavily on meditation, trance, and dissociative techniques is also likely to include elements of intense emotional arousal devices, and the reverse is also true. Some of the most intense emotional arousal responses can be produced by guided imagery, speaking in tongues, and other trance-inducing procedures. Thus it is important not to regard this heuristic division too rigidly, since the techniques readily overlap and can produce a range of responses.

Some aftereffects may be experienced by former members regardless of the kind of cult they were in. These general aftereffects are:

- Depression and a sense of alienation
- Loneliness
- Low self-esteem and low self-confidence
- Phobic-like constriction of social contacts
- Fear of joining groups or making a commitment
- Distrust of professional services
- Distrust of self in making good choices
- Problems in reactivating a value system to live by

Recovering from Cult Aftereffects

Once out of the cult, former cult members, although now free, face the challenge of reentering the society they once rejected. The array of necessary adjustments can be summed up as coming out of the pseudopersonality, or as others have termed it, dropping the synthetic identity or reuniting with the split-off old self. An additional helpful way to view the many problems faced by former cult members is to cluster them into the five major areas of adjustment: practical, psychological-emotional, cognitive, social-personal, and philosophical-attitudinal (see Table 12.1). Former cult members must

- Address *practical* issues related to daily living
- Face *psychological* and *emotional* stirrings that can cause intense agonies for a while
- Deal with *cognitive inefficiencies*
- Develop a new *social* network and repair old *personal* relationships, if possible
- Examine the *philosophical* and *attitudinal* content adopted during cult days

It is through dealing with all these areas that the former cult member gains insight into his or her experience and, over time, sheds the cult pseudopersonality.

In this chapter, I will explore each of these areas of adjustment, presenting them in a sequence that gives a feel for what must take place: a kind of peeling off of the outer layer of identity that was taken on while in the cult. The process is a matter of recovering one's self and one's value system, and of keeping whatever good was learned during cult days while discarding all the not-so-good. (Of course, in actuality, life and growth are multilevel and multidimensional, not the orderly sequence of compartmentalized events that I have adopted for convenience here.)

Table 12.1. Major Areas of Postcult Adjustment.

Practical	Psychological-Emotional	Cognitive	Social-Personal	Philosophical-Attitudinal
Makes living arrangements. Arranges financial support. Arranges medical & dental care. Examines nutrition & eating habits. Gets psychological examination, if needed. Makes career & educational plans, & gets vocational counseling, if needed. Explains the years in the cult. Structures daily life.	Feels depressed. Has feelings of loss. Feels guilt & regret. Lacks self-esteem & self-confidence; exhibits self-blaming attitudes & excessive doubts. Has panic attacks. Experiences relaxation-induced anxiety (RIA) & tics. Separates from family & friends still in the cult. Exhibits fear of the group.	Experiences indecisiveness. Experiences blurring of mental acuity. Has difficulty concentrating. Has memory loss. Cannot recall what was just read or heard. Must stop using cult language. Has sense of losing track of time. Experiences floating, slipping into altered states. Has poor & unreliable sense of judgment.	Has pervasive sense of alienation. Needs to reconnect with family & friends. Needs to make new friends. Distrusts own ability to make good choices. Has phobic-like constriction of social contacts; mistrusts/distrusts others. Feels loneliness. Is confused about sexuality & sexual identity & roles.	Has hypercritical attitude toward others & society. Needs to overcome aversions ingrained by the cult. Has condemning attitude toward normal human foibles & is harsh toward self & others; still judges by cult standards. Lacks satisfaction with the world & self; feels emptiness at no longer being a world saver.

Not all former cult members encounter all the problems listed in Table 12.1, nor do most have them in severe and extended form. Some individuals need only a few months to get themselves going again. After encountering some adjustment problems to life outside the cult, they make rather rapid and uneventful reintegrations into everyday life. Generally, however, it takes individuals anywhere from six to twenty-four months to get their lives functioning again at a level commensurate with their histories and talents. Even then, however, that functioning may not reflect what is still going on inside them. Many are still sorting out the

Table 12.1. Major Areas of Postcult Adjustment. (Cont.)

Practical	Psychological-Emotional	Cognitive	Social-Personal	Philosophical-Attitudinal
Copes with difficulties created by distrust of professional services: medical, dental, & mental health professionals & educators.	Feels generalized paranoia & fear of the world. Is overly dependent for age; submissive, suggestible. Worries over reality of past lives; must sort out true past from the one engendered by the cult.	Hears what others say uncritically & passively. Has recurring bizarre mental contents from the cult: for example, waking dreams, orange fog.	Faces dealing with marital, family/parental, & child custody issues. Fears making a commitment to another person. Feels unable to make & express opinions. Overextends self to make up for lost time; is unable to say no. Has sense of being watched all the time—the fishbowl effect. Is embarrassed & uncertain how or when to tell others about cult experience; fears rejection.	Is unable to be kind to or supportive of others. Fears joining any group or being active. Feels loss of sense of being elite. Needs to reactivate own belief system & moral code/values & sort them out from the ones adopted in the cult.

conflicts and harms that grew out of their cult experience long after two years have gone by.

In addition, no simple relationship between time of membership and time of recovery is apparent, for those who recover rapidly may have been in cults for either brief or long periods and vice versa. Also, in general, the issues identified in those who left cults in the sixties and seventies are similar to the problems I hear about today. Yet there are some changes: people in a wider age range seek consultation, and duration of cult membership has increased.

When I began working with former cult members and then writing about their recoveries, I saw primarily young adults who were coming out after two to six years in a cult. Now I meet with whole families, elderly persons, couples, children who have known no other life, and people who entered as young adults and are emerging in their forties and fifties, having spent half their lives in a cult. Today, many former cult members have spent fifteen to twenty-five years in a cult.

Each former member wrestles with a number of the problems I describe in this chapter. Some need more time than others to resolve all the issues they face, and a few never get their lives going again. I also have heard reports of walkaways who have committed suicide after leaving a cult. Of these, apparently none had talked with exit counselors. They were described as inaccessible to others in the family, and no one had a clue about their motivations for committing suicide.

Practical Issues

Most of the practical issues faced by former cult members, such as where to live, how to earn a living, and nutritional and medical concerns are nearly universal concerns and need little explanation.

Money

One issue that does bear some explanation is cult members' curious experience with financial matters, which may have left them unfamiliar with handling personal money, unaware of how to earn money legitimately, or full of resentment at having turned over family fortunes or money earned to their former cult.

Many former cult members, while in their cults, took in more per day fund-raising on the streets than they will ever be able to earn on any job. Most cults assign members daily quotas that usually start at $100 or $150. Skillful and dedicated solicitors say they can bring in as much as $1,500 day after day. One former member claimed to have raised $30,000 in a month, selling flowers, and another to have raised $69,000 in nine months. Yet another has testified in court to raising a quarter of a million dollars over a three-year period, selling flowers and candy and begging, and another testified that she collected $2 million for her cult in little more than a decade. Her guru said to his followers, "My heart is where your money is." This former member said that fund-raisers worked thirteen- or fourteen-hour days: "Sometimes we were exhausted, but we were encouraged to work bars late at night. That was pretty humiliating, but we'd do it."

After such experiences, it can be difficult to figure out how to recoup resources or make an honest living, not to mention coping with the guilt many former members feel at having taken part in such deceptions. These cult experiences may make it necessary for former members to contact career counseling or mental health services.

Education and Health Care

The role of professional services, in particular medicine and psychology, is important in postcult adaptation. Some cults put down modern medicine and psychiatry and psychology, along with education in general. A few New Age cults teach that one can just "will" not only perfect health but whatever one desires. Such cults have sessions in which you are to imagine desired items (chocolate bars, apples, or whatever), and if you do this correctly and are in a proper state, the items will materialize. When they don't, the reasons given are that you are impure, unworthy, or not doing the routine right. Keep practicing the cult routine, you are told, and soon the materialization will happen—if you just clean up the basic you.

Because the states of perfection the cults promise are impossible to attain, cult members feel continually defeated and like failures, but they can't let it show. Cult doctrine preaches that if they only follow certain instructions, they will never be ill, never feel blue, and will save the planet, attain nirvana, and become spiritually or politically perfect. Meanwhile cult chores and practices keep them tired, worn down, and often ill. But they have to hide these conditions and keep smiling and working.

When it comes to education, many cults teach that members should "get out of the mind," stop thinking, and get into the heart or the everyday work of the cult. Some leaders preach that we are born with "natural knowing" that has been impaired by school, parents, and society, and that followers should reject "old thinking" and live by the dictates of the leader who has "experienced life," or who claims to have visited God, Heaven, Jesus, Buddha, various saints, or sometimes planets. Afterward, former cult members of almost any age and background need some sort of education or training to update knowledge and skills and to expand their training.

After years of neglecting both their minds and their health, former cult members feel odd and possibly even guilty about their concern with illness, health issues, and their psychological states after leaving the group. They soon realize, however, that their education stopped when they joined the cult, that they have neglected their health, and that they are in emotional turmoil. Yet they have been turned against the very support systems they now need. As they struggle to sort out their personal views about education, medicine, and mental health care, often they may need urging and explanations about what happened in the cult to create their negative feelings and attitudes.

Explaining Time Spent in the Cult

As I wrote in Chapter One, most people think that cult members are a breed apart and that they must be an odd, dumb, and even crazy bunch. Thus former cult members need to prepare themselves to deal with the most frequent responses relatives, old friends, and new acquaintances make when they learn that the person was in a cult. They are likely to come forth with some version of "But you seem like such a nice person, so bright. How come you were in a cult? Were you really in a cult? You couldn't have been—only weirdos join cults."

Application forms for jobs, higher education, and professional schools will ask for an accounting of one's past education and time. One man asked me, with honest humor and genuine concern, "How can I explain that for years I was a public relations flak for a fraudulent guru, getting the press to interview him and print pictures of his faked skills, and now that I'm out I want to become a scientist?" The admissions committee apparently accepted his explanations, especially when he made it to the personal interview stage, where the committee could ask direct questions and get the information they needed to assess him for professional training. I know of only one man who had serious difficulty in pursuing a chosen career. He was not admitted to medical school soon after leaving a cult because the admissions committee felt his choosing to follow a bizarre cult leader for many years indicated that he needed more time to become autonomous and to learn to use his training and good sense in making judgments, just as he would have to use these qualities later in making medical judgments.

There have been no specific studies of this issue, but I have been told by many former cult members how embarrassed they are to tell prospective employers they were in a cult. They know how a blame-the-victim attitude colors the way they will be regarded. One man said, "It's difficult to explain just what I did as a Governor of Enlightenment." Another man said he could only put "office supervisor" on an application form to describe what he did in his old cult, where in actuality he had worked as a spy for the group.

People learn to deal creatively with all these issues as they reenter society, network with other former cult members, and get experience in making friends, applying for jobs, and telling their stories when they feel safe and comfortable doing so.

Psychological and Emotional Difficulties

With their twenty-four-hour regimes of ritual, work, worship, and community, cults provide members with tasks and purpose. When these members leave, a sense of meaninglessness surfaces. Leaving the cult means losing friends, a mission in life, and direction. Former members also soon realize that they have lost their innocence. They entered the cult full of reverential amazement and with wide-eyed naïveté only to discover that they had been deceived and betrayed. As a result, they may be pervaded with a feeling of mourning.

Former members have a variety of other losses to contend with. They often speak of their regret for the lost years during which they wandered off the main paths of everyday life. They regret being out of step and behind their peers in career and life pursuits. They feel the loss of a solid sense of self-esteem and self-confidence as they come to realize that they were used or that they surrendered their autonomy.

Guilt and Shame

Former cult members experience an overdose of guilt and shame. In the cult, most were obligated to enlist new members and to collect money in less than honest ways. They feel guilty about their treatment of parents, brothers and sisters, and friends; about having lied, having committed acts of violence, or having carried out illegal activities at the bidding of the cult leader. They feel guilty about having tricked others into supporting the cult in some way, and about those they recruited who are still in the cult or who never would have joined otherwise.

Former members may also feel extreme and unwarranted guilt over almost anything they thought or did, fears of all kinds of things, and intense doubt every time they try to make a decision. As they unearth the stark reality of the deception and dishonesty of cult life, many ex-members also feel great remorse over their actions and frequently worry about how to right the wrongs they did. They can overcome such guilt only by accepting what they did and forgiving themselves, making amends with others where possible.

Panic Attacks

Many former members experience panic attacks, defined as discrete periods of intense fear or discomfort in which any four of the following symptoms develop abruptly and reach a peak within about ten minutes:

- Pounding heart
- Sweating
- Trembling or shaking
- Shortness of breath or a feeling of smothering
- Feeling of choking
- Chest pain or discomfort
- Nausea or abdominal distress
- Feeling dizzy, unsteady, light-headed or faint
- Feelings of derealization (surroundings don't seem real)
- Depersonalization experiences (feeling detached, as though looking at oneself as an object)
- Fear of losing control or going crazy; fear of dying
- Numbness, tingling, and hot and cold flashes

Panic attacks and other panic disorders are commonly experienced by people coming out of the emotional arousal cultic groups, which tend to focus on stimulating fear and guilt.

Fear of Retribution

Fear of the cult is long lasting, especially if the group has a tendency toward violence. Many cult leaders threaten the lives of potential defectors. For example, Jeannie Mills, who was in the Peoples Temple more than six years said, "After 1973 we didn't stay in because we loved the group. We stayed in because we knew we could be killed if we left. Jones had told us hundreds of times, privately, publicly, in Planning Commission meetings—it was common knowledge—that if you left the church you'd be killed."

Some former members fear that zealous current members will harm them or their families to show the leader how devoted the current members are. A former member told me: "When I was involved in my lawsuit against the cult I had been in, I had to call the bomb squad to my parents' home to remove a fake bomb. Another time after I left the group, two strangers approached my sister in a department store and told her that her brother (me) would never live to collect on his lawsuit."

As I have described, some groups have specific derogatory labels for persons who criticize the cult, and they train their members to avoid or harass these stated "enemies." For such reasons, fear and anxiety are high in many former cult members from a variety of groups—and not without justification, although it appears that most cults soon turn their energies to recruiting new members rather than prolonging efforts to harass defectors. Nevertheless, even after the initial fear of retaliation has passed, ex-members worry about how to handle the inevitable chance street meetings with cult members, expecting these members to try to stir up the ex-members' feelings of guilt over leaving and to condemn their present life.

Fear of Self

Yet another kind of fear exists—a more inwardly focused fear that comes from believing that if you leave, you will be doomed to live a life of unenlightenment, will never be psychologically whole, never spiritually fulfilled, never healthy or able to live in peace.

Some cults inculcate their followers with notions that they contain hidden selves or hidden loads of stress that may erupt at any moment and destroy or at least severely damage them. Former members may worry indefinitely about their inner "ticking bomb" or the cult leader's dire predictions of the horrible events that will befall them and their families. Because they have been so well trained, former cult members may continue to see this possible fate as something they may bring on themselves by having left the group, given up on their faith, and betrayed the cause.

Often at the root of the fear is the memory of old humiliations administered for stepping out of line. A woman who had been in a cult for more than five years said: "Some of the older members might still be able to get to me and crush my spirit like they did when I became depressed and couldn't go out and fund raise or recruit. I was unable to eat or sleep. I was weak and ineffectual. They called me in and the leader screamed at me: 'You're too rebellious. I am going to break your spirit. You are too strong-willed.' They made me crawl at their feet. I still freak out when I think about how close they drove me to suicide that day; for a long time afterward, all I could do was help with cooking. I can hardly remember the details—it was a nightmare."

It is crucial to analyze and work through such fears objectively. The former member needs to learn that the cult does not hold magical powers over him or her.

Conflicts over Those Left Behind

Fear and anxiety may be most acute for former members who have left a spouse or children in the cult. Any effort to make contact risks breaking any remaining link to those left behind. Often painful legal actions ensue over child custody or conservatorships, fought out between the one who leaves and the spouse who remains loyal to the cult.

Even reporters who have gone into a cult for a few days as bogus recruits to get a story have felt a terrible compassion for the real recruits who stay behind. One reporter said it took him three and a half hours to extract himself from the group once he announced he wanted to leave. He was denied permission to go, pleaded with, and told the phone didn't work so he could not contact a ride. "Two steps beyond the gate," he wrote, "I experienced the sensation of falling and reached out to steady myself. My stomach, after churning for several hours, forced its contents from my mouth. Then I began to weep uncontrollably. I was crying for those I had left behind."

Lack of Understanding in the Outside World

A problem related to the fear and anxieties that former cult members experience is that often they find it difficult to get others, even helping professionals, to understand what they are going through. Some psychiatrists and psychologists who have ex-members as clients think that they are psychotic, brain damaged, or malingering when they report seeing fog or hearing the voice of Thor, their old leader in another life, or being unable to hold down a job.

When I am consulted on such cases, although I cannot make a diagnosis without seeing the person, I urge the therapists to listen, learn more, and see what happens when they allow a client to go over the details of cult life. As was described in Chapters Six and Seven, many of these phenomena are products of the odd, repetitive training that goes on in cults, and they generally go away with simple listening and helping the patient see how the behavior became conditioned. To diagnose these occurrences as a true hallucination or a sign of major mental disturbance can cause even more damage to the person than he or she has already suffered.

While a few cult members may actually have become psychotic in the cult, more typically, seemingly psychotic behavior is a result of cult conditioning. For example, someone once asked me during a consultation if I saw the Devil sitting across the room where he pointed. I looked over, told him no, and asked if he did. We then talked about the source of this idea and when it first happened. From that discussion, we learned that the cult leader often used the phrase, "I see the Devil beside you." He would say it to those being chastised or use it to convey that a person was not trustworthy but "of the Devil." When I commented to the man that maybe he wasn't able to fully trust me yet and that it was sensible to go slowly in trusting anyone, he was relieved. Further discussion revealed that he was not hallucinating (and never had), but he had been conditioned by his cult leader to associate feelings of distrust with ideas of the Devil.

So some odd events may well be leftovers from cult days. All such symptoms need to be checked out carefully, with warmth and compassion.

Cognitive Inefficiencies

Cult practices can cause members' mental skills to falter and become inefficient. Since all cult members learn that reflective thought gets them in trouble, it's no wonder that they emerge with some mental constrictions. Many ex-members experience difficulty concentrating, an inability to focus and maintain attention, and impaired memory, especially short-term memory. It is reassuring for them to know that these aftereffects will pass. General explanations of what they are going through will help them.

Most of us who work with people soon after they emerge from cultic groups note that a lack of humor is almost universal until they have been away from the group for some time. In cults, people do not laugh, joke, and think at the multiple levels that other people ordinarily do and that allow them to grasp the incongruities central to much humor.

Many former members are also unable to comprehend what they read for some time. Many are forgetful, fail to meet deadlines, lose jobs because of inefficiency, and miss appointments. Some become very literal in their thinking. They've been so obedient and nonreflective that, like "Jack" in the following example, they are now highly concrete and literal in the ways they deal with what they hear, see, or read.

Jack, a former graduate student in physiology had been in a cult for several years. When he went to see his dissertation advisor back at the university, he reported that, as they talked, "the advisor wrote ideas on the board. Suddenly he gave me the chalk and said, 'Outline some of your ideas.' He wanted me briefly to present my plans. I walked over and drew a circle around the professor's words. I was like a child doing it. I heard his words as a literal command: I drew a line around the outside of the ideas written on the board. I was suddenly embarrassed when I saw what I had done. I had spaced out, and I keep doing little things like that."

Uncritical Passivity

Many former members find themselves accepting almost everything they hear, just as they were trained to do. They cannot listen and judge; they listen, believe, and obey. As a result, simple remarks by friends, family, dates, and co-workers are taken as commands, even though the person may not feel like doing the task or dislikes whatever it is. One woman, for example, got up in the middle of the night to respond to the request of someone she hardly knew. She said: "I borrowed my dad's car and drove sixty-five miles out into the country to help this guy I had just met once to transport some stolen merchandise because he spoke in such a strong and authoritarian manner on the phone. I can't believe how much I still obey people."

Leftover Cult Language

A prime hurdle for former cult members is to overcome speaking and thinking in the cult's special language. As we have seen, each group has its own jargon, usually based on applying new and idiosyncratic meanings to regular words and phrases. The jargon creates a sense of eliteness, solidarity, and belonging among those in the in-group; at the same time, it cuts people off from easy conversation with outsiders. This is true even in the live-out cults, whose members work at outside jobs but put in most of their free time with the cult; during that time with the cult, they speak the group jargon. In certain groups, the loaded language is more centrally encompassing than in others and thus harder to shed afterward. That is, it supplies new terms for practically everything and thereby controls more of the members' thinking.

Communication with others is naturally hindered as long as former members continue to use cult terminology. They don't make sense when they speak to others, and sometimes they can't make sense out of their own internal thoughts.

Memory Loss and Altered Memories

The distorted personal history gradually built up in the cult is not quickly removed. Perhaps this is nowhere more apparent than in the recent controversy over "recovered" memories of child abuse and other highly painful events. Stories of *false memory syndrome*, or as researchers in hypnosis have called them for decades, pseudo-memories, are frequently in the news.

A *pseudomemory* is a fictitious experience induced in a person's memory, either by design or inadvertently, through the use of guided imagery, hypnosis (ranging from light to deep trance states), and direct and indirect suggestions. During the trance state, or even without trance via carefully constructed suggestions, individuals can be led to construct scenes in their minds. They experience these fabricated, or confabulated, images as vividly as, or even more vividly than, real-life memories, even though the events never happened and are products of the interaction between a manipulative operator and a dependent subject.

In Chapter Six, I described a woman who saw orange fog and another who spoke to the deities who appeared in her daily life like dream figures. These women's visions were the constructions of cult practices that combined trance induction with the suggestion that seeing deities or fog was a good thing. Cult members may be trained to have specific visualizations and then be praised and rewarded and feel self-fulfilled when they achieve the goal.

Some cults specialize in creating purely fictional personal identities through emphasizing how bad the member's past was, as discussed in Chapter Seven. Cults that focus on past-lives regression and getting members to think they are communicating with entities from past lives build into their followers rather firm and puzzling revisions of history. In such cults, long-term members lead newer members through processes in which they are encouraged to locate events and imagine experiences and past lives that date back millions of years. In all these cases, the revised personal history becomes part of the pseudoidentity the cult member adopts during cult life.

Cults have been leading followers to create revised histories for some years now. Members have been made to gradually accuse parents and family and separate from them, then they are repeatedly rewarded for these actions and statements. This practice leaves many former members deeply conflicted. One woman sobbed, "How could I have denied so many years of happiness and love and told the tales about my family that I did in the cult? They got me to actually rave and rant in rage about my parents, especially my father, calling him an infidel capitalist."

Many times, former cult members will have written hateful, accusatory letters—the so-called disconnect letters—to parents and relatives at the direction of the cult after they were led to believe that their parents acted in accordance with the fabrications concocted during history revision. Within the cult milieu, these "mystical manipulations" are very believable. One man later asked, "How can I face how much I hurt my family? I really obeyed the leader. I sent back birthday gifts with hate letters. I didn't visit my dying grandfather, whom I really loved. I didn't go to my sister's wedding or write or call when her husband was killed in a logging accident. They may say they forgive me, but I can't forgive myself. How could I have allowed anyone to control me like that?"

Eventually former cult members realize that their life history was distorted and manipulated by cult practices, and they will want to sort out the truth from fabrication. They will desire to reconnect with what was real and rid themselves of nagging guilt and anxiety and distorted self-images engendered by the cult.

Triggers, Flashbacks, and Floating

A number of cult practices tend to produce varying degrees of trance states, disrupt normal reflective thought, and interrupt a person's general reality orientation (GRO). After practicing or participating in certain exercises and activities for years, some of these undesirable habits become ingrained. Both while in the cult and after leaving, a number of persons involuntarily enter dissociative states and have difficulty maintaining reflective thinking and concentration. Time goes by without their being aware of it. During these periods, they have certain kinds of memories and slip into altered states of consciousness, which they sometimes call *flashbacks* or *floating*. But these are, in fact, forms of dissociation.

Dissociation is a normal mental response to anxiety. A momentary anxiety arises when internal or external cues (*triggers*) set off a memory, a related idea, or a state of feeling that has anxiety attached to it. This brief anxiety experience alerts the mind to split off—that is, the mind stops paying attention to the surrounding reality of the moment. The person becomes absorbed and immersed in some other mental picture, idea, or feeling. This dissociation occurs unexpectedly and unintentionally and it is this dissociation that can be experienced as a floating effect.

Most of the time the floating is described by former cult members as "how I felt while in the group." Sometimes the feeling is one of nostalgia for some aspect of the cult. Sometimes it is a feeling of fear that the person should go back to the cult. Most of the time, people describe it as being suspended between the two worlds of present life and the past cult life.

Triggers, flashbacks, and floating are part of the normal reper-
toire of the human mind, but usually people experience them as
brief, infrequent episodes. Because certain cult practices tend to
produce hypnotic states and are used extensively for prolonged periods, people emerge with years of practice in how to dissociate.
What are transient, brief mental moments for the ordinary person
become practiced and reinforced behaviors for cult members. The
moments of dissociation become intensified, prolonged, and dis-
ruptive experiences; they prevent sustained reflective thinking,
concentration, and the ability to plan ahead.

Because these dissociative responses are overlearned, they
become distracting, immobilizing habits. They often occur when a
person has to shift from one task to the next. It's as though the
choice of what to do next sets off the act of spacing out. In the cult,
that moment of what to do next was stressful: you had to make a
decision knowing that all decisions had to be "right" and that you
could get into trouble if your decision was wrong. This experience
is perhaps the source of the apparent conditioning that causes decision making to trigger a dissociation.

Consequently, great difficulty in making decisions is common
among ex-members. At times they do not know what to do, say, or
think. It is as though they suddenly become dependent and childlike, looking for direction. In the cult, they followed a predeter-
mined path of obedience. Now they find themselves fearful, feeling
stupid and guilty, and not knowing what to do. The newly found
independent decision-making process becomes riddled with fears
and anxieties—all ripe moments for floating.

Floating episodes occur more frequently when someone is tired
or ill, at the end of the day, on long highway drives, or doing highly
repetitive tasks—that is, when the person feels weary and unfo-
cused but must also think. A period of dissociation and a puzzled
moment of wondering, What just happened to my thoughts and
feelings? will arrive at such times. It helps if former members can
learn to recognize those vulnerable moments in their lives for the
conditioned responses that they are.

Social and Personal Relations

A majority of former cult members experience varying degrees of *anomie*, or alienation, for some period of time. This sense of alienation and confusion results from the loss and then the reawakening of previous norms, ideals, and goals. It is exacerbated as the individual tries to integrate three cultures: the culture he or she lived in before joining the cultic group, the culture of the group itself, and the culture of the general society encountered now that the person is out of the group. The theories learned and held to so strongly in the cult need to be reconciled with the person's precult past as well as the postcult present. In a sense, the former member is asking, Who am I? in the midst of three sets of competing value systems.

For this reason, former cult members often feel like immigrants or refugees entering a foreign culture. In most cases, however, they are actually reentering their own former culture, bringing along a series of cult experiences and beliefs that may conflict with the norms and expectations of society in general. Unlike the immigrant confronting novel situations, the person coming out of a cult is confronting the society she or he once rejected.

Building a New Social Network

Many friends, a fellowship with common interests, and the intimacy of sharing a significant experience are all left behind when members walk away from the cult. A cult is a world of its own. Leaving such an all-encompassing experience means having to look for new friends in what you were taught is an uncomprehending or suspicious world. Moreover, a prominent characteristic of cult members, particularly in those who were in a cult for a long time, is a developmental lag in their social and experiential lives.

Gradually former members need to start making friends, dating, and having a social life, as well as either working for a living or returning to college or both. It's important to give them enough time to make this adjustment and to catch up. It doesn't have to be a great deal of time but enough so that they can pull themselves together in various ways before attempting complicated mental, social, and business enterprises.

Loneliness

Upon leaving the group, a person usually discovers that the group practices shown toward outsiders are now turned on him or her—that is, he or she is scorned and ostracized. Also, there is no hope of retaining cult friendships because cult members have been trained to hate defectors, and because members may try to pull the former member back in. In addition, the former member may not easily resume relationships with former friends and family because of the harsh way these relationships were most likely broken off when he or she joined the cult.

Leaving is a final door slam: the past is behind, and the exiting cult member is heading forward—but alone—toward an uncharted future in which the former member has to start all over at creating a friendship network.

Dating and Sexuality

Some people try to make up for lost time through binges of dating, drinking, and sexual adventures. However, this behavior often produces overwhelming guilt and shame when former members contrast the cult's prohibitions to their new freedom. It also can lead to some uncomfortable, regrettable experiences. "Valerie," a twenty-six-year-old former teacher, commented, "When I first came out, I went with any guy that seemed interested in me—bikers, bums. I was even dating a drug dealer until I crashed his car on the freeway. I was never like that before."

Others simply panic and avoid dating altogether. One man remarked, "I had been pretty active sexually before I joined. Now it's as if I'd never had those experiences because I'm more inhibited than I was in junior high. I feel sexual guilt if I even think of asking a woman out. They really impressed upon me that sex was wrong."

Often people were struggling with issues of sexuality, dating, and marriage before they joined a cult, and the cult artificially alleviated such struggles by restricting sexual contact and pairing, ostensibly to keep the members targeted on doing the "work of the master." Even marriage and parenthood, if permitted, are subject to cult rules. Sexuality in cults is almost always monitored or controlled in some way. Pairing off with another means you may care more for that person than for the leader or group mission. So cult leaders develop ways to ensure that allegiance goes to the top, not sideways in pair bonding. Another result of this control of sexuality is that cult friendships become sexually neutral and nonthreatening; rules that permit only brotherly and sisterly love can take a heavy burden off a conflicted young adult.

In some instances, highly charged interpersonal manipulations performed in the cult have long-lasting consequences. "Jennifer" said she was often chastised by a prestigious female cult member for "showing lustful thoughts toward the brothers. She would have me lie face down on the floor. She would lie on top of me and massage me to drive Satan out. Soon, she began accusing *me* of being a lesbian!" After leaving the cult, Jennifer felt conflicted about her sexual preferences.

Some groups promote a level of membership made up of renunciates, individuals who are akin to monks in the Far East. Some of these men and women do not engage in heterosexual lives when they leave the group, nor are they homosexual. The cult has so affected their outlook that they simply avoid issues of sexuality.

Orgiastic cults enforce sexuality rather than celibacy, and this too affects departing individuals. Describing her cult leader, one woman said, "He used orgies to break down our inhibitions. If a person didn't feel comfortable in group sex, he said it indicated a psychological hang-up that had to be stripped away because it prevented us from all from melding and unifying." A few cults practice child-to-child and adult-to-child sexual encounters and forms of prostitution or sexual slavery, sometimes combined with neo-Christian philosophy. There are also a few aberrant Mormon-based cults that practice polygamy. In some of the guru-based cults, the guru teaches and demands celibacy but has sexual liaisons with male or female members.

Upon leaving groups with unusual sexual practices, ex-members often are hesitant to talk about their experiences lest the listener be critical of them for participating. This is a case where good therapeutic counseling—or the sympathetic ear of a trusted friend—may be beneficial.

Marital Issues

When one partner of a married pair is recruited into a cult, pressure is put on that person to get the partner to join. If the partner doesn't, most of the time the cult, in effect, breaks up the marriage. Leaders give talks about how sinful, how suppressive, how negative the partner is, and the combination of keeping members busy with cult work while denigrating nonmember partners wrecks many marriages.

If both partners have joined the cult, they do not feel able to talk with one another about plans to escape the cult because loyalty to the leader supersedes marital obligations. Therefore one partner might leave without letting the other know, rather than run the risk of being stopped because the other had told the leadership. A number of marriages break up because the ones who leave are crushed when they realize that love and marital loyalty are nothing compared to their partner's fear and duty to the cult and that the partner has chosen loyalty to the cult leader over loyalty to the spouse.

A number of groups arrange members' marriages. The most publicized are the mass weddings in Moon's Unification Church, such as one in which 5,150 members were united in a group ceremony. Smaller groups do the same on a reduced scale. Legal consultation is needed for those who leave a spouse and/or children back in the cult or who simply no longer wish to remain married to a partner they didn't choose.

Trust

Former cult members find themselves feeling phobic in many social situations. They tend to withdraw and to stay away from crowds and gatherings of more than several people. Feeling badly ripped off by the cult experience, they don't trust their own judgment, and they don't trust other people. Additionally, they lack self-esteem and self-confidence; they feel incompetent, clumsy, and undesirable as a consequence of their cult training.

Former members' inability to trust is one of their most frequent and vivid problems. Not only do they realize that they trusted too much, but also they often end up blaming themselves for ever joining the cult and for feeling inadequate about their own decision-making abilities and judgment.

The "Fishbowl" Effect

A special problem for cult veterans is the constant watchfulness of family and friends, who are on the alert for any signs that the difficulties of real life may send the former member back to the cult. Mild dissociation, deep preoccupations, mood swings, and positive talk about the cult tend to cause alarm in a former member's family. Both new acquaintances and old friends can also trigger a former member's feeling that people are staring, wondering why he or she joined a cult. Often neither the ex-member nor family and friends know how to open up a discussion of this topic. The best advice I can give for dealing with this is for ex-members to focus on the reality of their surroundings and details of the current conversation until the sense of being under scrutiny gradually fades.

Former members sometimes want to talk to people about positive aspects of the cult experience. Besides acknowledging the seriousness of having made a commitment, the sense of purpose and accomplishment, and the simplicity of life in the old regime, they generally want to discuss a few warm friendships or romances, as well as their unique travels, experiences, or personal insights. Yet they commonly feel that others, especially family, want to hear only the negative.

As one man exclaimed, "How can I get across the greatest thing—that I no longer fear rejection the way I used to? While I was in the group and selling on the streets, I was rejected by thousands of people I approached, and I learned to take it. Before I went in, I was terrified that anyone would reject me in any way!" This experience, in fact, did help him in his life after the cult, but his being aware of that positive aspect of his cult experience certainly didn't drive him back into the cult.

Former members need to talk about their experiences as they wish, explaining to those around them that this talk doesn't mean they're running back to the cult. Part of shedding the cult's black-and-white thinking is learning to see all sides of an issue, and that learning will apply to the way the cult experience is seen as well.

Fear of Commitment

Many people coming out of cults want to find ways to put their altruism and energy back to work without becoming pawns in another manipulative group. Some fear they have become "groupies," defenseless against entanglements with controlling organizations or people. They feel a need for affiliations, yet wonder how to select properly among the myriad contending organizations—social, religious, philanthropic, service, and political—choosing a group in which they can continue to be their own bosses.

For a period of time, most will experience this reluctance to join any type of group or to make a commitment to another person or an activity or life plan. They will fear going back to their old church, old club, or old college; they will avoid social activities and volunteer organizations.

This may, in fact, be a healthy reaction. Those of us helping ex–cult members advise caution about joining any new uplift group and suggest, instead, purely social, work, or school-related activities, at least for the time being, until the person is more fully distanced from the cult experience and better understands the recruitment phenomenon.

Philosophical and Attitudinal Issues

Most cults claim their members are the elite of the world, even though individual members may be treated subserviently and degraded. While in the cult, members identify with this claim and display moral disdain toward others. They internalize the group's value system and its sense of moral pretentiousness, intellectual superiority, and condescension toward the outside world. In the cult, members get points for showing moral disdain for nonmembers and for members who faltered or left the group.

Aversions and Hypercritical Attitudes

Aversions and loathing are taught by many cults, sometimes in subtle forms. Ex-members of various cults talk about how they must struggle to not fuss at women in pants suits, not rage at relatives who eat meat, and not scoff at mainstream political or social advances. They may find themselves clinging to cult ways, such as wanting to wear dark, dingy clothes to avoid looking like a "harlot," wanting to be on the side of righteousness in their thinking, wanting never to spend money, show closeness, or have fun.

Some are taught prejudices toward certain races, religions, ethnic groups, or social classes, or even something as simple as people who wear clothing of the "wrong" color. While in the group, members are praised for sounding off about these pet hates of the leader.

Out of the cult now, the person wants desperately to stop spewing hatred.

Teenagers raised in such groups need considerable training in how to live in a multiethnic, multicultural, multiracial world with ecumenical practices. Never instructed in how to live in a democratic world, they learned instead to exist in a fascist one, where followers echo the leader's values. One teenager and his parents came to me for help because the boy had attended only cult schools. Now out of the cult, he spouted the venom of the cult leader and was being beaten and ostracized by others at school; he was terribly confused. He sobbed as he told me, "I told the class what the leader taught us—that the Pope and the United States Postal Service were part of a Communist conspiracy—and everybody laughed at me and said, 'There goes crazy ["Joey"] again.' After school they beat me up and say they will get me." Through the school principal and teacher, we worked out an educational program for him, and eventually he and his parents instructed the class about cults, showed educational films on cults, and discussed how to avoid getting recruited.

To newly emerged ex–cult members, people on the outside do not seem dedicated or hardworking enough. They appear lazy and uncaring about the world. Cults preach perfection and condemn members for not being perfect, and cult members spend years trying to live up to the ideal of perfection, always failing because the standards are beyond human capabilities. Conditioned by their cult's condemnation of the beliefs and conduct of outsiders, former members tend to remain hypercritical of much ordinary human behavior.

While in the cult, members not only learned to be harsh to those under them who were not perfect, but were sometimes punished for the shortcomings of others as well their own. Upon entering the general society, some former members continue to be punitive, critical, confrontational taskmasters. The simple human errors and forgetfulness of others can bring an ex–cult member to look down on them. One woman said about her relations with fellow employees, "It's all I can do to not put my face in theirs at work and scream at them and yell like we used to do back in the cult." Cults organized around paramilitary, political, and psychological themes tend to teach some of the harshest and most confrontational practices.

No Longer a World Saver

Nothing on the outside seems as vital and grand as life was supposed to be in the cult. Members were told they were doing "world-class work." Upon emerging, the ex-member looks at the jobs people do, and sees them as hopelessly small and without meaning compared to his or her work for a group that was purportedly saving souls or the world itself.

One former member said, "It was like I thought I was an astronaut while I was in the cult, and here I am driving a tour bus around San Francisco." But another woman said, "There I was saving the world, and kicking the nearest person out of the way, so that I could get on with saving the universe. That is, until I realized that the cult never saved the world either."

Helpful Tasks for Individuals Leaving Cults

Knowing that others before you have experienced many of the symptoms you may now be experiencing as a former member is a great source of comfort and relief for many. Rather than thinking that you're hopeless or going crazy, you can educate yourself so that you will see that the experiences you are going through are recognizable consequences of having been in a cult.

My understanding of former members' experiences in this area was assisted by three former members I worked with some years ago. They had decided to heed advice and get rather undemanding jobs for a few months, to give themselves time to regain their health and get their minds squared away. One of them went to a rural area and found work as a dock loader, putting big sacks of potatoes on trucks. He called me and said, "Dr. Singer, you know I'm just spacing out. I keep loading these sacks and I float out somewhere. I'm really not paying attention to loading these sacks of potatoes. I'm floating into meditating again." I also heard complaints from the other two in their routine jobs, loading a lumber truck and doing house painting. Unfortunately, I don't find that I can advise recent cult members any differently than I advised these three, since often these recently exited members simply cannot concentrate enough to get more demanding jobs. However, I do now advise that they be alert to the possibility of dissociation and try to find activities that will break the rhythm of monotonous work, so they will not fall into cult habits and periods of floating. These early insights also cued me to start looking more precisely at some of the effects on people of the highly repetitive activities typically found in cults and the power of thought-reform processes.

When I lecture about these things, I know there are people sitting in the room thinking, "Oh, my gosh, I've got everything she's talking about."

"Don't worry," I say. "It eventually all goes away." And it does. It's a matter of time, plus learning to label what you are experiencing and hearing some good explanations for what's happening to you, including your physiological reactions and the up-and-down process of recovery.

Recovery is a psychoeducational process—the more you learn about the cult and what to expect afterward, the quicker your healing process and integration into a new life outside the cult.

Past Lives and Altered Histories

In sorting out past lives from real-life experiences or recapturing your history and family connections, part of the recovery work is to remember and review life experiences before you joined the cult and to compare them with the specific attitudes and contents inculcated by the cult. Working actively to ascertain what was real before, during, and after cult life, and thinking over how to reestablish family connections is crucial work for most former members.

Cognitive Inefficiencies

I often recommend to ex-members with the kinds of cognitive inefficiencies described earlier that they take time out and give themselves a break, and that they not enroll immediately in college or graduate school, because their reading retention, ability to sit, and capacity to recall and reflect will get better in a few months. To attempt high-level functioning in a demanding and competitive situation like graduate school may create undue stress.

Reversing the loss of mental acuity takes time and effort—you may want to try reading again, going back to activities that interested you before you joined the cult, or taking some relatively less demanding evening classes for a start. Making lists and keeping a notebook are two of the most useful and most popular remedies for cognitive difficulties. You can make detailed plans of everything you need to do and everything you want to do, day by day. Then you follow your plan, checking off items as you go along, so you can see your progress.

When passive behavior or troublesome indecisiveness comes up, it can be helpful to dissect the cult's motives and injunctions against questioning doctrines or directives. This will shed light on the effects of your having lived for months or years in a situation that encouraged acquiescence, and also help you to think on your own once again and voice opinions. During this process, the cult and its power become demystified as you realize that leadership's orders were meant primarily to reinforce the closed, controlled cult environment and keep tabs on members.

How to Stop Floating

Behaviorally oriented educational techniques are the best methods of counteracting and dealing with floating episodes. The triggers are just associations and memories, and only that. They are not arcane implants put in your mind by others; they do not reflect uncontrollable suggestions. Floating is simply getting stuck for a few minutes, or sometimes hours, in a familiar, detached, and conflicted state, such as you experienced while in the cult.

Three types of remembrances are experienced by ex–cult members during floating episodes:

- *Contents* from the cult days: jargon, dogma, practices, songs, rituals, certain clothing
- *Feeling states* that were vivid and frequent during the time in the group: gnawing inner doubt, inadequacy, unmitigated fear, unending hidden tension
- Strange *wordless states*, sometimes given denigrating labels by the cult (for example, "bliss ninny," "space cadet"): referred to as floating, involuntary meditation, and wavy states by former members

Often former cult members don't distinguish among the array of remembrances from cult life. But learning to recognize and identify the types just described is helpful in the process of getting rid of them for good. It demystifies your cultic experience and the power you think it holds over you. You will no longer feel you are at the mercy of some strange phenomenon that you cannot control.

Some cults even have their own terms, such as *restimulation*, which they use to predict the recurrence of these episodes (both while in the cult and later). This, of course, sets members up to expect what does occur once in a while. The cult that uses this particular term also imbues the involuntary state with the implication that "you can't help it because it's in your wiring." This frightens members, who then carry this notion with them when they leave. Myths such as this cause former members to become very anxious when the dissociative episodes occur.

Remember, there are no mysterious, mechanical, out-of-our-control events. No cult and no person has the power or skill to implant such things in the minds of their members or to cause these episodes to happen after members leave. There is no scientific evidence, no valid clinical observation that such a possibility exists.

Individuals newly emerging from a cult can almost expect and need not be alarmed by periods of seeming to lose track of time or where they are. It's normal for them to think often about various experiences from cult days and to sometimes feel as they felt back in the cult. During exit counseling, families should be told that floating is likely to occur for a time after the cult member leaves the group. They are advised to allow the ex-member to talk about and deal with these episodes.

Floating does not mean you want to return to the cult. As described earlier, floating is most likely to happen when you are stressed, anxious, uncertain, lonely, distracted, fatigued, or ill. Once you recognize when these episodes may occur, you can prepare for them. Then the event will be less distressing when it happens. Realizing that floating is a dissociative moment will help. Once you understand that you are merely temporarily psychologically disengaging, you won't think that your memory is shot or that you are losing your mind. You can say to yourself, "I'm not damaged for life. This is just a momentary dissociation. I can pick up where I was. It's just a thought, just a memory. I don't have to act on it."

Here are some helpful antidotes:

• Keep a written log of the happenings so that you can talk about them and come to understand what happens. Write down the simple word, event, voice, sound, smell, motion, expression, or memory; that is, trace back and recall what set you off so that you can begin to comprehend what occurred. Why that thing? Why that moment? What was the state you were in?

• Divert yourself when you are about to fall into a dissociative state. Sometimes a friend or co-worker will notice that you are beginning to space out, and she or he may offer companionship or listening time or divert you into an activity. You can also create your own activities that you set into motion when you recognize a trigger or start to float. Turn on the radio, listen to the news, call someone on the phone, write in your journal, play with the dog.

• Suppress the feeling. You do not have to act on it, you do not have to let the cult-related feeling overwhelm you. Push it away and go on to something else. Later, at a more appropriate moment, you may want to talk with someone about the situation.

• Learn to minimize the frightening leftovers from cult days. You might be flooded with feelings, but say to yourself, "I'm not going crazy. I'm just a little anxious." Focus on the present, on today, on getting your life back together.

• If you do fall into a dissociative state, bring yourself back with a sensory change. Pinch yourself. Rub your hand. Do something that will provide sensory input and break the feeling of being in limbo. Focus your eyes on something directly in front of you.

All these techniques will help break up the floods of emotion and emotional memories that come in at you. Taking a down-to-earth and aggressive stance against triggers and floating will propel you to take great leaps forward in your recovery.

Combatting Aversions

Former cult members remain rigid in their attitudes for some time. This rigidity is a remnant of the cult's moral relativism, which provided reasons to hate and condemn. It takes much constant personal monitoring of your attitudes to change these ingrained reactions. It is necessary to make a conscious effort to understand human frailties. Reactivating a personal sense of values and good standards without being maniacally condemning of everyday human failures and foibles in yourself or others is a needed step in recovery.

Learning to Trust Again

Regaining your sense of trust will grow partly out of the gradual awakening of your ability to tolerate thinking about and discussing the abuse and betrayal you experienced. Members' massive anger over injustices and abuses is kept hidden in the cult. This anger surfaces in ex-members, along with anger over the dishonesty and deceptions that had to be ignored or the facts that weren't known until the individuals left the group.

Trust is difficult to reestablish. Regaining trust is sometimes easier for those who have the chance to speak with exit counselors, to spend some time at a rehabilitation center (see Chapter Eleven), or to engage in psychotherapy after leaving the cult. The knowledge and insights gained through these opportunities generally help former members move along more quickly in adapting to a new life and building new relationships outside the shadow of the cult experience.

One of the most poignant aftereffects of cult life is the distrust of the self. Many people start blaming themselves, asking, "Why ever did I join?" Part of exit counseling and the subsequent psychoeducational work is helping former cult members analyze their involvement. As they recognize the deceptive, step-at-a-time influence program that led them into the group, they will be less hard on themselves. As they discern the social and psychological situation that retained them once they were in the cult, they will be able to forgive themselves and carry on with life.

Regaining a Sense of Satisfaction

Most of us get a sense of satisfaction from doing life's little tasks well—taking care of the family, being supportive of friends, doing a good job at work, cooking a grand meal, creating a work of art, or growing plants in the window box. Early every morning a few of my closest friends call or I call them, and our brief phone conversations are mutually supportive. All of us get some sense of satisfaction out of these simple conversations. After leaving a cult, people take a while to learn that such little things are where satisfaction lies.

Learning that life's small kindnesses and pleasures are satisfying and worthwhile may be an arduous journey. Many ex-members describe struggling along, feeling they are wasting time by being nice to fellow employees or watering flowers for a neighbor or visiting a sick aunt. They don't allow themselves to feel any satisfaction, since they are still judging by the cult's standards, and visiting Aunt Betsy isn't equal to saving the world. I try to nudge them along the path they were on before the cult: seek pleasure from simple things.

One woman shared with me some observations she learned from her father. He pointed out to her that she seemed not to realize that helping clean the garage, taking care of young relatives while parents went shopping, and advancing in her job were making the world a better place—that doing good nearby was visibly helping to improve the world. She said she finally got the point: "It is all right to enjoy once more. It is all right to be kind to one person at a time. In fact, it is impossible to do whatever 'save the world' means. Such abstract goals are just that—abstract—and keep you from living and doing good day by day."

The discussion in this chapter does not cover all the conflicts, turmoils, and disturbing aftereffects that ex–cult members have struggled with. But it should help the reader begin to understand the breadth of the recovery from cult conditioning and cult experiences that must occur.

Some of the adults I have counseled had spent one of every two days of their lives in a cult. Some of the young adults had spent every day in a cult until a few weeks before I met them. Coming out of a cult identity is not like popping out of an eggshell. It is a relearning process and a period of growing up—with educational help from others who have trod the same path.

Coming out of the cult pseudopersonality is about reeducation and growth. Self-help through reading can be invaluable for those who live far from knowledgeable resources such as exit counselors, cult information specialists, former member support groups, and mental health professionals who have educated themselves about the cult phenomenon. At the end of this book, the reader will find a list of helpful books and articles, as well as names, addresses, and phone numbers of agencies that can provide information, resource networks, and contacts.

There Is Life After the Cult

I recall as a little girl going to the railroad stations in small Colorado towns and watching the new streamlined trains either stop or slow down to toss off mail bags, then speed on into the distance. The Chief and the SuperChief roared past. My high school graduating class was even named the Zephyr, after the sleek silver Burlington train that symbolized progress, glamour, technology, and the future. There was perfection implied in that future and in the faraway places the train was headed to. There were places where there was no dust bowl with sand blowing across the dried fields, places where there were bright lights and ice cream all the time, libraries filled with colorful new books, and playgrounds all over.

From working with so many former cult members, I have a new picture of the railroad station and the tracks. I think of people standing alongside the railroad tracks, watching the various trains come and go, while at each stop, hucksters, pied pipers, scam artists, and self-avowed saviors of the world hop off the trains and display their enticing wares, trying to get as many as possible of the people at the stations to hop on board and go with them into that vision of perfection.

When a cult leader, a guru, a trainer, or any self-proclaimed pied piper asks you to jump on the train because he or she claims to have the "one way," watch out! That can be the last train stop on the way to hell on earth.

Down through the ages, people have helped the sick, the poor, the downtrodden. Let us not forget also to help those who have suffered at the hands of mental abusers, tyrants, and manipulators who take away the freedom of human minds to reason, create, criticize, and change.

As we end this book's journey, I want to share my fascination and admiration for the humans who have lived through the utter disappointment and the shocking, eye-opening experience of seeing how a dream of making the world a better place merely helped a selfish leader feather his nest and go laughing off to the bank. I've heard the broken dreams of the young who joined cults, the adults who got hooked into New Age thought-reform groups, the elderly who come to realize all too late that they gave all their savings to a seductive young person from a cult.

All of the persons I have worked with who went into and came out of the kinds of experiences this book has described were among the most inspiring persons I have ever met. They wanted to make themselves better, and they wanted to make the whole world better. They were altruistic, caring, and wanted to help, and they were taken in—they believed a charlatan.

I'm inspired by the fact that former devotees could spring back after the bitter disillusionment of learning that their leader had lied, had bought cocaine with the money his followers begged on the street, had abused children or murdered enemies, and that nothing these persons were doing in the cult had anything to do with their original lofty goals. I'm inspired by those elderly folks who bounce back after coming to learn that the sweet young person who seemed so eager to help with a few chores has really just tricked them.

When people say, "I was scammed, I was tricked, and now I see it. And I am going to get up, come back, and still try not to become so embittered that no one wants to be around me"—these people are inspiring.

I also want to pay my respects to the memories of all those who died at the hands of cult leaders, including those who committed suicide when they were so harmed and bereft by what happened that they could not go on. I want to have others join me in remembering those who died from carrying out the regimens prescribed by quacks, those who died while driving without sleep to get to the next town to raise money for the leader who drove fancy cars and slept at leisure, those who died from lack of medical care because it was disparaged by the cult or because they were so busy carrying out the leader's bidding that they couldn't get to a doctor.

I want to applaud all of those who keep on wanting to try to do good, and to be good to their families, friends, and humankind. I applaud them for springing back after the betrayal of a spiritual abuser, a psychological exploiter, or a political fraud and for not allowing a fascistic pseudo-guru to keep on controlling them. I applaud those who speak out and believe that we all need to continue trying to prevent these abusers from taking over more of the world. Truly, the price of freedom is eternal vigilance, and the ability to recover from defeats, scams, and harassment.

A free mind is a wonderful thing. Free minds have discovered the advances of medicine, science, and technology; have created great works of art, literature, and music; and have devised our rules of ethics and the laws of civilized lands. Tyrants who take over our thinking and enforce political, psychological, or spiritual "correctness" by taking away our freedoms, especially the freedom of our minds, are the menace of today, tomorrow, and all eternity.

Postscript:
The Millennium, Cults, and
the End of the Century

As this book went to press, we learned that fifty-three members of a cult died together in a series of explosions and fires in Canada and Switzerland. The group held among its beliefs a doomsday outlook. Those who died were affluent, educated, and accomplished adults: businesspeople, a mayor, a journalist, a civil servant, and the leader himself a physician. This was not a ragtag youth cult, or a collection of people living an alternative life-style. These people lost their lives in fancy Swiss chalets. But their deaths were bizarre and violent and remain a mystery to many.

The dead were members of a cultic group following a man named Luc Jouret, a forty-six-year-old Belgian homeopathic doctor whose body was also eventually found. Jouret was described as having been charismatic, learned, energetic. Playing the role of a priest, he was known to have preached an amalgam of apocalyptic visions and health awareness set against a backdrop that some call *eco-fatalism*.

The group was known as the Order of the Solar Temple. After the fires from the explosions were extinguished, the bodies of men, women, and children were discovered. According to reports, they died of various combinations of bullets, fire, stabbings, plastic bags over their heads, and injected drugs. Some had their hands tied behind their backs. A complex system of electrical wiring had triggered flaming blazes in the expensive buildings where the dead were found. Some were dressed in ceremonial white, red, gold, or black robes, arranged in a circle facing a portrait of a Christ-like figure resembling Jouret. At a Swiss farmhouse owned by one of the victims, champagne bottles were found scattered about a basement room with mirror-covered walls that served as the temple.

Former members of the group report that Jouret had urged them to prepare for the end of the world, which he described as a fiery annihilation. Jouret recruited people of affluence, with property, who retained their jobs. Reportedly he recruited about a dozen members at a Canadian public utility plant where he was paid to speak on the meaning of life and "self-realization." Sources say he gathered about seventy-five members in Quebec and two hundred more in Switzerland and France. A former member speaking on Swiss television summed up their life: "We went about our daily lives, but we didn't belong to this world. . . . Jouret made us feel we were a chosen and privileged congregation." Former members also stated that followers gave large amounts of money and property to Jouret.

In early October 1994, at the time of these dreadful events, a wire service report proclaimed, "Once again, mass death in an apocalyptic sect. This time it was murder." When I read this, I thought, for once they got it right.

Because the tragedy at Jonestown was portrayed in the media as a "mass suicide," most people never bothered to analyze what had happened: Jones had *murdered* his followers. He may have labeled it "revolutionary suicide," but in reality Jones orchestrated a mass murder. It was through his commands, his power, and his control that 912 lives were lost; it was not the vote of his followers to die.

Again in 1993 when the Koresh group met its fiery end in Waco, Texas, I balked at the use of the term *suicide*. Once more a cult leader had orchestrated a mass murder.

The fate of these three groups led by Jones, Koresh, and Jouret—and others that received only brief public attention because they existed, and in some cases died, in places far from North America like Vietnam and the Ukraine—illustrates all too forcefully the power of cult leaders. Recent events again remind us that some cults come to violent endings. When groups include a doomsday doctrine among their beliefs, we must be particularly alert to the potential for mass murder.

Because it is near the end of the century and the end of a millennium, we can expect to hear of other groups following leaders who predict the end of the world. This pattern has recurred with astonishing regularity throughout history.

For this reason many cult watchers and journalists are calling attention to a phenomenon happening today across the United States. Numerous families are selling their homes; many single or widowed women are uprooting their lives to move to the Pacific Northwest or other sparsely populated areas to follow a variety of cult leaders. The preaching is a mix of old-fashioned doomsday predictions, New Age mysticism, radical environmentalism (or eco-fatalism), survivalist philosophy, and the narrow worldview of identity groups who want to live only with their kind. While saying the end is near—whether from crime, disease, natural disaster, economic collapse, failure to follow particular religious doctrines, or failure to make changes in personal lifestyle—this transcontinental movement appears to offer inspiration to form utopian communities around a guru, cult leader, survivalist leader, or channeler. These leaders are encouraging their followers to join them in preparing for the end.

Some groups are predicting the traditional end-time apocalypse in which the forces of good and evil battle. Some predict a group of earthlings will battle each other in a final struggle. But others foresee that the end of the world will be caused by killer-bee plagues, planetary chaos and earthquakes, space aliens and spaceships invading the world, or an evolutionary recycling in which civilization will be "spaded under." Still others say that we have already been invaded by space alien walk-ins who are just waiting for a cue to take over.

The more cultic and controlling such groups are, the more risk there is for those who become involved. In general, the personality and fantasies of the leader are key to how a group will evolve and how it will end up. If the leader gets backed into a corner—either because of illegal and threatening behavior or because he or she may no longer be able to play god on earth—and has already prepared the group to die by fire or shooting, the likelihood of a tragic ending has obviously increased for that group.

We hope such occurrences do not happen, but if they do, let us not call these deaths "suicide." Let's view them for what they are: the sad, lonely, dreadful ending of life for people who trusted too much, followed too long, and could not get away from a self-serving and murderous leader.

Chapter Notes

Chapter One

P. 3, *The Rajneesh cult in Oregon:* F. FitzGerald, "Rajneeshpuram—II," *New Yorker,* Sept. 29, 1986, pp. 108–116; W. McCormack (ed.), "The Rajneesh Files 1981–86," *Oregon Magazine Collector's Edition* (Portland: New Oregon Publishers, 1985), p. 5; "Oregon's Bhagwan Dies of Heart Failure," *Livingston* (Montana) *Enterprise,* Jan. 19, 1990.

P. 12, *between two million and five million Americans:* Suggested membership figures appear in Russell Chandler, *Understanding the New Age* (Grand Rapids, Mich.: Zondervan, 1993); G. A. Mather and L. A. Nichols, *Dictionary of Cults, Sects, Religions and the Occult* (Grand Rapids, Mich.: Zondervan, 1993); B. Larson, *Larson's New Book of Cults* (Wheaton, Ill.: Tyndale House, 1989); J. G. Melton, *Encyclopedic Handbook of Cults in America* (New York: Garland, 1986); E. Barker, *The Making of a Moonie* (New York: Basil Blackwell, 1984); and W. Martin, *The New Cults* (Santa Ana, Calif.: Vision House, 1980).

P. 13, *cults can be classified:* This list is quoted from L. J. West and M. T. Singer, "Cults, Quacks, and Nonprofessional Therapies," in H. I. Kaplan, A. M. Freedman, and B. J. Sadock (eds.), *Comprehensive Textbook of Psychiatry,* Vol. 3 (3rd ed.) (Baltimore: Williams & Wilkins, 1980), p. 3249. The subsequent examples of cults in different categories are also taken from this work.

P. 17, *two-thirds . . . who have joined cults:* M. T. Singer, "Cults," in S. B. Friedman, M. Fisher, and S. K. Schonberg (eds.), *Comprehensive Adolescent Health Care* (Norwalk, Conn.: Appleton & Lange, 1992), p. 700.

Chapter Two

P. 32, *These sects of the 1800s can be categorized:* These categories of sects are described by L. K. Pritchard, "Religious Change in Nineteenth Century America," in C. Y. Glock and R. N. Bellah (eds.), *The New Religious Consciousness* (Berkeley: University of California Press, 1976).

P. 33, *fifty . . . utopian cults were established*: R. V. Hine, *California's Utopian Colonies* (San Marino, Calif.: Huntington Library Publications, 1953).

P. 33, *the Oneida Community and the Amana Society*: Information about the two groups is taken from J. Gutin, review of *Without Sin: The Life and Death of the Oneida Community*, by Spencer Klaw, *East Bay Express*, October 1993, Express Books section, pp. 1, 10; R. M. Kanter, *Commitment and Community: Communes and Utopias in Sociological Perspective* (Cambridge, Mass.: Harvard University Press, 1972); *Encyclopedia Americana* (1992 ed.).

P. 37, *three popular rebellions*: L. J. West and J. R. Allen, "Three Rebellions: Red, Black, and Green," in J. Masserman (ed.), *The Dynamics of Dissent*: (New York: Grune & Stratton, 1968).

P. 39, *communes . . . differentiated from cults*: West and Singer, "Cults, Quacks, and Nonprofessional Therapies," pp. 3247–3248.

P. 44, *Occult groups espouse*: B. Alexander, "Occult Philosophy and Mystical Experience," *Spiritual Counterfeits Journal*, 1984, 6(1), 13–19.

P. 45, *Controversial channeler J. Z. Knight*: H. Gordon, *Channeling into the New Age* (Buffalo, N.Y.: Prometheus Books, 1988), pp. 95–101; J. Klimo, *Channeling* (Los Angeles: Tarcher, 1987), pp. 42–45; Larson, *Larson's New Book of Cults*, pp. 418–419; Ramtha, with D. J. Mahr, *Voyage to the New World* (New York: Ballantine, 1985).

P. 45, *with the tightening of the economy*: M. T. Singer, "Consultation with Families of Cultists," in L. C. Wynne, S. H. McDaniel, and T. T. Weber (eds.), *Systems Consultation: A New Perspective for Family Therapy* (New York: Guilford Press, 1986), p. 281.

P. 48, *"Mary Jo"*: This example is quoted from Singer, "Consultation with Families of Cultists," pp. 273–274.

Chapter Three

P. 53, *(see Table 3.1)*: This table originally appeared in M. T. Singer and M. E. Addis, "Cults, Coercion, and Contumely," in A. Kales, C. M. Pierce, and M. Greenblatt (eds.), *The Mosaic of Contemporary Psychiatry in Perspective* (New

York: Springer-Verlag, 1992), p. 133, and is reprinted with permission. The sources for items in the table, in order of appearance, are: T.E.H. Chen, *Thought Reform of the Chinese Intellectuals* (New York: Oxford University Press, 1960); E. Hunter, *Brainwashing in Red China* (New York: Vanguard, 1951); R. J. Lifton, *Thought Reform and the Psychology of Totalism: A Study of Brainwashing in Red China* (New York: W. W. Norton, 1961); I. E. Farber, H. F. Harlow, and L. J. West, "Brainwashing Conditioning and DDD: Debility, Dependency, and Dread," *Sociometry,*1956, 20, pp. 271–295; E. H. Schein, with I. Schneier and C. H. Barker, *Coercive Persuasion: A Socio-psychological Analysis of the "Brainwashing" of American Civilian Prisoners by the Chinese Communists* (New York: W. W. Norton, 1961); Anonymous, 1980; M. T. Singer, "The Systematic Manipulation of Psychological and Social Influence," paper presented at the Cult Awareness Network annual meeting, Washington, D.C., Oct. 23, 1982; R. Ofshe and M. T. Singer, "Attacks on Peripheral Versus Central Elements of Self and the Impact of Thought-Reforming Techniques," *Cultic Studies Journal*, 1986, 3(1), pp. 3–24; Singer and Addis, "Cults, Coercion, and Contumely."

P. 56, *accused of a spanking:* State of West Virginia v. *Stuart Green* (involuntary manslaughter), Civil Action No. 92-M-1; *State of West Virginia* v. *Leslie Green* (involuntary manslaughter), Civil Action No. 92-M-5; *State of West Virginia* v. *Dorothy McClellan* (2 counts conspiracy), Civil Action N. 83-F-11 (involuntary manslaughter), Civil Action No. 83 (2 counts conspiracy), Civil Action No. 83-F-60.

P. 57, *Ron Luff . . . was convinced by his cult leader:* P. Earley, *Prophet of Death* (New York: Morrow, 1991), pp. 431, 435.

P. 60, *others who study these programs emphasize:* Lifton, *Thought Reform and the Psychology of Totalism*; Schein, Schneier, and Barker, *Coercive Persuasion*.

P. 60, *attacking . . . a person's sense of self:* Ofshe and Singer, "Attacks on Peripheral Versus Central Elements of Self and the Impact of Thought-Reforming Techniques."

P. 61, *Cardinal Mindszenty wrote:* J. Mindszenty, *Memoirs* (New York: Macmillan, 1974), p. 114.

P. 61, *Patty Hearst said:* P. C. Hearst, with A. Moscow, *Every Secret Thing* (New York: Doubleday, 1982), pp. 95, 98, 240.

P. 62, *summarized in Table 3.3:* The sources of this table are: Lifton, *Thought Reform and the Psychology of Totalism*, pp. 419–437; Schein, Schneier, and Barker, *Coercive Persuasion*, pp. 117–139; M. T. Singer and R. Ofshe, "Thought Reform and Brainwashing," document offered as proof of testimony, Queens High Court, London, on behalf of the *London Daily Mail*, 1980; M. T. Singer, "Group Psychodynamics," in R. Berkow (ed.), *The Merck Manual of Diagnosis and Therapy* (15th ed.) (Rahway, N.J.: Merck Sharp & Dohme Research Laboratories, 1987), p. 1470; M. T. Singer and R. Ofshe, "Thought Reform Programs and the Production of Psychiatric Casualties," *Psychiatric Annals*, 1990, 20(4), pp. 189–190.

P. 69, *For example, "heavenly deception" and:* Barker, *The Making of a Moonie*, p. 22; D. G. Bromley and A. D. Shupe, Jr., *Strange Gods: The Great American Cult Scare* (Boston: Beacon Press, 1981), pp. 171–172; R. Enroth, *Youth, Brainwashing and the Extremist Cults* (Grand Rapids, Mich.: Zondervan, 1977), p. 115; Larson, *Larson's New Book of Cults*, pp. 163, 259, 441; Mather and Nichols, *Dictionary of Cults, Sects, Religions and the Occult*, p. 55.

P. 69, *psychiatrist Robert Lifton:* Lifton, *Thought Reform and the Psychology of Totalism*, pp. 419–425.

P. 71, *the group's founder has stated:* R. Wallis, *The Road to Total Freedom* (New York: Columbia University Press, 1976), p. 106.

P. 74, *psychologist Edgar Schein:* Schein, Schneier, and Barker, *Coercive Persuasion*.

P. 78, *We see from years of research:* Lifton, *Thought Reform and the Psychology of Totalism*; R. Ofshe, "Coercive Persuasion and Attitude Change," in E. F. Borgatta and M. L. Borgatta (eds.), *Encyclopedia of Sociology*, Vol. 1 (New York: Macmillan, 1992).

P. 78, *The phenomenon has been . . . described:* R. J. Lifton, *The Future of Immortality and Other Essays for a Nuclear Age* (New York: Basic Books, 1987), pp. 195–208; L. J. West, paper presented at the American Family Foundation Conference, Arlington, Va., May 1992.

P. 79, *impermissible experiments:* J. Clark, personal communication, Sept. 1981.

Chapter Four

P. 84, *The most cogent analysis:* L. J. West, "Persuasive Techniques in Contemporary Cults: A Public Health Approach," *Cultic Studies Journal*, 1990, 7(2), 126–149.

P. 84, *what happened in Antelope:* J. W. Anderson, "Bhagwan Is 'Back' With Club Meditation," *San Francisco Examiner,* Feb. 20, 1994; "Oregon's Bhagwan Dies of Heart Failure," *Livingston* (Mont.) *Enterprise,* Jan. 19, 1990.

P.86, *one large group operated a cleaning firm:* C. Williams, "How Cults Bilk All of Us," *Reader's Digest* (reprint), Nov. 1979, pp. 1–6.

P.86, *evangelist Tony Alamo:* D. Hughes, "Judge Blasts Alamo Conduct," *Southwest Times Record* (Fort Smith, Ark.), Nov. 29, 1989, pp. 1A, 5A; D. Hughes, "Alamo Leader Portrayed as Tyrant," *Southwest Times Record,* Nov. 28, 1989, pp. 1A, 5A; H. Tobar, "Jewish Group Sued by Alamo Jacket Firm," *Los Angeles Times,* Dec. 21, 1989, pp. B1, B3; Williams, "How Cults Bilk All of Us"; "Deal Makes Alamo pay $5 Million," *Tennessean* (Fayetteville, Ark.), June 16, 1992, pp. 1A, 2A; "Jury Convicts an Evangelist in Tax Evasion," *New York Times,* June 12, 1994.

P. 87, *William A. Lewis:* C. Thompson, "Michigan Trial Precedes Ecclesia Case," *Oregonian,* Feb. 10, 1991, pp. D1, D13.

P. 87, *fifty-three children were removed:* J. Painter, "7 Ecclesia Members Plead Guilty, Sentenced," *Oregonian Metro,* Jan. 18, 1992, pp. D1, D8; "Indicted Cult Leader Found Dead in Oregon," *New York Times,* Sept. 6, 1991.

P. 87, *Tony Alamo, leader:* Hughes, "Alamo Leader Portrayed as Tyrant"; "Jury Convicts an Evangelist"; J. Bravin, "Boy Tells of Abuse, Isolation at Alamo Commune," *Los Angeles Times,* Mar. 26, 1988, pp. 3–4; Tobar, "Jewish Group Sued by Alamo Jacket Firm."

P. 89, *a polygamy sect:* "3 Members of Polygamous Sect Face Prison Terms for 4 Killings," *Chicago Tribune,* Jan. 22, 1993, p. 12; "Ex-Member of Cult Sentenced for Killing Man Who Left Cult," *Savannah* (Ga.) *News Press,* Dec. 3, 1993.

P. 89, *a faith-healing cult:* J. Melvoin, "No Peace in the Valley," *Time,* Nov. 8, 1982, p. 35.

P. 89, *Keith Ham:* L. O'Dell, "New Trial Ordered for Head of Krishnas," *Charleston* (S.C.) *Gazette,* Jul. 7, 1993, p. 1A, 11A.

P. 89, *Yahweh Ben Yahweh:* "Sect Leader, Follower Convicted of Conspiracy," *Chicago Tribune,* May 28, 1992, p. 2; M. Warren, "Prosecutor Says Yahweh Ordered Slayings to Intimidate Followers," *Tampa Tribune,* Jan. 8, 1992, p. 4.

P. 89, *a federal appeals court:* P. McMahon, "U.S. Says Scientology Hasn't Really Reformed," *St. Petersburg Times*, Dec. 11, 1981; "U.S. Appeals Court Upholds Convictions of Scientologists," *Calgary* (Canada) *Herald*, Oct. 3, 1981.

P. 90, *Bhagwan Shree Rajneesh was deported:* "Oregon's Bhagwan Dies of Heart Failure," *Livingston* (Mont.) *Enterprise*, Jan. 19, 1990.

P. 90, *Lyndon LaRouche, Jr., and six:* I. VonZahn, "Retirees Fall into LaRouche's Camp," *Loudon* (Leesburg, Va.) *Times-Press*, Oct. 27, 1993, p. A3; Associated Press, "LaRouche Wins Parole in January," *Chicago Tribune*, Dec. 1, 1993, p. 18; C. Babcock, "Door Left Ajar for LaRouche Matching Funds," *Washington Post*, Nov. 30, 1993, p. A7; R. F. Howe, "Appeals Court Upholds LaRouche Conviction on Mail Fraud, Conspiracy," *Washington Post*, Jan. 23, 1990, p. A8.

P. 90, *Ed Francis:* T. Egan, "Thousands Plan Life Below, After Doomsday," *New York Times*, Mar. 15, 1990, pp. A1, B6; Enterprise Staff and Associated Press, "Francis Pleads Guilty," *Livingston* (Mont.) *Enterprise*, Oct. 13, 1989.

P. 90, *Church of Scientology:* B. Brent, "Church Can Pay $1 Million Fine, Lawyer Tells Court," *Toronto Star*, Aug. 14, 1992, p. A18; T. Claridge, "Church of Scientology Fined $250,000 for Breaches of Trust," *Globe and Mail* (Toronto), Sept. 12, 1992; T. Claridge, "Church of Scientology Found Guilty," *Globe and Mail* (Toronto), July 27, 1992, p. A17; J. Kavanagh, "Conviction 'Frightening' for Religions, Lawyer Says," *Toronto Star*, Jun. 29, 1992, p. A4; N. van Rijn, "Scientology Church Sues OPP Ministry," *Toronto Star*, Sept. 15, 1992, p. A10.

P. 91, *George Jurcsek:* S. McKeel and S. Friedman, "Cult Leader Due for Parole," *Daily Record* (Morris, N.J.), Mar. 1, 1993, pp. 1, 5.

P. 91, *a doctor who allegedly had sex:* A. Goldstein, "Doctor's License Is Suspended," *Washington Post*, May 1, 1993, p. D3; B. J. Blackledge, "Patient Backs G'burg 'Cult' Doctor," *Montgomery Journal*, May 3, 1993, p. A1; B. J. Blackledge, "Gaithersburg CFS Doc Taped Offbeat Sessions," *Montgomery Journal*, May 11, 1993, p. A1; "Md. Doctor's License Taken Away," *Washington Post*, Jul. 29, 1993; S. Roffe, "The Secret Life of Robert Hallowitz," *Bethesda* (Md.) *Gazette*, Jul. 14, 1993, p. A46.

P. 91, *a man . . . giving five-day seminars:* J. B. Quinn, "Lawsuit Claims Guru's Road to Riches Has Dead End," *San Francisco Chronicle*, June 2, 1992, p. B3.

P. 94, *political science professor:* J. Hulse, "Ominous Cult or Quiet Study Group?" *Santa Barbara News-Press*, Mar. 26, 1989, pp. A1, A6; and author interviews.

P. 95, *Helen Overington:* A. Howard, "LaRouche Still Is Finding Contributors," *Washington Post,* May 21, 1990, p. A1, A6.

P. 95, *Luther Dulaney:* D. Lattin, "The Guitar That Speaks for God," *San Francisco Chronicle,* Dec. 31, 1991, p. 1; and author interviews.

P. 96, *Betsy Dovydenas:* D. T. Keating, "The Bible Speaks Loses Again," *Berkshire* (Pittsfield, Mass.) *Eagle,* Jan. 26, 1988, pp. A1, B4; "Bible Speaks Must Return $6.5 Million," *New Haven* (Conn.) *Register,* Oct. 3, 1989.

Chapter Five

P. 105, *a recent survey of 381 former members:* M. D. Langone, "Former Cult Member Survey," *Cultic Studies Journal,* in press.

P. 108, *43 percent were students:* Langone, "Former Cult Member Survey."

P. 119, *Eventually, they no longer call:* Singer, "Cults," p. 701.

P. 120, *"I liken it to a compass . . .":* R. W. Dellinger, "Elderly Are a New Target for Cults," *National Catholic Register,* Jul. 6, 1986, p. 1.

P. 120, *clients are . . . trying to extricate their mothers:* B. Barol and N. Joseph, "Getting Grandma Back Again," *Newsweek,* Oct. 23, 1989, p. 4.

P. 120, *cults have gone directly into nursing and retirement homes:* Dellinger, "Elderly Are a New Target for Cults"; C. Collins and D. Frantz, "Let Us Prey," *Modern Maturity,* June 1994, pp. 22–32.

P. 121, *Once, Chuck performed:* C. P. Brown, "The Body Electric," *Forever Alive,* Sept. 1992, pp. 19–20; D. and L. Bardin, "Jews in Cults: Hanging by a Thread," *Moment,* Aug. 1993, pp. 28–29, 56; J. M. Laskas, "Never Say Die," *Gentleman's Quarterly,* Aug. 1993, pp. 126–133, 171, 196.

P. 122, *"we have the ability . . .":* C. P. Brown, BernaDeane, and J. R. Strole, *Together Forever: An Invitation to Physical Immortality* (Scottsdale, Ariz.: Eternal Flame Foundation, 1990), pp. 35–36.

P. 124, *"We were being deculturized . . .":* T. Brooke, *Riders of the Cosmic Circuit* (Batavia, Ill.: Lion Publishing Corporation, 1986), p. 37.

Chapter Six

P. 129, *physicians explained that continuous overbreathing:* Ben Kliger, M.D., personal communication, Feb. 6, 1994; Edward Lottick, M.D., telephone conversation, Feb. 7, 1994; Harold Scales, M.D., letter to author, Oct. 1985.

P. 135, *studies have shown that high-strength niacin:* J. E. Bishop, "Niacin, Used for Cholesterol Called Toxic," *Wall Street Journal,* Mar. 2, 1994, p. B4; J. M. McKenney, J. D. Proctor, S. Harris, and V. M. Chinchill, "A Comparison of the Efficacy and Toxic Effects of Sustained-vs-Immediate-Release Niacin in Hypercholesterolemic Patients," *Journal of the American Medical Association,* 1994, *271*(9), 672–677.

P. 138, *relaxation-induced anxiety:* F. J. Heide and T. D. Borkovec, "Relaxation-Induced Anxiety: Mechanisms and Theoretical Implications," *Behavioral Research Therapy,* 1984, *22,* 1–12.

P. 138, *RIA symptoms fall into three clusters:* Heide and Borkovec, "Relaxation-Induced Anxiety: Mechanisms and Theoretical Implications."

P. 140, *One former devotee . . . was told:* S. Gervasi, "Grounding the Guru," *City Paper* (Wash., D.C.), July 13, 1990, pp. 14, 16.

P. 140, *more than one million persons:* Larson, *Larson's New Book of Cults,* pp. 423–424; R. Thomson, "Meditation Urged for Student Ills," *Sarasota Herald Tribune,* Feb. 19, 1993; E. Garcia, "TM Leaders Chant Mantra to Schools: Try Meditation," *San Jose Mercury News,* Mar. 1, 1993, pp. 1B, 2B; L. Goodstein, "Karmic Convergence, the Sequel," *Washington Post,* June 9, 1993, pp. B1, B5; L. Goodstein, "Meditators See Signs of Success," *Washington Post,* Jul. 30, 1993, pp. B1, B6; S. Saperstein, "Transcendental Meditation on Trial," *Washington Post,* Dec. 12, 1986; D. Thompson, "The Maharishi's Search for Heaven on Earth Pays Off," *Daily Telegraph* (London), Apr. 7, 1993; S. S. Sadleir, *The Spiritual Seeker's Guide* (Costa Mesa, Calif.: Allwon, 1992), p. 216.

P. 140, *the multitude of courses meditators:* L. Kadaba, "Good Vibrations," *Philadelphia Inquirer Magazine,* Jan. 11, 1993, pp. E1, E4; S. Gervasi, "Wasted Away in Maharishiville," *City Paper* (Wash., D.C.), Dec. 22, 1989, p. 10.

P. 141, *clinical reports of negative outcomes:* A. P. French, A. C. Schmid, and E. Ingalls, "Transcendental Meditation, Altered Reality Testing, and Behavioral Change: A Case Report," *Journal of Nervous and Mental Disease,* 1975, *161,* 55–58; R. B. Kennedy, "Self-Induced Depersonalization Syndrome," *American Journal of Psychiatry,* 1976, *133,* 1326–1328; A. A. Lazarus, "Psychiatric Problems Precipitated by Transcendental Meditation," *Psychological Reports*, 1976, *39*, 601–602.

P. 141, *his research proved otherwise:* L. S. Otis, "Adverse Effects of Transcendental Meditation," in D. Shapiro and R. Walsh (eds.), *Meditation: Classic and Contemporaneous Perspectives* (New York: Alden, 1984); N. Mead, "Why Meditation May Not Reduce Stress," *Natural Health*, Nov./Dec. 1993, pp. 80–85, 122.

P. 141, *findings are consistent with those of a variety of studies:* D. S. Holmes, "Meditation and Somatic Arousal Reduction," *American Psychologist*, 1984, *39*, 1–10.

P. 141, *professor of psychology Michael Persinger:* M. A. Persinger, "Transcendental Meditation and General Meditation Are Associated with Enhanced Complex Partial Epileptic-like Signs: Evidence of 'Cognitive Kindling'?" *Perceptual and Motor Skills*, 1993, *76*, 80–82; M. A. Persinger, "Enhanced Incidence of 'The Sensed Presence' in People Who Have Learned to Meditate: Support for the Right Hemispheric Intrusion Hypothesis," *Perceptual and Motor Skills*, 1992, *75*, 1308–1310; M. A. Persinger, N. J. Carrey, and L. A. Suess, *TM and Cult Mania* (North Quincy, Mass.: Christophe, 1980); M. A. Persinger and K. Makarec, "Temporal Lobe Epileptic Signs and Correlative Behaviors Displayed by Normal Populations," *Journal of General Psychology*, 1987, *114*(2), 179–195.

P. 142, *researchers Michael Murphy and Steven Donovan:* M. Murphy and S. Donovan, *The Physical and Psychological Effects of Meditation* (Big Sur, Calif.: Esalen Institute, 1989).

P. 142, *"a depersonalized state can become . . . ":* R. J. Castillo, "Depersonalization and Meditation," *Psychiatry*, 1990, *53*, 158–168.

P. 142, *legal suits for damages: John Doe I–VI and Jane Doe v. Maharishi Mahesh Yogi; World Plan Executive Council-United States; Maharishi International University*, U.S. District Court for the District of Columbia, 85–2848, 2849, 2850, 2851, 2852, 2853, 2854 (consolidated); *Jane Green v. Maharishi Mahesh Yogi et al.* U.S. District Court for the District of Columbia, 87–0015-OG. *Patrick Ryan v. World Plan Executive Council-United States et al.* U.S. District Court for the District of Columbia, 87–0016-OG.

P. 142, *my observations based on . . . seventy persons:* Singer and Ofshe, "Thought Reform Programs and the Production of Psychiatric Casualties."

P. 149, *the popular book:* H. Benson, *The Relaxation Response* (New York: Morrow, 1975).

Chapter Seven

P. 153, *work of Milton Erickson . . . provides an excellent compilation of the methods:* J. Miller, "The Utilization of Hypnotic Techniques in Religious Conversion," *Cultic Studies Journal*, 1986, *3*(2), 243–250.

P. 155, *Her findings . . . showed:* M. A. Kim, "Communication and the Psychology of Charisma." Unpublished doctoral dissertation, Department of Psychology, University of California, Berkeley, 1984.

P. 155, *described in the work of Hillel Zeitlin:* H. Zeitlin, "Cult Induction: Hypnotic Communication Patterns in Contemporary Cults," in J. Zeig (ed.), *Ericksonian Psychotherapy* (New York: Brunner/Mazel, 1985).

P. 156, *First, the picture is not mine:* Quoted from B. S. Rajneesh, *I Am the Gate* (New York: HarperCollins, 1975, pp. 45–46), by Zeitlin, "Cult Induction: Hypnotic Communication Patterns in Contemporary Cults."

P. 157, *people used . . . to read trance poetry:* E. D. Snyder, *Hypnotic Poetry: A Study of Trance-Inducing Techniques in Certain Poems and Its Literary Significance* (Philadelphia: University of Pennsylvania, 1930).

P. 157, *six qualities of trance-inducing poetry:* E. D. Snyder and R. E. Shor, "Trance-Inductive Poetry: A Brief Communication," *International Journal of Clinical and Experimental Hypnosis*, 1983, *31*(1), 1–7.

P. 160, *the picture had been staged:* "L.A. Times Says Fire Photo Was Staged," *San Francisco Chronicle*, Feb. 2, 1994.

P. 160, *After Synanon leader Chuck Dederich:* W. Olin, *Escape from Utopia: My Ten Years in Synanon* (Santa Cruz, Calif.: Unity Press, 1980), p. 274; D. Gerstel, *Paradise Incorporated: Synanon* (Novato, Calif.: Presidio Press, 1982), p. 268; D. Mitchell, C. Mitchell, and R. Ofshe, *The Light on Synanon: How a County Newspaper Exposed a Corporate Cult* (New York: Seaview Books, 1982), p. 201.

P. 163, *Sathya Sai Baba . . . is described:* J. Hawley, *Reawakening the Spirit in Work* (San Francisco: Berrett-Koehler, 1993), pp. 84–85, 94, 187–202.

P. 166, *described her experience this way:* M. L. Tobias and J. Lalich, *Captive Hearts, Captive Minds: Freedom and Recovery from Cults and Abusive Relationships* (Alameda, Calif.: Hunter House, 1994), pp. 25–26.

P. 166, *an informant who told her of three past lives:* H. Whitehead, *Renunciation and Reformulation: A Study of Conversion in an American Sect* (Ithaca, N.Y.: Cornell University Press, 1987), p. 90.

P. 168, *Robert Lifton speaks of the totalism of the person:* Lifton, *Thought Reform and the Psychology of Totalism.*

P. 169, *Robert Cialdini, a social psychologist:* R. B. Cialdini, *Influence: The New Psychology of Modern Persuasion* (New York: Quill, 1984).

P. 172, *Two colleagues and I studied:* M. T. Singer, M. K. Temerlin, and M. D. Langone, "Psychotherapy Cults," *Cultic Studies Journal,* 1990, 7(2), pp. 101–125.

P. 176, *"longest, costliest, and most complex psychotherapy malpractice case . . .":* L. Timnick, "Psychologists in 'Feeling Therapy' Lose Licenses," *Los Angeles Times,* Sept. 30, 1987, pp. 1, 4.

P. 176, *the civil cases were settled for more than $6 million:* C. L. Mithers, *Therapy Gone Mad: The True Story of Hundreds of Patients and a Generation Betrayed* (Reading, Mass.: Addison-Wesley, 1994), p. 377.

P. 176, *The administrative law judge wrote:* The relevant legal cases are: *State of California, Department of Consumer Affairs, Board of Behavioral Science Examiners,* No. M-84, L-31542 v. *Cirincione, Franklin, Gold, Gross, Swanson* (1985); *State of California, Department of Consumer Affairs, Psychology Examining Committee Division of Allied Health Professionals, Board of Medical Quality Assurance,* L-30665, D-3103–3107 v. *Corriere, Gold, Hart, Hopper and Karle* (1985); *State of California, Division of Medical Quality, Board of Medical Quality Assurance, Department of Consumer Affairs,* D-3108, L-30664 v. *Woldenberg* (1985); *State of California, Department of Consumer Affairs, Board of Vocational Nurse and Psychiatric Technician Examiners,* No. T-300, L-31451 v. *K. S. Corriere* (1985); *State of California, Department of Consumer Affairs, Board of Medical Quality Assurance, Division of Allied Health Professionals, Psychology Examining Committee,* No. A-392, L-33445 v. *Binder* (1985); *Superior Court of the State of California for the County of Los Angeles, Jean Rains et al. v. Center Foundation, etc., et al.,* Case No. C 372 843, consolidated with C 373 272, C 389 178, C 388 681, C 379 789, C 388 882, C 384 972, C 388 512, C 388 362, C 388 683, C 388 334 (1981, 1983).

Chapter Eight

P. 182, *$150 million was being spent annually:* J. Borden, "'New Age' Training Furor: Illusion or Reality?" *Human Resources Exchange,* June 1989, p. 4.

P. 183, *A 1992 Gallup Poll reveals:* A. Goldman, "Religion Notes," *New York Times,* Apr. 24, 1993.

PP. 183–184, *89 percent of Americans single out a religious preference:* Cited in D. Lattin, "Religions of the World Gather in Chicago," *San Francisco Chronicle,* Aug. 27, 1993, p. A4.

P. 188, *The statement reads in part:* Equal Employment Opportunity Commission, "EEOC's Policy Statement on Training Programs Conflicting with Employees' Religious Beliefs," *EEOC Notice No. N-915,* Feb. 22, 1988, pp. 6276–6277.

P. 189, *said to be at the Wilson Learning Corporation:* J. Main, "Trying to Bend Managers' Minds," *Fortune,* Nov. 23, 1987, pp. 77–88; A. Johnson, "Mind Cults Invade the Boardroom," *Canadian Business,* Jan. 1992, pp. 38–42.

P. 191, *a $30,000 settlement . . . was reached:* American Jewish Congress, "$30,000 to Health Food Employee Who Alleged Employer Coercion to Join Unification Church," Press release, Dec. 11, 1989.

P. 191, *complaints to the EEOC:* M. D. Langone, "Beware of 'New Age' Solutions to Age-old Problems," *Business and Society Review,* Spring 1989, pp. 39–41; Main, "Trying to Bend Managers' Minds"; P. Waldman, "Motivate or Alienate? Firms Hire Gurus to Change Their 'Cultures,'" *Wall Street Journal,* Jul. 24, 1987, p. 19; R. Watring, "New Age Training in Business: Mind Control in Upper Management," *Eternity,* Feb. 1988, pp. 30–32; R. Watring, "Producing Results: Fact and Fantasy—A Review of *Enhancing Human Performance: Issues, Theories, and Techniques* by the National Research Council," *Spiritual Counterfeits Journal,* 1990, 9(1), pp. 28–33.

P. 196, *John-Roger Hinkins . . . his story is an interesting one:* R. Flynn, "Insight Out," *City Paper* (Wash., D.C.), Dec. 7–13, 1990, pp. 20–31; P. Kingston, "TV Chief's Link to Sect Worries His Staff," *London Evening Standard,* Mar. 25, 1987; M. Yaple, "Candlelight Path to the 'Messiah,'" *Sun Chronicle* (Attleboro, Mass.), Dec. 18, 1987; B. Sipchen and D. Johnston, "John-Roger: The Story Behind His Remarkable Journey from Rosemead Teacher to Spiritual Leader of a New Age Empire," *Los Angeles Times,* Aug. 14, 1988, pp. 1, 10–12; B. Sipchen and D. Johnston, "Negativity Shakes the Movement," *Los Angeles Times,* Aug. 15, 1988, pp. 1–3, 6; R. Storm and I. Pollard, "False Messiah," *City Limits* (London), Sept. 13–20, 1990, pp. 8–10.

P. 199, *employees also objected to specific:* Main, "Trying to Bend Managers' Minds."

P. 199, *From a tire factory:* R. Lindsey, "Gurus Hired to Motivate Workers Are Raising Fears of 'Mind Control.'" *New York Times,* Apr. 17, 1987; M. Brannigan, "Employers' New Age Training Programs Lead to Lawsuits Over Workers'

Rights," *Wall Street Journal*, Jan. 9, 1989, p. B1; P. Galagan, "The Transformers," *Training and Development Journal*, Jul. 1987, p. 4; R. Zemke, "What's New in the New Age?" *Training*, Sept. 1987, pp. 25–33.

P. 199, *one lawsuit filed by three dentists alleged:* E. McCormick, "A Bittersweet Mix," *San Francisco Examiner*, Mar. 21, 1993, pp. E1, E5, E8; G. Power, "Cocolat Plans to Close All of Its Stores," *San Francisco Chronicle*, Apr. 7, 1993, pp. D1, D4; R. Weizel, "A Tale of Capture and Brainwashing," *Akron* (Oh.) *Beacon Journal*, Jan. 21, 1990, pp. A1, A4; S. Cartwright, "Definitely Not the First, Probably Not the Last," *El Vaquero* (Glendale, Calif.), Mar. 23, 1990, p. 1.

P. 200, *Sterling representatives assert that the training is:* McCormick, "A Bittersweet Mix," p. E5.

P. 200, *a "ground-breaking precedent . . .":* H. L. Rosedale, cited in "Protection Against Cultic Influence in the Workplace," *Cult Observer*, 1993, *10*(10), 7, in reference to State of New York, New York State Division of Human Rights, Complaints of Karen Webster and Maryann Slutsky, Case No. 2-EC91–35000 64–67E.

P. 200, *Applied Materials . . . settled out of court:* D. Machan, "Scientologizing," *Forbes*, Sept. 14, 1992.

P. 201, *admitted it had "lacked sensitivity . . .":* A. Gathright, "Scientology, Intimidation at Heart of Applied Materials Suit, *Mercury News* (San Jose, Calif.), Jul. 28, 1992, pp. 1E, 10E; A. Gathright, "Applied Materials Loses Ruling Involving Scientology," *Mercury News*, Aug. 5, 1992, pp. 1E, 7E; Machan, "Scientologizing."

P. 201, *writer commented that the case "is a typical one . . .":* C. Cooper, "Is Firm Teaching Skills or Religion? EEOC to Decide," *Sacramento* (Calif.) *Bee*, June 25, 1989, p. A9; Machan, "Scientologizing."

P. 201, *management and administrative employees told local newspapers:* McCormick, "A Bittersweet Mix"; Power, "Cocolat Plans to Close All of Its Stores."

P. 201, *According to a 1990 lawsuit filed against this . . . company:* S. Cartwright, "Student Alleges Local Company Is a Front for Scientologists," *El Vaquero* (Glendale, Calif.), Mar. 23, 1990, p. 1; "Pair Sue, Say Bosses Forced Faith Upon Them," *Miami Herald*, Feb. 16, 1990, p. 2A; McCormick, "A Bittersweet Mix."

P. 202, *est . . . reemerged as the Forum:* Chandler, *Understanding the New Age*, p. 70.

P. 202, *was targeted by Landmark Education International:* R. Clancy, "Professionals Fall Prey to New Age Gurus," *Times* (London), Jul. 21, 1992, p. 4; "Mind Game Courses Aimed at Public Sector Workers," *Times* (London), Jul. 22, 1992, p. 4; "Mercenary Mindbogglers," *Times* (London), Jul. 23, 1992; "Seminars Leave Firms Divided," *Times* (London), Jul. 23, 1992.

P. 203, *Erhard franchised Transformational:* R. Zemke, "What's New in the New Age?"; Main, "Trying to Bend Managers' Minds"; G. White, "'New Age' Pep Talks: A Backlash," *Los Angeles Times,* Mar. 25, 1989, pp. 16–17; S. Pressman, *Outrageous Betrayal: The Dark Journey of Werner Erhard from est to Exile* (New York: St. Martin's Press, 1993), p. 218.

P. 204, *staff members at the Ohio Children Services Agency complained:* S. Brooks, "Agency Spends $4,800 on 'Cultlike' Seminars," *Columbus Dispatch,* Feb. 10, 1992, pp. 1A, 2A; "Erhard's Mind-sets Made Him Millions," *Columbus Dispatch,* Feb. 10, 1992, p. 2A; "'Cult' Seminar Brings Call for Firing," *Columbus Dispatch,* Feb. 11, 1992; "Few Agencies Interested in est-Like Program," *Columbus Dispatch,* Feb. 13, 1992, pp. 1C, 2C; "Forum Grads Say Seminars Helped Them," *Columbus Dispatch,* Feb. 14, 1992, p. 6C; R. Ruth and S. Brooks, "Consultant Sticks to Guns on Training Seminar Issue," *Columbus Dispatch,* Feb. 12, 1992, p. 6B.

P. 204, *one of the most celebrated cases related to workers' rights:* Brannigan, "Employers' New Age Training Programs Lead to Lawsuits over Workers' Rights"; "'New Age' Training Suit Against Market Settled Out of Court," *Wall Street Journal,* May 31, 1989, p. B10.

P. 205, *One of the most notorious New Age employee programs:* K. Pender, "Pac Bell's New Way to Think," *San Francisco Chronicle,* Mar. 23, 1987, pp. 1, 6.

P. 206, *Outside evaluators . . . reported:* California Public Utilities Commission, Public Staff Division, *Report on Pacific Bell's Leadership Development Program* (San Francisco, California: California Public Utilities Commission, June 10, 1987), chap. 5, p. 3.

P. 206, *Pacific Bell had spent $50.6 million:* K. Pender, "Pacific Bell Dumps 'Krone' training," *San Francisco Chronicle,* Oct. 30, 1987, p. 1.

P. 206, *a case that involved PSI World:* White, "'New Age' Pep Talks: A Backlash."

P. 206, *Lifespring's philosophy:* M. Fisher, "Inside Lifespring," *Washington Post Magazine,* Oct. 25, 1987, p. 23.

P. 210, *laws that protect human rights:* National Commission for the Protection of Human Subjects of Biomedical and Behavioral Research, *Ethical Principles and Guidelines for the Protection of Human Subjects* (The Belmont Report) (Wash., D.C.: Government Printing Office, 1983).

Chapter Nine

P. 217, *ex-members of a health-fad . . . group reported: Bellak v. Murietta Foundation, Inc. (a.k.a. Alive Polarity Fellowship, a Washington Corporation)*, United States District Court for the Central District of California, Civil Case No. 87–08597(CBM)(Kx).

P. 218, *Although some men in the group:* Gerstel, *Paradise Incorporated: Synanon*, pp. 217–224; Mitchell, Mitchell, and Ofshe, *The Light on Synanon*, p. 218.

P. 219, *Massive amounts of medicines were procured:* T. Reiterman and J. Jacobs, *Raven: The Untold Story of Jim Jones and His Temple* (New York: Dutton, 1982), pp. 449–450, 452, 539; K. Wooden, *The Children of Jonestown* (New York: McGraw-Hill, 1981), pp. 16–18.

P. 221, *the Nazi doctors of whom Robert Jay Lifton has written:* R. J. Lifton, *The Nazi Doctors: Medical Killing and the Psychology of Genocide* (New York: Basic Books, 1986).

P. 221, *Eileen Barker, a London sociologist, wrote a book:* Barker, *The Making of a Moonie*, pp. 178–179.

P. 221, *recruits join freely:* See, for example, Barker, *The Making of a Moonie*, pp. 122–125, 136–139, 254–255.

P. 222, *the Religious News Service carried a story:* A. Carley, "Government Grant to Cult Watchdog Stirs Flap in Britain," *Religious News Service*, Jul. 10, 1989, pp. 6–7.

P. 222, *According to a press release from a member of the House of Commons:* A. Meale, "INFORM—Cut in Funding by the Home Office," Press Release, House of Commons, London, Nov. 15, 1993.

P. 223, *sociologists David Bromley and Anson Shupe published the book:* Bromley and Shupe, *Strange Gods*, pp. 199–201.

P. 227, *Journalists Marshall Kilduff and Ron Javers wrote about the ordeal:* M. Kilduff and R. Javers, *The Suicide Cult* (New York: Bantam Books, 1978), p. 76.

P. 228, *The National Council on Health Fraud said:* "Rampant Deception by Maharishi Ayur-Veda Promoters Exposed," *NCAHF Newsletter,* Nov./Dec. 1991, vol. 14(6).

P. 228, *St. Martin's Press, was greeted with "blasts of hostility . . .":* J. M. Hall, "Erhard Book Draws Threat of Legal Action," *San Francisco Daily Journal,* Mar. 31, 1993, pp. 1, 9; A. S. Ross, "Libel Suit Threat by est Founder Erhard," *San Francisco Examiner,* Apr. 6, 1993.

P. 228, *Not long ago a large:* "Reader's Digest Foils Scientologist Appeal; Libel Suit Still Active," *Publish,* June 1992; B. Steffens, "Scientology's Current Target: Reader's Digest," *Quill,* Nov./Dec. 1991, p. 39; J. H. Richardson, "Catch a Rising Star," *Premiere,* Sept. 1993, p. 91.

P. 228, *what she describes as "a nightmare":* R. Behar, "The Thriving Cult of Greed and Power," *Time,* May 6, 1991, p. 57; author interview with P. Cooper, Jul. 13, 1994.

P. 229, *As two authors wrote:* Bromley and Shupe, *Strange Gods,* p. 67.

P. 230, *The article cited Price's presence:* "'God Sir' at Esalen East," *Time,* Jan. 16, 1978, p. 50.

P. 230, *Price wrote to both the editors of* Time *and Rajneesh:* D. Boadella, "Violence in Therapy," *Energy and Character* (Dorset, England) (Jan. 1980), *11,* 1–20; letters from Richard Price to *Time* magazine, Jan. 21, 1978, to Rajneesh Ashram dated Feb. 23, 1978, and to Rajneesh dated Jul. 7, 1978.

P. 231, *Kilduff and Javers reported that "Al Mills . . .":* Kilduff and Javers, *Suicide Cult,* p. 72.

P. 233, *A psychiatric social worker . . . was a steady target:* A. MacRobert, "Uncovering the Cult Conspiracy," *Mother Jones,* Feb./Mar. 1979, p. 8.

P. 234, *"A severely sick, extremely troubled member . . .":* J. Clark, "Problems in Referral of Cult Members," *NAPPH Journal* (National Association of Psychiatric Health Systems), 1978, 9(4), 28.

P. 234, *a California lawyer was attacked by a rattlesnake:* Mitchell, Mitchell, and Ofshe, *The Light on Synanon,* p. 125.

P. 234, "Once inside Synanon . . .": Mitchell, Mitchell, and Ofshe, *The Light on Synanon*, p. 177.

P. 234, "Her hair had been . . .": Mitchell, Mitchell, and Ofshe, *The Light on Synanon*, pp. 178–179.

P. 235, *Two of the Imperial Marines*: Mitchell, Mitchell, and Ofshe, *The Light on Synanon*, p. 299; Olin, *Escape from Utopia*, p. 287.

P. 235, *with Charles Dederich speaking of*: Olin, *Escape from Utopia*, p. 288.

P. 236, *Among the more litigious stances . . . was that shown by Synanon*: Gerstel, *Paradise Incorporated: Synanon*, pp. 197, 258; Mitchell, Mitchell, and Ofshe, *The Light on Synanon*, p. 167.

P. 236, *Ralph Craib wrote, "Major news organizations . . ."*: Mitchell, Mitchell, and Ofshe, *The Light on Synanon*, pp. 284–285.

P. 236, *did the National News Council . . . investigate*: Mitchell, Mitchell, and Ofshe, *The Light on Synanon*, p. 298.

P. 237, *These events . . . were turning points*: Gerstel, *Paradise Incorporated: Synanon*, p. 269.

P. 237, *Patricia Ryan . . . said, "The American courts . . ."*: Cult Awareness Network, "Non-profit Sues Controversial Church of Scientology for Millions—Claims Scientology Backed Dozens of Lawsuits to Bankrupt It," Press release, Feb. 9, 1994.

P. 239, *Those who criticize or oppose cults become accustomed*: MacRobert, "Uncovering the Cult Conspiracy."

Chapter Ten

P. 248, *At one memorial, a girl*: Wooden, *The Children of Jonestown*, pp. 208–209.

P. 248, *It has been estimated that there are thousands*: M. Rudin, "Women, Elderly, and Children in Religious Cults," *Cultic Studies Journal*, 1984, *1*, 8–26.

P. 248, *the work of a number of researchers attests*: S. Landa, "Hidden Terror: Child Abuse in Religious Sects and Cults," *Justice for Children*, 1985, *1*, 2–5; "Warning Signs: The Effects of Authoritarianism on Children in Cults," *Areopagus*, 1989, 2(4), 16–22; S. Landa, "Children and Cults: A Practical Guide," *Journal of Family Law*, 1991, 29(3), 591–634.

P. 250, *Jones had begun to plan the ending . . . five years before:* Wooden, *The Children of Jonestown*, p. 172.

P. 251, *Clayton reported that "the nurses . . ."* : Wooden, *The Children of Jonestown*, p. 187; E. Feinsod, *Awake in a Nightmare, Jonestown: The Only Eyewitness Account* (New York: W.W. Norton, 1981).

P. 252, *These freed children have been carefully studied:* This information is based on an audiotape of Dr. Bruce Perry's presentation, "Raised in Cults: Brainwashing or Socialization?" at the Cult Awareness Network annual conference, Minneapolis, Nov. 1993.

P. 254, *Five-year-old Luke Stice died of a broken neck:* L. D. Hatfield, "Killing Fields, U.S. Style: Right Wingers on Trial," *San Francisco Examiner*, Mar. 9, 1986, p. A6; J. Gauger, "Dennis Ryan Conviction Upheld by Nebraska Court," *Omaha World-Herald*, Jul. 24, 1987; N. Schinker, "Rulo Witness Withheld His Story, 'Who Would Have Believed It?'" *Omaha World-Herald*, Mar. 26, 1986, pp. 17–18.

P. 254, *Twelve-year-old John Yarbough allegedly was beaten to death:* K. DeSmet, "Witness Details Beatings at House of Judah Camp," *Detroit News*, Aug. 15, 1986, p. 3B; K. DeSmet, "Ex-cultist Describes Torture," *Detroit News*, Aug. 16, 1986, p. 4A; J. Swickard, "Brother Beaten by Sect Elders, Boy Testifies," *Detroit Free Press*, Aug. 20, 1986.

P. 256, *an Indiana judge ordered four children removed:* T. Shands, "CUT Member Loses Custody of Children," *Livingston* (Mont.) *Enterprise*, Aug. 26, 1992.

P.257, *members testified that they sing to their children:* A. Rochell, "Discipline or Abuse?" *Atlanta Journal-Constitution* (Ga.), Jul. 31, 1993, pp. B1, B10.

P. 257, *A former member of Moon's Unification Church wrote:* D. Durham, *Life Among the Moonies: Three Years in the Unification Church* (Plainfield, N.J.: Logos International, 1981), pp. 73–75.

P. 258, *one case in which I testified: Miller et al. v. The Tony and Susan Alamo Foundation et al.*, U.S. District Court, Western District of Arkansas, Fort Smith Division, 88–2206 (1990).

P. 259, *"We were taught . . . ," wrote a mother:* Durham, *Life Among the Moonies,* p. 105.

P. 261, *One example of this thinking is found in the Sullivanians:* E. Henican, "Dads Battle 'Cult' for Children," *New York Newsday,* May 31, 1988, pp. 9, 23; T. Lewin, "Custody Case Lifts Veil on a 'Psychotherapy Cult,'" *New York Times,* June 3, 1988, pp. B1–B2; F. McMorris, "Cultism and Sex May Hype Trial," *Daily News* (Brooklyn, N.Y.), June 3, 1988, p. 27; S. Reed, "Two Anxious Fathers Battle a Therapy 'Cult' for Their Kids," *People,* Jul. 25, 1988, pp. 47–48.

Chapter Eleven

P. 271, *to keep the cult member from seeing:* I would like to thank my colleague, Janja Lalich, for the use for this section of her notes from her lecture "Why It's Not Easy to Leave Cults," presented at a public education seminar sponsored by the Northern California chapter of the Cult Awareness Network, San Francisco, Nov. 17, 1993.

P. 282, *Robert Dole . . . responded to a petition signed by fourteen thousand citizens:* R. Delgado, "Religious Totalism: Gentle and Ungentle Persuasion Under the First Amendment," *Southern California Law Review,* 1977, *51*(1), 5.

P. 282, *brought out descriptions of the way cult members' "dependence . . .":* Delgado, "Religious Totalism: Gentle and Ungentle Persuasion Under the First Amendment," p. 5.

P. 282, *These changes included:* Delgado, "Religious Totalism: Gentle and Ungentle Persuasion Under the First Amendment," pp. 70–71.

P. 285, *On the Fourth of July:* Patrick's story appears in T. Patrick with T. Dulack, *Let Our Children Go* (New York: Dutton, 1976), pp. 36–39.

P. 290, *most exit counselors agree:* D. Clark, C. Giambalvo, N. Giambalvo, K. Garvey, and M. D. Langone, "Exit Counseling: A Practical Overview," in M. D. Langone (ed.), *Recovery from Cults: Help for Victims of Psychological and Spiritual Abuse* (New York: W.W. Norton, 1993), p. 163.

P. 291, *families begin their search for assistance:* This discussion of choosing an exit counselor draws upon M. T. Singer, "Cults and Families," in R. H. Mikesell, D. D. Lusterman, and S. H. McDaniel (eds), *Family Psychology and Systems Ther-*

apy: A Handbook (Wash., D.C.: American Psychological Association Press, in press); Singer, "Consultation with Families of Cultists," pp. 270–283.

P.294, *Books and other material written by exit counselors are available:* Clark, Giambalvo, Giambalvo, Garvey, and Langone, "Exit Counseling"; C. Giambalvo, *Exit Counseling: A Family Intervention* (Bonita Springs, Fla.: American Family Foundation, 1992); S. Hassan, *Combatting Cult Mind Control* (Rochester, Vt.: Park Street Press, 1988).

P. 296, *people suffer spiritual abuse in cults:* R. M. Enroth, *Churches That Abuse* (Grand Rapids, Mich.: Zondervan, 1992); Singer, "Cults and Families."

P. 296, *A group . . . has formed an association with bylaws:* "Bylaws of the Association of Thought Reform Consultants," adopted Sept. 19, 1993.

P. 297, *Other professionals have found the same thing:* S. M. Ash, "Cult-Induced Psychopathology, Part I: Clinical Picture," *Cultic Studies Journal,* 1985, *2,* 31–90; L. Goldberg and W. Goldberg, "Psychotherapy with Ex-Cultists," *Cultic Studies Journal,* 1988, *5,* 193–210; P. Martin, Personal communication, Jan. 7, 1992; M. T. Singer, "Coming Out of the Cults," *Psychology Today,* Jan. 1979, pp. 72–82.

Chapter Twelve

P. 299, *those who help former cult members have seen certain patterns:* Singer and Ofshe, "Thought Reform Programs and the Production of Psychiatric Casualties," 188–193.

P. 301, *as others have termed it:* West, Presentation at the American Family Foundation Conference; Lifton, "Doubling: The Faustian Bargain," in *The Future of Immortality,* pp. 195–208.

P. 309, *panic attacks, defined as discrete periods of intense fear:* American Psychiatric Association, *Diagnostic and Statistical Manual of Mental Disorders* (DSM-III-R) (3rd ed. rev.) (Wash., D.C.: Author, 1987), pp. 235–238.

P. 310, *Jeannie Mills . . . said, "After 1973 . . .":* F. Conway and J. Seigelman, *Snapping: America's Epidemic of Sudden Personality Change* (New York: Dell, 1981), p. 238.

P. 311, *One reporter said:* Singer, "Coming Out of the Cults," p. 80.

PP. 321–322, A *few cults practice child-to-child:* L. B. Davis, *The Children of God* (Grand Rapids, Mich.: Zondervan, 1984).

P. 322, *aberrant Mormon-based cults:* "3 Members of Polygamous Sect Face Prison Terms for 4 Killings," *Chicago Tribune*, Jan. 22, 1993, p. 12; "6 in Sect Indicted in Deaths, Polygamous Clan Eliminated Foes," *Mesa* (Ariz.) *Tribune*, Aug. 25, 1992.

P. 322, *weddings . . . in which 5,150 members were united:* M. Galanter, *Cults, Faith Healing and Coercion* (New York: Oxford University Press, 1989).

Resources and Organizations

Publications

CAN News (monthly newsletter)
Cult Awareness Network
2421 W. Pratt Blvd., Suite 1173
Chicago, IL 60645

Cultic Studies Journal (semiannual journal)
American Family Foundation
P.O. Box 2265
Bonita Springs, FL 33959

The Cult Observer (ten issues yearly newsletter)
American Family Foundation
P.O. Box 2265
Bonita Springs, FL 33959

FOCUS NEWS (quarterly newsletter for former cult members)
c/o Cult Awareness Network
2421 W. Pratt Blvd., Suite 1173
Chicago, IL 60645

Organizations

This is an abbreviated list. For organizations in specific locales or with a special interest, contact the American Family Foundation or the Cult Awareness Network for referrals.

American Family Foundation (AFF)
P.O. Box 2265
Bonita Springs, FL 33959
(212) 249–7693

Commission on Cults and Missionaries
Jewish Federation Council of Greater Los Angeles
6505 Wilshire Blvd., Suite 802
Los Angeles, CA 90048
(213) 852–1234, ext. 2813

Cult Awareness Network (CAN)
2421 W. Pratt Blvd., Suite 1173
Chicago, IL 60645
(312) 267–7777

FOCUS (Former cult members support group)
c/o Cult Awareness Network
2421 W. Pratt Blvd., Suite 1173
Chicago, IL 60645
(312) 267–7777

International Cult Education Project (ICEP)
P.O. Box 1232 Gracie Station
New York, NY 10028
(212) 439–1550

Task Force on Cults and Missionaries
Greater Miami Jewish Federation
4200 Biscayne Blvd.
Miami, FL 33137
(305) 576–4000

Counseling Services

In addition to the following services, the American Family Foundation maintains a list of mental health professionals around the country with cult-related expertise.

Cult Clinic
Jewish Family Service
6505 Wilshire Blvd., 6th Fl.
Los Angeles, CA 90048
(213) 852–1234

Cult Clinic & Hot Line
Jewish Board of Family and Children's Services
120 W. 57th Street
New York, NY 10019
(212) 632–4640

Wellspring Retreat & Resource Center
P.O. Box 67
Albany, OH 45710
(614) 698–6277

International Organizations

This is an abbreviated list. For additional organizations in these and other countries, contact the American Family Foundation.

ADFI (Association pour la défense de la famille et l'individu)
10 rue du Pere Julien Dhuit
75020 Paris
France
33–47–97–96–08

Asociacion Pro Juventud, A.I.S. (Asesoramiento e informacion sobre sectas)
Aribau, 226
08006 Barcelona
Spain
34–32–014–886

Family Action Information and Rescue (FAIR)
BCM Box 3535, P.O. Box 12
London WC1N 3XX
United Kingdom
44–1–539–3940

Info-Cult
5655 Park Avenue, Suite 305
Montreal, Quebec H2V 4H2
Canada
(514) 274–2333

Further Reading

Books

Captive Hearts, Captive Minds: Freedom and Recovery from Cults and Abusive Relationships, by Madeleine Landau Tobias and Janja Lalich. Alameda, Calif.: Hunter House, 1994.

Churches That Abuse, by Ronald Enroth. Grand Rapids, Mich.: Zondervan, 1992.

Coercive Persuasion: A Socio-psychological Analysis of the "Brainwashing" of American Civilian Prisoners by the Chinese Communists, by Edgar H. Schein, with Inge Schneier and Curtis H. Barker. New York: W.W. Norton, 1961.

Combatting Cult Mind Control, by Steve Hassan. Rochester, Vt.: Park Street Press, 1988.

Cults: What Parents Should Know, by Joan C. Ross and Michael D. Langone. Secaucus, N.J.: Lyle Stuart, 1989.

Exit Counseling: A Family Intervention, by Carol Giambalvo. Bonita Springs, Fla.: American Family Foundation, 1992.

Influence: The New Psychology of Modern Persuasion, by Robert Cialdini. New York: Quill, 1984.

Recovery from Cults: Help for Victims of Psychological and Spiritual Abuse, edited by Michael D. Langone. New York: W.W. Norton, 1993.

Thought Reform and the Psychology of Totalism: A Study of Brainwashing in China, by Robert Jay Lifton. New York: W.W. Norton, 1961.

Articles and Pamphlets

"Attacks on Peripheral Versus Central Elements of Self and the Impact of Thought-Reforming Techniques," by Richard Ofshe and Margaret T. Singer. *Cultic Studies Journal*, 1986, 3(1), 3–24.

"Coming Out of the Cults," by Margaret Thaler Singer. *Psychology Today*, Jan. 1979, pp. 72–82.

"Cults in America," by Charles C. Clark. *The CQ Researcher*, 1993, 3(17), 385–408. (Available from American Family Foundation)

"Cults, Quacks, and Nonprofessional Therapies," by Louis J. West and Margaret Thaler Singer. In *Comprehensive Textbook of Psychiatry*, Vol. 3 (3rd ed.), edited by Harold I. Kaplan, Alfred M. Freedman, and Benjamin J. Sadock. Baltimore: Williams & Wilkins, 1980.

"Cults: Religious Totalism and Civil Liberties." Chapter in *The Future of Immortality*, by Robert J. Lifton. New York: Basic Books, 1987.

"Group Psychodynamics," by Margaret T. Singer. In *The Merck Manual of Diagnosis and Therapy* (15th ed.), edited by Robert Berkow. Rahway, N.J.: Merck Sharp & Dohme Research Laboratories, 1987.

"Persuasive Techniques in Contemporary Cults: A Public Health Approach," by Louis J. West. *Cultic Studies Journal*, 1990, 7(2), 126–149.

"Psychotherapy Cults," by Margaret T. Singer, Maurice K. Temerlin, and Michael D. Langone. *Cultic Studies Journal*, (1990), 7(2), 101–125.

Special Issue on Cults. *Psychiatric Annals*, 1990, 20(4), 171–216. (Available from American Family Foundation)

"Thought Reform Programs and the Production of Psychiatric Casualties," by Margaret T. Singer and Richard Ofshe. *Psychiatric Annals*, 1990, 20(4), 188–193.

"Undue Influence and Written Documents: Psychological Aspects," by Margaret T. Singer. *Journal of Questioned Document Examination*, 1992, 1(1), 4–13.

"Undue Influence in Contract and Probate Law," by Abraham Nievod. *Journal of Questioned Document Examination*, 1992, 1(1), 14–26.

"The Utilization of Hypnotic Techniques in Religious Cult Conversion," by Jesse S. Miller. *Cultic Studies Journal*, 1986, 3(2), 243–250.

The Authors

Margaret Thaler Singer is a clinical psychologist and emeritus adjunct professor of the Department of Psychology, University of California, Berkeley. She received her Ph.D. degree in clinical psychology from the University of Denver, and she has been a practicing clinician, researcher, and teacher for nearly fifty years. Singer's major area of work—how people influence one another—grew directly out of her undergraduate and graduate work in speech and psychology, and the study of cults has been a special area of her research. Over the years Singer has counseled and interviewed more than three thousand current and former cult members. In 1978 she was awarded the Leo J. Ryan Memorial Award, named in honor of the U.S. Representative murdered in Jonestown, Guyana.

Over the past two decades Singer has been an active consultant and expert witness in many legal cases and has appeared frequently on television discussing influence and persuasion. The author of more than one hundred articles published in professional journals, she has received numerous national honors for her various research work, including awards from the American Psychiatric Association, the American College of Psychiatrists, the National Mental Health Association, the American Association for Marriage and Family Therapy, and the American Family Therapy Association. She also held a Research Scientist Award from the National Institute of Mental Health and was the first woman and first clinical psychologist elected president of the American Psychosomatic Society.

Singer lives in Berkeley with her husband, Jay, a physicist whose special contributions have been in the development of magnetic resonance imaging. Her son is a public relations and political consultant, and her daughter is a resident in orthopedic surgery. Singer is the happy grandmother of twin boys.

Janja Lalich received her B.A. degree in French from the University of Wisconsin, Madison, and spent the following year as a Fulbright Scholar doing postgraduate research at the Université d'Aix-en-Provence, France. She is a writer, editor, and publishing and marketing consultant.

A member of a political cult for more than ten years, Lalich has been studying the cult phenomenon since she left the group in 1986. She has written, lectured, and been interviewed in the media about both her personal cult experience and cults in general, and she offers preventive-education workshops and training seminars to campus, religious, civic, and professional organizations.

She is coauthor of *Captive Hearts, Captive Minds: Freedom and Recovery from Cults and Abusive Relationships* (Hunter House, 1994), and author of the chapter "A Little Carrot and a Lot of Stick," in *Recovery from Cults: Help for Victims of Psychological and Spiritual Abuse* (W.W. Norton, 1993). Lalich is also associate editor of the *Cultic Studies Journal*, and an advisory board member and research associate of the American Family Foundation, a tax-exempt research and educational organization founded in 1979 to assist former cult members and their families.

She is coordinator of a San Francisco Bay Area support group for former cult members, and is a cult information specialist and consultant, working with families and friends of those involved with cults.

Lalich lives in Alameda, California, with her partner, Kim, and their two dogs, Rikki and Lucy.

Index

Commitment, exploited by cult, 10, 92–93, 271–272

Communes, versus cults, 39–40

Communication, in totalistic environment, 69–70, 116, 273–274. *See also* Language and jargon

Complex marriage, 34–35

Compliance, Cialdini's six categories of, 169–171; example of, 171–172

Confession process, 72

Conservatorships, 283–284

Conspiracy and fraud, 89–90

Cooper, P., 228–229

Counterculture of 1960s, and emergence of cults, 37–40

Course in Miracles, 43

Covenant, the Sword, and the Arm of the Lord, 42

Critics. *See* Harassment and intimidation

Cult(s); of 1880s, 31–37; of 1960s, 5, 37–40; of 1970s, 5, 40–43; of 1980s, 43–46; apologists, 23–25, 221–223; categories, 4; characteristics, 6–12; as consumer issue, xx–xxi, 127; definition of term, xix–xx, 6–7, 11; history of, 29–51; image manipulation, 229–231; versus legitimate groups, 11–12, 96–102; myths about who joins, xxi, 15–28; names, significance of, 14–15; as negative utopias, xxi–xxiii; origins, 8; purpose, 11; statistics, 5, 12; structure, 8–9; types, 13–15; use of thought-reform processes, 4, 7, 10, 52–82

Cult Awareness network (CAN), 237, 239

cult ideology, as sacred science, 73–74

Cult indoctrinee syndrome, 282–283

Cultic relationships, 7

D

Debriefing, postcult, 290, 297, 304. *See also* Exit counseling

Deception, 9, 105, 117–118, 123–124, 161–163

Decreeing, 257

Dederich, C., 41, 160–161, 235, 236

Defectors, 276–279; harassment of, 309–310; punishment of, 257, 278–279

Democratic Workers Party, 41, 256

Depersonalization, and meditation, 141–142

Deprogramming, 280–287. *See also* Exit counseling

Diet and dietary requirements, 132–135

Direct centering, 42, 191

Discipline, as control mechanism, 56–57, 254, 257–258, 276–277, 278–279; aftereffects, 300

Disconnect letters, 168, 316

Dissociation, 317–318

Dissociative techniques, aftereffects, 299–300

Donovan, S., 142

Doomsday ideology, XXX

Doubling, 77–79

Drescher, T., 89

Drug, dealing and use, 89, 255

E

Eastern-based groups, 13, 14, 38, 40, 43; dissociative techniques in, 300; experiential rituals in, 126–128

Ecclesia Athletic Association, 15, 87

Eckankar, 197

Education, lack of, 254–255, 305–306; versus thought reform, 58–59

Elderly, recruitment of, 88, 95, 119–122

Emotional arousal techniques, aftereffects, 299, 300

Emotional manipulation, 169–172

Encounter groups, 41, 42, 45

Enforced dependency, 10, 27, 277–278

Equal Employment Opportunity Commission (EEOC), training programs policy, 85, 188–189, 181, 211

Erhard, W., 42, 202–203, 205, 228

Erickson, M., 153–154

Esalen Institute, 230

Est, 14, 42, 191, 197, 202, 205, 228

Ethics, double set in cults, 9

Exhaustion, as control technique, 274

Exit counseling, 286–290, 296–298; family participation in, 286–287, 291; value of, 297–298; versus therapy, 295–296

Exit counselor: background, 290–291, 296–297; choice of, 291–294; clergy as, 294–295; harassment of, 293–294;